HABERMAS

Key Contemporary Thinkers

Published

Peter Burke, *The French Historical Revolution: The Annales School 1929–1989*
Simon Evnine, *Donald Davidson*
Phillip Hansen, *Hannah Arendt: Politics, History and Citizenship*
Christopher Hookway, *Quine: Language, Experience and Reality*
Douglas Kellner, *Jean Baudrillard: From Marxism to Post-Modernism and Beyond*
Chandran Kukathas & Philip Pettit, *Rawls: A Theory of Justice and its Critics*
Lois McNay, *Foucault: A Critical Introduction*
Philip Manning, *Erving Goffman and Modern Sociology*
Michael Moriarty, *Roland Barthes*
William Outhwaite, *Habermas: A Critical Introduction*
Georgia Warnke, *Gadamer: Hermeneutics, Tradition and Reason*
Jonathan Wolff, *Robert Nozick: Property, Justice and the Minimal State*

Forthcoming

Jeremy Ahearne, *Michel de Certeau*
Alison Ainley, *Irigaray*
Michael Best, *Galbraith*
Michael Caesar, *Umberto Eco*
James Carey, *Innis and McLuhan*
Colin Davis, *Levinas*
Eric Dunning, *Norbert Elias*
Jocelyn Dunphy, *Paul Ricoeur*
Judith Feher-Gurewich, *Lacan*
Kate and Edward Fullbrook, *Simone de Beauvoir*
Andrew Gamble, *Hayek and the Market Order*
Graeme Gilloch, *Walter Benjamin*
Adrian Hayes, *Talcott Parsons and the Theory of Action*
Christina Howells, *Derrida*
Simon Jarvis, *Adorno*
Paul Kelly, *Ronald Dworkin*
Susan Sellers, *Hélène Cixous*
Geoff Stokes, *Popper*
Ian Whitehouse, *Rorty*
James Williams, *Lyotard*

HABERMAS
A Critical Introduction

William Outhwaite

Stanford University Press
Stanford, California
1994

Stanford University Press
Stanford, California
© 1994 William Outhwaite
Originating publisher: Polity Press
   in association with Blackwell Publishers, Oxford
First published in the U.S.A. by
   Stanford University Press, 1994
Printed in Great Britain
Cloth ISBN 0-8047-2478-4
Paper ISBN 0-8047-2479-2
LC 94-67173
This book is printed on acid-free paper.

For Laura, who was also there

Contents

Acknowledgements

I would like to thank John Thompson for his enormous help and patient encouragement throughout the long preparation of this book. I have also benefited from discussions with a number of Sussex University students and colleagues working on Habermas – in particular Angela Clare, Christy Swords, Simon Hollis, Julien Morton and Catherine Skinner. Roy Bhaskar and others took time off from their own work to read the manuscript and encourage me to finish it, and Barbara Kehm in Kassel and Stefan Müller-Doohm in Oldenburg generously kept me up to date with Habermas's output over the past few years. My thanks also to Diane Jordan, who typed the greater part of the manuscript, and to Linden Stafford for her meticulous copy-editing.

Table 1: from *The Critical Theory of Jürgen Habermas* by Thomas McCarthy, (Polity 1984). Reprinted by permission of Polity Press and MIT Press.

Introduction

Any account of such an active and richly developing thinker as Jürgen Habermas can only be provisional. Since the publication of David Held's *Introduction to Critical Theory* (1980) and Thomas McCarthy's *The Critical Theory of Jürgen Habermas* (1978), the overall shape of Habermas's work has been altered by his *Theory of Communicative Action* (1981), *The Philosophical Discourse of Modernity* (1985) and *Faktizität und Geltung* (*Between Facts and Norms*) (1992). And it is only since the beginning of the 1980s that he has dealt systematically with the complex issue of the relationship of his thought to that of the earlier generation of critical theorists, notably Max Horkheimer and Theodor Adorno.

The Theory of Communicative Action and *Faktizität und Geltung* also recall some of the themes of one of his earliest works, *The Structural Transformation of the Public Sphere*. Finally, the issue of his relationship to the history of Germany and the development of the Federal Republic has been given a new twist by his edited volume on the 'Spiritual Condition of the Age', his critical interventions in the so-called 'Historians' Dispute' over the interpretation, forty years on, of the Third Reich, and his discussion of the 1989 revolutions and of the reunification of Germany.

Habermas has described modernity as an incomplete project, and the same is true of his own work. In this book, I attempt to bring out the continuities in Habermas's developing work, while paying due regard to the shifts of orientation and emphasis and the reasons for them. My aim is to present his thought and indicate its interest and importance, rather than to argue for an alternative theoretical model; the more important criticisms will, however, be noted, especially where they have led to modifications of Habermas's own position.

Compared to the dramatic experiences of exile forced upon the first-generation members of what came to be called the Frankfurt School, Habermas's life has been relatively uneventful – at least after the overthrow of the Nazi regime. Born in 1929, he grew up in the small town of Gummersbach, some 35 miles east of Cologne, where his father was director of the Chamber of Commerce. He describes the political climate in his family as one of 'bourgeois adaptation to a political environment with which one did not fully identify, but which one didn't seriously criticize either', and recounts 'the impression of a normality which afterwards proved to be an illusion'.[1]

As Habermas notes, the shock of the Nuremberg revelations and the fact that his first education in liberal democratic theory was in the context of 'reeducation' separates his generation from those who had known the 'half-hearted bourgeois republic' of Weimar,[2] which made some of them impatient with the elements of restoration in post-war western Germany. It also separates his from the later generation, growing up under a democratic regime which some of them were quick, in the late 1960s, to dismiss as an illusory democracy (*Scheindemokratie*). Habermas himself soon became anxious about the continuities in personnel between the Nazi regime and the emergent West German state, as it rearmed in the 1950s.

Habermas studied philosophy, history, psychology and German literature at the University of Göttingen, and then in Zurich and Bonn, where he obtained his doctorate in 1954 with a rather traditional dissertation on Schelling. After some time as a journalist, which perhaps still shows in the vigorous style of some of his later newspaper polemics, he became, in 1956, Adorno's assistant at the reconstituted Institute for Social Research, where he participated in an empirical study on the political awareness of students, published in 1961. From 1959 to 1961 he worked on his *Structural Transformation of the Public Sphere* (1962); this was rejected by Adorno as a *Habilitation* thesis and supported instead by Wolfgang Abendroth in Marburg.

After a period as Professor of Philosophy at Heidelberg, Habermas returned to Frankfurt in 1964 as Professor of Philosophy and Sociology, where he delivered the inaugural lecture on 'Knowledge and Interest', reprinted with other essays in his *Technik und Wissenschaft als Ideologie* (*Technology and Science as Ideology*) of 1968 and in English in *Knowledge and Human Interests*. His other works of this period are the essays entitled *Theory and Practice* (1963) and a survey work on *The Logic of The Social Sciences* (1967).

The year 1968 was of course the time of major student-led protest, in West Germany as elsewhere. Habermas participated fully in the movement, welcoming its intellectual and political challenge to the complacency of West German democracy (and incidentally to the gloomy diagnosis in *Student und Politik* of the unpolitical orientation of West German students). As Habermas put it in his introduction to his essays *Protestbewegung und Hochschulreform*,[3] 'the SDS [the Socialist Student Association] was the motor of a "movement" which opened up an unforeseen political terrain and thus the prospects of enlightenment for the purposes of a radical reformism.' But the movement went too far for Habermas and in what he considered to be unrealistic directions, dangerous both politically, given the repressive capacities of the state, and intellectually, in its tendency to reject scholarship as bourgeois. Although Habermas saw his criticisms as coming from within the movement, his relationship with the activists turned increasingly sour. He has, however, continued to give a very positive view of the long-term effect of the movement on the political culture of the Federal Republic, while deploring the short-term legacy of its failure: a decline into apathy and desperate terrorism.

In 1971 Habermas left Frankfurt for Starnberg, Bavaria, to take up, along with the natural scientist C. F. von Weizsäcker, the directorship of the newly created Max Planck Institute for the Study of the Conditions of Life in the Scientific-Technical World. In an environment which attracted some of the most brilliant younger sociologists in the country, he published an enormous amount of material, including the well known *Legitimation Crisis* (1973) and culminating with *The Theory of Communicative Action* (1981). In 1982 he returned to Frankfurt, to the chair in sociology and philosophy which he still occupies.

Habermas's massive intellectual achievement will be discussed in detail in the following chapters. In concluding this biographical introduction, it may be appropriate to make some general remarks about his role as an intellectual. If Max Weber has been described as a bourgeois Marx, Habermas might be summarily characterized as a Marxist Weber. His Marxism, as will be seen in the next chapter, is anything but orthodox, but he continues to describe himself as a

Marxist, and not only out of solidarity with others and as a provocation to the circumscribed political culture of the Federal Republic. The reference to Weber is justified by Habermas's role as one of the leading intellectuals in Germany. Like Weber, he is basically a thinker rather than a man of action but one who intervenes in political issues when something, as he often puts it, 'irritates' him. His collected 'political writings' – a broad category which includes occasional lectures and interviews – run to several hundred pages. Although he rejects Weber's doctrine of the value-freedom of science, like Weber he insists on the distinction between scholarly and political discourse.[4] Like Weber, and Karl Jaspers[5] in the post-war period, he has operated in some way as the intellectual conscience of Germany, with a public profile higher than one would expect of someone who has not sought out a political role.

The comparison with Weber is perhaps also not inappropriate in intellectual terms. In my view, Habermas is the most important social theorist of the second half of the twentieth century – a judgement shared by contemporary sociologists much less enthusiastic than I am about the content of his work. The remainder of this book attempts to justify such an assessment.

1

The Roots of Habermas's Thought

Habermas combines a deep grounding in the philosophical tradition with a remarkable openness to a wide variety of contemporary philosophical and social theories.[1] Entire books could be written about the respective influences of Kant and Hegel, Marx and Weber, Parsons and Piaget, and so on. The most important source is, however, without question the broad Marxist tradition which also inspired the original Frankfurt Institute for Social Research.

The history of Marxist thought in the twentieth century is in large part a process for which the pejorative term is revisionism, involving the abandonment or relegation of certain Marxian principles, the incorporation of, or at least engagement with, non-Marxist theories such as those of Kant, Nietzsche or Freud and a tendency to pay more attention to superstructural processes, whether political, ideological or more particularly artistic, than to the so-called 'base'.[2]

The Hungarian Marxist György Lukács can be seen as a crucial figure in this development: one channel at least through which German idealism, with important modifications by the sociologist Georg Simmel, was transmuted into 'critical theory'. This term is used in two main ways: first, to refer to a tradition beginning with Simmel and Lukács; second, more narrowly, to refer to the work of some of the writers associated with the Frankfurt Institute for Social Research. (The term 'Frankfurt School', which tends to be used interchangeably with 'critical theory' in the English-speaking world, was used in West Germany to refer to the Institute after its re-establishment in 1950.)

The history of the Institute, and its relationship to the Marxist tradition, have been thoroughly discussed in a variety of books, and it has become clear that Habermas's relationship to Frankfurt critical theory was rather less immediate than is often assumed.[3] Max Horkheimer, the Director of the Institute, seems not to have been at all concerned to establish a continuity with its pre-war interdisciplinary Marxist research; indeed he kept the back numbers of the Institute's *Zeitschrift für Sozialforschung* locked away in a cellar.[4] His interests, like those of Theodor Adorno, had become increasingly philosophical, and their critique of instrumental reason, expressed in *Dialectic of Enlightenment* (1947), suggested a considerable scepticism about empirical social research. In intellectual terms, Habermas is closer to the Institute's earlier programme, with its emphasis on the interdisciplinary appropriation of material drawn from various social sciences.

But, if Habermas was dissatisfied with the form of Adorno and Horkheimer's thought from *Dialectic of Enlightenment* onwards, he shared their substantive preoccupation with the way in which enlightenment, in the form of instrumental rationality, turns from a means of liberation into a new source of enslavement: 'Already at that time [the late 1950s] my problem was a theory of modernity, a theory of the pathology of modernity, from the viewpoint of the realization – the deformed realization – of reason in history.'[5]

In Habermas's early work this preoccupation took three forms. First, a working-through of the classical philosophical texts: Marx and Weber, but also Kant, Fichte and Hegel – not to mention the Greeks. Second, a preoccupation with technology and the attempt to construct a 'left' alternative to the technological determinism arising in part from Heidegger and in post-war Germany from Arnold Gehlen and Helmut Schelsky. Third, and relatedly, a concern with the conditions of rational political discussion or, more grandiosely, practical reason, in the conditions of modern technocratic democracy. The first of these themes predominates in *Theory and Practice*; the second can be found in Habermas's early journalism and in *Technology and Science as Ideology*; the third theme occurs in both these works, but is first addressed in *Student und Politik* and *Structural Transformation of the Public Sphere*.

Student und Politik is based on an empirical study carried out in 1957 on a sample of Frankfurt students: Habermas was responsible for the theoretical introduction on the concept of political participation and the sections on the students' 'political habitus' and 'image of society'. Habermas argues, in a move which may seem obvious but is actually not so common in the literature on participation, that this should not be considered as a value in itself but related to the conditions in which it occurs. His account of the contemporary situation in West Germany and related state-forms prefigures that given in his later book on the public sphere. With the partial resolution of the 'social question' in a welfare state with a fully democratic franchise, and with the decline of open class antagonism, the contradiction 'has changed its form: it now appears as the depoliticization of the masses coinciding with the progressive politicization [in the sense of party political and parliamentary incorporation] of society itself'.[6] This society 'increasingly functionalizes its citizens for various public purposes, but it privatizes them in their consciousness'.[7] It is thus not surprising that a large proportion of students, even those who consider themselves to be 'good citizens', are relatively distanced from politics.

The results of the survey caused a certain amount of public anxiety, in a country with a tendency to pull up its newly planted democracy to see how it was growing. The analysis of the limitations of German democracy, however, seems to have had a more lasting influence on the political consciousness of students and other radicals.

The public sphere

The same is true of Habermas's first major book, *Strukturwandel der Öffentlichkeit* (1962), translated after a long delay as *The Structural Transformation of the Public Sphere*. In this book, Habermas applies, at much greater length, to the concept of public opinion the kind of analysis which he had earlier given of political participation.

> 'Public opinion' takes on a different meaning depending on whether it is brought into play as a critical authority in connection with the normative mandate that the exercise of political and social power be subject to publicity or as the object to be molded in connection with a staged display of, and manipulative propagation of, publicity in the service of persons and institutions, consumer goods, and programs.[8]

Habermas's strategy is to relate the concept of public opinion back to its historical roots in the idea of public sphere or public domain (*Öffentlichkeit*) in the hope of 'attaining a systematic comprehension of our own society from the perspective of one of its

central categories' (p. 5). The literate bourgeois public (*Öffentlichkeit*
again) of the eighteenth century, which had cut its teeth in literary
discussion, took on a political role in the evaluation of contemporary affairs and, in particular, state policy. The clubs, salons and
coffee-houses (there were 3000 of the latter in London in the early
1700s) supported by the growing and increasingly free press
formed a critical forum, in which gentlemen independent of the
court and other political institutions could get together on a basis of
relative equality and discuss the great events of the day.

Among the causes of this development was a shift in the relationship between state and society which prefigures the later one described in *Student und Politik*. With the growth of trade and
industry, state policy came to have an importance for the growing
bourgeoisie which it had not had in a society of small-scale house-
hold production and retailing; hence the enormous growth in the
newspaper market. In addition to any independent desire for
greater democratic influence, people needed to know what the state
was doing or failing to do and to influence it as far as they could.
Habermas's explanation of this process may be a rather materialist
one, but the ideal of rational, informed discussion of public policy is
one which runs like a red thread through the whole of his later
work.[9]

Of course, Habermas admits, the idealized concept of public
opinion as it was incorporated into constitutional theory was not at
all fully realized; he notes, somewhat casually, the limitations of
class and gender (pp. 85ff) and the tendencies to commercialization
in the press (pp. 181ff). The second of these processes forms part of
what Habermas calls the transformation of the public sphere – a
shift from publicity in the abstract sense of what Gorbachev called
glasnost, openness, to the modern sense of the term in journalism,
advertising and politics (p. 140). In addition to these trends, there is
the expansion of the state's role as it develops into a welfare state,
and the growth of large private concerns with a 'quasi-political
character' (p. 148). Private law, expecially in relation to property
rights, is transformed as it necessarily becomes relevant to public
law, in, for example, labour law or the law of tenancy, or in increasingly frequent contracts between the public authorities and private
individuals or corporations. This blurring of the distinction between public and private law corresponds to a changed relationship
between state and society (see e.g. pp. 151, 231).

Interestingly, Habermas does not put much emphasis on
the general process which he and others have come to call

Verrechtlichung – the trend to legal regulation of private life in, for example, family law. The 'hollowing out' of the intimate sphere of the family, as outside influences on family members become stronger, with the growth of labour markets and social insurance, and developments in suburban architecture tending to open up the family house to public gaze, is discussed in language which anticipates the later theme, in *The Theory of Communicative Action*, of the 'colonization' of the lifeworld by the market economy and legal-bureaucratic regulation.

In *Structural Transformation*, however, Habermas focuses on the role of publicity and public opinion in these changed conditions. The principle of critical publicity gets watered down as it expands into wider and wider areas of modern life. The reading public, which had prefigured the political public, also prefigures the latter's decline into 'minorities of specialists who put their reason to use publicly and the great mass of consumers whose receptiveness is public but uncritical' (p. 175). 'Whereas the press could previously merely mediate the reasoning process of the private people who had come together in public, this reasoning is now, conversely, only formed by the mass media' (p. 188). The same is true of the political process, split between a small number of party activists and a basically inactive mass electorate; public opinion ceases to be a source of critical judgement and checks, and becomes a social-psychological variable to be manipulated. The result is a 'gap between the constitutional fiction of public opinion and the social-psychological dissolution of its concept' (p. 244; cf. section 24, pp. 236–44).

> The contradiction is obvious: a proliferation of the social conditions of private existence that are maintained and secured by public authority, and therefore ought to be clarified within the communication process of a politically autonomous public of citizens, that is, should be made a topic for public opinion. Although objectively greater demands are placed on this authority, it operates less as a *public* opinion giving a rational foundation to the exercise of political and social authority, the more it is generated for the purpose of an abstract vote that amounts to no more than an act of acclamation within a public sphere temporarily manufactured for show or manipulation. (p. 222)

Habermas writes at times of a dialectic of *Öffentlichkeit*, and it is not too far-fetched to see *Structural Transformation* as a social-scientific remake of Horkheimer and Adorno's *Dialectic of Enlightenment*.

Just as the enlightenment critique of myth turned into another myth, the principle of the bourgeois public sphere, the critical assessment of public policy in terms of rational discussion oriented to a concept of the public interest, turns into what Habermas calls a manipulated public sphere in which states and corporations use 'publicity' in the modern sense to secure for themselves a kind of plebiscitary acclamation. Habermas's version, however, is both more carefully grounded in the results of historical, sociological and political scientific research, and also somewhat less pessimistic in its conclusions. If some of his younger readers drew the conclusion that there was nothing for it but to join the SDS, Habermas envisaged certain counter-tendencies to, and opportunities in, the process he described.

When the liberal constitutional state develops into a welfare state and thus massively extends the range of its activity, 'the requirement of publicity is extended from the organs of the state to all organizations acting in relation to the state' (p. 232). These organizations are thus opened up to scrutiny by, and dialogue with, a corresponding variety of interest groups which link together members of the public concerned with specific aspects of welfare state provision.

Although the bureaucratization of administration seems, as Max Weber had noted in relation to parliamentary politics, to remove the activity of specialists from rational control, it might yet be possible to create, by means of public communication within these organizations, 'an appropriate relation between bureaucratic decision and quasi-parliamentary deliberation' (p. 234). This cautious conclusion seems to point in two main directions: (1) the critique of technocratic ideology and (2) the attempt to work out an intellectual and practical basis for public discussion and effective control of public policy. The first theme points towards Habermas's essays in *Technology and Science as Ideology* and the philosophical critique of positivism; the second theme finds its full development in *The Theory of Communicative Action* and in *Between Facts and Norms*.

Strukturwandel der Öffentlichkeit sparked off a considerable discussion in West Germany. One possible response for those who wholly accepted Habermas's diagnosis of the disintegration of the bourgeois public sphere was to join the revolutionary student movement. Along with Marcuse's *One Dimensional Man*, published in 1964 and translated into German in 1965, the book was a central text for radical critics of West German society, even after

Habermas's own relations with the student movement had become strained and discussion of his work increasingly hostile.[10]

Most critics of the book, from whatever direction, shared an anxiety at Habermas's rather idealized account of the bourgeois public sphere. Marxists pointed out its limitations in terms of class, and feminists in terms of gender, while liberal-conservative critics also tend to stress the importance of private interests as against a warmed-up notion of the general will. Wolfgang Jäger argued this in historical terms, referring especially to English interest-group politics,[11] while the system theorist Niklas Luhmann roundly dismissed, in the name of sociology, the very idea 'that the individual . . . can find something common to all humanity, that he can reach a consensus, even truth'.[12]

For all these lines of criticism, the historical doubts feed into a critique of Habermas's diagnosis of the present and his proposed solutions. For the liberal-conservatives, the present situation is not as bad as Habermas, following too closely the old Frankfurt critique of the 'culture industry', presents it; and his alternatives are utopian, if not Jacobin or terroristic. For Luhmann, for example, public opinion as a sphere of communication becomes, like most things, more and more differentiated, specialized, institutionalized and professionalized. It is no longer appropriate, if it ever was, to think in terms of a subject of public opinion, the 'public' whose opinion it is claimed to be. For Marxist critics, Habermas's account is either just insufficiently materialist, too concerned with 'superstructural' issues or, in the more positive critique presented by Oskar Negt and Alexander Kluge,[13] insufficiently sensitive to the prospects for the promotion of an alternative, proletarian public sphere.

Feminist critiques of Habermas appeared rather later, and thus tended to focus more on his recent work than on *Structural Transformation*. Feminists have pointed out that Habermas's 'sex-blind' categories fail to thematize the exclusion of women from the bourgeois public sphere and, more generally, the gender dimension of the public – private split. For some critics, this leads into a far-reaching and powerful critique of the abstract character of the Enlightenment (and Habermasian) model of the egalitarian interaction of rational citizens. This 'excludes bodily and affective particularity, as well as the concrete histories of individuals that make groups unable to understand one another'.[14] The feminist critique of Habermas's theorization of the private–public division takes on a new form in relation to the opposition between 'system' and 'lifeworld', which is the dominant motif of Habermas's later work, and the contrast between an abstract ethics of duty and one which is grounded more substantially in notions of human community and solidarity.

I shall not discuss these three lines of criticism in detail here. Luhmann's sceptical position has been a major preoccupation for Habermas, both in his exchange at the beginning of the seventies[15] and in substantial discussions in *The Theory of Communicative Action* and *The Philosophical Discourse of Modernity*, as well as in shorter essays such as 'Can complex societies construct a rational identity?' As we shall see, Habermas takes Luhmann very seriously indeed. His own rejection of neo-Marxist 'praxis philosophy' is based in good part on a Luhmannian doubt about the possibility of collective self-reflection – though Habermas continues to see a problem here, where Luhmann's 'sociological enlightenment' suggests that one should simply reformulate the problem in terms of institutional specialization and technocratic management.

The negative Marxist critique which saw Habermas as just another bourgeois ideologist has lost what credibility it ever had with the demise of Marxism-Leninism, at least in Europe, as a political project. The more positive approach of looking towards the growth of a proletarian public sphere also seems less promising than it did in the 1970s. A more fruitful prospect is provided by the new social movements, though their 'alternative public sphere' is hardly distinct from that of the wider society and the movements' efficacy depends largely on this close interaction.[16]

At a more empirical level, it is clear that Habermas's thinking about the mass media was heavily influenced by *Dialectic of Enlightenment*'s model of the 'culture industry' and other models dominant in the 1960s. Media analysts have moved away from the conception of the public as passive recipients of commercial and political messages, as Habermas himself has noted in his occasional references to this issue, notably in his introduction to the second German edition of *Structural Transformation*. If this has taken some of the sting out of Habermas's critique of the disintegration of the public sphere, his diagnosis of the limitations of mass representative democracy seems as relevant as ever. Although rather few politically active members of modern societies would uphold the ideas of council democracy or radical participatory models in the way that was common in the 1960s and 1970s, these themes have had a substantial influence on thinking about ways in which representative democracy might be radicalized and developed.

In his introduction to the second German edition, Habermas takes up the question of the exclusion of sub-bourgeois strata and women from the liberal public sphere. He concedes that he might have said more about the existence of various forms of 'plebeian' public sphere, and notes that the exclusion of subordinate strata from the bourgeois public sphere leads paradoxically to the latter's pluralization, thus casting further doubt on his tendency to present it as a homogeneous entity. This process of exclusion remains fundamentally different, he insists, from that found in the 'representative' public sphere of traditional societies, in which the people are merely a background to royal, ecclesiastical and aristocratic displays of status.[17]

The exclusion of women, Habermas now believes, had more radical consequences. Just as popular culture, as described by Mikhail Bakhtin, operated as a counter-culture to the hierarchical and disciplined official culture, so the exclusion of women defined the public and private sphere in gendered terms, showing up the former as based on a 'fraternal' social contract, in Carole Pateman's phrase.[18] As his work moved on, Habermas did not respond systematically to criticisms of *Structural Transformation* until the publication of the second edition, but the main critical thrust of the book will be seen to return throughout his later work, notably *Legitimation Crisis, On the Reconstruction of Historical Materialism, The Theory of Communicative Action* and *Between Facts and Norms.*

Theory and practice

Habermas's first volume of essays, *Theory and Practice*, was published in 1963 and contains material written over the previous six or seven years. [19] In the preface, Habermas described these studies as 'historical preliminaries to a systematic investigation of the relationship between theory and practice in the social sciences'. In the introduction to the fourth edition, he describes them somewhat more ambitiously as an attempt 'to develop the idea of a theory of society conceived with a practical intention, and to delimit its status with respect to theories of different origins' (p. 1).

Taken as a whole, the book has three main themes which recur in Habermas's later work: (1) a critical evaluation of the Marxist tradition; (2) some reflections on the possibility of what he later called the 'reconstruction' of historical materialism; (3) a methodological comparison between the unity of empirical and normative, or technical and 'practical' issues to be found in Aristotle, in natural-law theory and in Marxism, and the scientistic, ostensibly value-free approach of the modern social sciences. The second and third of these themes lead us into Habermas's subsequent work, where they are more systematically discussed; his early account of Marxism is, however, of considerable interest in delimiting his attitude to this body of theory.

The essay 'Between philosophy and science: Marxism as critique' begins with 'four facts' often held to count 'against Marx'. First, the interpenetration of state and society in organized capitalism means that one can on longer treat political phenomena as simply dependent on an economic base. Second, the very widespread increase in prosperity in these societies means that 'the interest in the emancipation of society can no longer be articulated directly in economic terms' (p. 195). The crude power relation embodied in the wage labour contract has been overlaid by more complex forms of indirect manipulation. Therefore, thirdly, 'the designated executor of a future socialist revolution, the proletariat *as* proletariat, has been dissolved . . . the exclusion from control over the means of production is no longer bound up to such an extent with deprivation that this objective situation would still in any way be expressed subjectively as proletarian' (p. 196). Finally, Soviet Marxism, in both theoretical and practical forms, has 'paralysed' 'systematic discussion of Marxism, and with Marxism' (p. 197).

These phenomena (noted long before in the earlier phase of critical theory) 'form an insuperable barrier to any theoretical acceptance of Marxism' (p. 198), and perhaps also to the 'hidden orthodoxy' (p. 203) which applies Marxist value theory to the cultural sphere.[20] But Habermas is equally hostile to the attempt, represented here by Schumpeter, to separate Marxism into economics, sociology, philosophy and political prescription. This kind of asset stripping 'only ends up with *disjecta membra*, torn out of the context of a theory envisaging society as a totality and related to practice' (p. 205). The concept of society as a totality unites 'the economic and sociological aspects', but Marxism contains two further themes:

> the dialectical conception of society as a historical process . . . which in the conflict of specifiable tendencies drives forward to produce one situation out of the other; and finally, a relation between theory and praxis which Marxism explicitly incorporates into reflection. For Marxism's structure, from the perspective of the philosophy of sci-

ence, corresponds to that of a philosophy of history with practical intentions. (p. 205)

It therefore cannot be reduced to 'pure' science, nor to 'pure' philosophy, but lies somewhere in between.[21] Thus it takes up the philosophical concept of critique; it is 'explicitly undertaken with political aims, and yet scientifically falsifiable'.

It is the latter point which comes to the fore in Habermas's exposition of Marxism. The politicization of capitalist economies renders the base–superstructure distinction 'problematic' (p. 235), and thus raises problems for Marxism seen as a science, but a second area of difficulty concerns the conception that Marx's critique of ideology is nothing more than a *science*. The dependence of ideas on interests arising from a system of production is originally a dialectical notion, linking ideas and material interests in a model of the process of social reproduction. But Engels, and Marx from 1859 onwards, turn this into a naturalistic theory. Thus 'the correct ideology was distinguished from the false solely according to the criteria of a realist theory of knowledge' (p. 238).[22] Marxism, in other words, failed to uphold its 'philosophical' content in setting itself up as one positive science among others. 'Marx never explicitly asked himself the epistemological question concerning the conditions of the possibility of a philosophy of history with a political intent' (p. 242).

This conception forms the basis of what Habermas later came to call the reconstruction of historical materialism. The 'presuppositions of a materialist philosophy of history' are, at their most general, 'the consciousness of global unity which arose in the eighteenth century' (pp. 249–50) and, secondly, the idea, coming from Vico and Hegel, that 'Human beings can only rationally appropriate their history insofar as it is their own work' (p. 250). These two themes are now more compelling than ever in the age of nuclear weapons: 'mankind has never before been confronted so sharply by the irony of a capacity to make its own history, yet still deprived of control over it. . . . On the other hand . . . the framework which philosophy has taken over from theology, of history as totality, becomes questionable' (p. 251). The unity of history is a fiction, as is that of a unified historical subject.[23]

An important element of Habermas's reformation of Marxism is the distinction between work and interaction. Hegel's early lectures in Jena, Habermas argues, contain a valuable model of 'the interrelation of work and interaction' (p. 159) which is abandoned in his later works. At this time, Hegel was studying political economy, and Marxist commentators have welcomed the concrete and almost materialist emphasis at this stage of his work, before he came to treat real-world processes as mere aspects of the self-development of mind or spirit (*Geist*). In Hegel's early work, it is, so to speak, the other way round:

> it is not the spirit in the absolute movement of reflecting on itself which manifests itself in, among other things, language, labor, and moral relationships, but rather, it is the dialectical interconnection between linguistic symbolization, labor and interaction which determine the concept of spirit. (p. 143)

Work and interaction, the latter analysed in terms of a struggle for recognition,[24] are two interrelated processes by which human beings come to terms with external nature and internal or human nature. Whereas Kant's principles of moral action are those which a human subject can adopt on his or her own or, as Habermas puts it, 'monologically', morality for Hegel involves the mutual recognition of socialized human beings; this, rather than an abstract 'practical reason', is the real source of ethical norms.[25] Already at this early stage in Habermas's work we find him distinguishing between strategic action, including both the self-interested action of *homo economicus* and, 'as a special case', moral action as described by Kant on the one hand, and 'communicative actions under common traditions' on the other (p. 151).

This distinction between work and interaction runs right through Habermas's writings; it also forms, along with the methodological issues discussed above, the main structuring element of Habermas's critical appropriation of Marxism. Marx, in Habermas's view, reduces communicative action to 'instrumental action, the productive activity which regulates the material interchange of the human species with its natural environment' (p. 169). This encourages a 'misinterpretation' of Marxism in terms of a mechanistic relationship between forces and relations of production which affects it both as an explanatory theory and as a theory of human liberation:

> to set free the technical forces of production . . . is not identical with the development of norms which could fulfill the dialectic of moral relationships in an interaction free of domination. . . . *Liberation from hunger and misery* does not necessarily converge with *liberation from*

servitude and degradation; for there is no automatic developmental relation between labour and interaction. (p. 169)[26]

Habermas's relationship to Marxism may perhaps best be described as one of positive critique. It embodies a qualified acceptance of historical materialism and the Marxist project of human liberation. This is, however, coupled with a strong sense of what has changed since Marx's time, putting his substantive analyses in need of major revision, and a rejection of two sets of reductionist tendencies within Marxism; first, its methodological or metatheoretical reduction to science; second, its theoretical reduction to a technological determinism which replaces Marx's dialectical conception of the interrelation between forces and relations of production.

Although the work/interaction distinction runs through Habermas's work, and is most systematically expressed in *The Theory of Communicative Action*, in the contrast between strategic and communicative action, it is worth noting here some of the criticisms which have been addressed to it. First, one may question the value of separating out in this way two elements which are fused together in the Marxian concept of praxis; these doubts are shared by orthodox Marxists and, for example, by Anthony Giddens.[27] Second, McCarthy and other critics have pointed to ambiguities in Habermas's formulations; in particular, he tends to slide between the common-sense notions of work and interaction as concrete forms of human activity and a more abstract conception of them. ('By "work" or *purposive-rational action* I understand either instrumental action or rational choice or their conjunction.'[28]) In a third line of criticism, which I shall discuss in more detail later and which goes to the heart of Habermas's project, Giddens argues that Habermas's concept of communicative action is too closely related to speech and to normative frameworks, and insufficiently oriented to 'the production and reproduction of society'. This omission Giddens calls the 'absent core in Habermas' writings'. And, although Habermas denies Giddens's charge that he assimilates the work/interaction distinction to that between forces and relations of production, his gloss on relations of production seems likely only to reinforce Giddens's anxiety: 'They make up the core component of a political, legal and social order that provides contexts for action orientated to reaching understanding.'[29]

Axel Honneth, in an article published (in *New German Critique*) in the same year as Giddens's, usefully locates Habermas's account of the concept of work in the context of twentieth-century social theory, in which the degradation of work in Taylorism is parallelled by a theoretical abandonment of the notion found in Marx (especially in his earlier writings) of work as self-fulfilment. At first sight this might seem a welcome exercise in demythologization on the part of people whose preferred form of work involves reading and, from time to time, speaking and writing. And there is surely much to be said for the view that what people value in their work is often precisely its communicative aspect. The force of Honneth's point emerges in its negative form, when he points to the very substantial resistance offered to the rationalization of work processes where this involves a reduction in the workers' autonomy in the direction of their work. The resistance to external interference with one's work is a form of 'practical rationality' which 'corresponds neither to the logic of acts of communication arrived at the coordination of actions via mutual understanding, nor to the logic of instrumental actions aimed at the technical domination of actual processes'.[30]

Whatever the analytical merits, then, of Habermas's categories of instrumental and stratetic action, they do not amount, as they might have seemed to in his earlier writings, to a concept of work.[31] And, whatever may have been said about the end of the 'work society' and the decreasing importance of work for social identities,[32] it remains a central aspect of life for most people. Honneth puts it neatly:

> The foundation of historical materialism upon communication theory has at least the advantage of diverting attention to the structures of an evolutionary process of communicative liberation which is no longer attributable to a specific class. But its categorial weakness, as I see it, is that its basic concepts are laid out from the beginning as though the process of liberation from alienated work relations, which Marx had had in mind, were already historically complete.[33]

Having noted these objections, it is worth recalling the central purpose which the work/interaction distinction serves, for better or worse, in Habermas's work. McCarthy expresses it well:

> The point of insisting on the 'heterogeneity' or 'irreducibility' of work and interaction is to avoid just that conflation of *techne* and *praxis*, of technical progress and the rational conduct of life, that we found to be at the roots of the technocratic ideology. Rationalization is not emancipation. The growth of productive forces and adminis-

trative efficiency does not of itself lead to the replacement of institutions based on force by an organization of social relations bound to
communication free from domination. The ideals of the technical
mastery of history and of liberation from the quasi-natural forces of
social and political domination, as well as the means for their realization, are fundamentally different. For this reason it is of decisive
importance for a critical theory of society that the different dimensions of social practice be made explicit; only then can we comprehend their inter-dependence.[34]

This passage both marks the status of the work/interaction distinction in relation to the overall purpose of Habermas's historical
essays and points us forward to the reflections on positivism and
technocracy which form the subject of the next chapter.

2

Scientism in Theory and Practice

Habermas inherited from the first generation of critical theorists a concern with the dominance of instrumental reason. In the more limited sense of the technocratic manipulation of public opinion, this forms a main theme of *The Structural Transformation of the Public Sphere*. Habermas's work of the middle and late 1960s is centrally concerned with the philosophical and sociological issues raised by scientism, the reduction of all knowledge to that furnished by the empirical sciences, where these are conceived as an unproblematic reflection of reality.[1] At the theoretical end of the spectrum, we have his contributions to the 'positivism dispute', his 'literature review' on *The Logic of the Social Sciences* and his major historical and philosophical study, *Knowledge and Human Interests*. In a more 'applied' mode, there are the essays in *Technik und Wissenschaft als Ideologie*, published in English in *Toward a Rational Society*. This separation is, however, only an approximate one, and several works span both areas: notably the essay from *Theory and Practice* entitled 'Dogmatism, reason and decision: on theory and practice in a scientized civilization'. I shall look first at Habermas's more practically oriented essays, then at the methodological issues in the 'positivism dispute' and the 'logic of the social sciences', and finally at Habermas's more systematic discussion in *Knowledge and Human Interests*, which in a sense brings to a close this period of his work.

Students of the sociology of science are often disappointed to find that Habermas has relatively little to say about science and technology as such. His assertion that in advanced industrial societies

science and technology have become a (or even the) leading productive force, whatever its consequences for more orthodox versions of Marxism, is not particularly contentious; nor is his claim
that 'science, technology, industry and administration interlock in a
circular process.'[2] Habermas's concern, as the titles of his essays
indicate, is with scient*ism* rather than science as such, with the
relation between theory and practice in a scientific civilization, between technical progress and the social lifeworld, with the
'scientization' of politics and with technology and science as ideology. His position is best understood as a left critique of theories of
technocracy current in West Germany in the 1950s and 1960s.[3] The
'technocracy thesis' associated with Hans Freyer and Helmut
Schelsky was that technological development is an autonomous
and self-sustaining process, setting its own goals and applications:
'Political norms and laws are replaced by objective exigencies of
scientific-technical civilization. . . . In place of the political will of
the people emerges an objective exigency, which man produces
himself as science and labor.'[4]

Not surprisingly, Habermas firmly rejects this notion, arguing
that it 'serves in the end merely to conceal pre-existing, unreflected
social interests and prescientific decisions.[5]' In other words, it is an
ideology:

> technology and science themselves in the form of a positivistic way
> of thinking, articulated as technocratic consciousness, began to take
> the role of a substitute ideology for the demolished bourgeois
> ideologies. . . . [What Horkheimer and Adorno called the dialectic of
> enlightenment] has been refined by Marcuse as the thesis that tech-
> nology and science themselves become ideological.[6]

Marcuse, however, puts too much weight on science and technology as intrinsically linked to domination, so that 'social emancipation could not be conceived without a complementary
revolutionary transformation of science and technology themselves'.[7] But the idea which Marcuse flirts with, of a science which
'would arrive at essentially different concepts of nature and establish essentially different facts',[8] is not just utopian but categorically
impossible; it confuses the sphere of symbolic interaction, possible
only with human partners, and that of work or purposive-rational
action.[9] Rightly or wrongly, Habermas believes that modern natural
science is 'inherently oriented to possible technical control'.[10] What
is at issue, rather, is how the rationality of science and technology
has come to pervade the whole of our world.[11]

It is only later, in the *Theory of Communicative Action*, that Habermas fully works out the implications of this project, and then in a form which puts science and technology somewhat into the background compared to more general processes of market and administrative rationalization. For the present, he concentrates on two more specific issues, the nature of technocratic ideology and the scientization of politics.

'Technocratic consciousness' is 'less ideological than all previous ideologies', since it does not simply falsify reality to serve particular interests, yet it also is 'more irresistible and farther-reaching than ideologies of the old type . . . it not only justifies a *particular class's* interest in domination and represses *another class's* partial need for emancipation, but affects the human race's emancipatory interest as such.'[12] It does this by the scientization of politics, the transformation of practical, i.e. moral-political questions, into technical ones. In technocratic politics, 'The depoliticization of the mass of the population and the decline of the public realm as a political institution are components of a system of domination that tends to exclude practical questions from public discussion.'[13]

It might seem that the next step to take would be to investigate the possibilities for the diffusion of scientific competence and the reanimation of the public sphere and democratic control. Habermas briefly canvasses these possibilities at the end of the essay on the 'scientization of politics', but in an indecisive and rather negative manner. The main thrust of his work in this period takes two other, complementary directions: the historical critique of positivism and a more specific examination of methodological issues in the social sciences, with the aim of developing a concept of emancipatory social science which might unite reason and interest and underpin an alternative conception of the relation between theory and practice.[14]

Although Habermas has since come to view *Knowledge and Human Interests* as something of a detour, it is easy to see why he felt compelled to offer a fuller critique of positivism than is provided in his two contributions to the positivism dispute[15] and the various essays in *Theory and Practice* and *Technik und Wissenschaft als Ideologie*. It was important to show that the positivist conception of science, which excludes ideas of critique and emancipation, was not after all obligatory.[16]

Thus although 'The positivistically cleansed demarcation set between knowing and evaluating . . . represents less a result than a problem',[17] in that it makes values the objects of arbitrary decisions or reduces them to imperatives arising from the need for survival, we cannot simply ignore the fact–value distinction and return to earlier traditions, such as those of Hegelian philosophy and political theory.

The logic of the social sciences

Habermas has always been even more than usually modest about his book *On the Logic of the Social Sciences*, resisting its republication for some time on the grounds that one should not confuse processes of self-clarification with their results.[18] In fact, however, the book is more than just a superb survey of the state of social scientific methodology in the mid-1960s; it remains an important contribution to subsequent debates.

Habermas believes that, while the traditional discussion in Germany about the differences between the human sciences and the sciences of nature has rightly been abandoned, it points to the ongoing conflict in the social sciences of 'heterogeneous aims and approaches'.[19] The positivist thesis of unified science, which assimilates all the sciences to a natural-scientific model, fails, in Habermas's view, because of the intimate relationship between the social sciences and history, and the fact that they are based on 'a situation-specific understanding of meaning that can be explicated only "hermeneutically"'.[20] As he put it some ten years later, 'access to a symbolically prestructured reality cannot be gained by observation alone.'[21]

This also rules out the possibility of methodological dualism, the separation and peaceful coexistence of the natural and the human sciences, since the social sciences have to 'resolve the tension between the two approaches under one roof'.[22] The book might therefore be described as a positive critique of interpretative sociological methodologies. Like his friend Karl-Otto Apel, whose short monograph *Analytic Philosophy of Language and the Geisteswissenschaften* had appeared in 1965,[23] Habermas was struck by the convergence between Wittgenstein's later philosophy, whose implications for the social sciences had been brought out by Peter Winch,[24] and the German tradition of the human sciences or *Geisteswissenschaften*, now put into a Heideggerian philosophical framework by Hans-Georg Gadamer.[25] The phenomenological philosophy of Edmund Husserl had also been brought into the centre of sociological debate by the republication in 1960 and the English translation in 1967 of

Alfred Schutz's *Phenomenology of the Social World*[26] and the publication, also in the early 1960s, of his *Collected Papers*.[27]

Schutz's major work was subtitled 'An introduction to *verstehende* sociology', and can be understood as answering the question how a sociology of the kind advocated by Max Weber is possible. Schutz's answer, in a nutshell, is that the 'ideal types' of understandable human action used by the Weberian social scientist are based on processes of typification carried out in everyday social life by ordinary members of society. The social world is 'constructed' out of action based on these typifications, as when you go into a shop and correctly distinguish between the sales assistants and the other customers. The phenomenological sociology of everyday life, which has affinities with the earlier and continuing pragmatist tradition of symbolic interactionism, was continued and developed, by Harold Garfinkel and others, in 'ethnomethodology' and 'cognitive sociology'.

From Wittgenstein, via Winch, comes the related notion of 'language-games' embedded in forms of life. To understand the sentence 'God will forgive you for laughing during mass' is to be able to step, however provisionally, into a universe of religious discourse and practice. (A strict logical positivist would of course reject such a statement as meaningless, in the absence of any possible evidence for this claim and for its presuppositions.) Finally, Gadamer's reinterpretation of hermeneutics stresses the element of existential encounter involved in understanding texts or other people: a 'fusion of horizons' between our background assumptions and theirs. We understand the Other, so far as we do, from within our own framework or 'tradition', whose 'pre-judgements' or 'prejudices' are not just obstacles to our understanding but, when reflected on, a possible means towards it. We cannot jump out of our tradition into a pure, value-free state of immaculate perception.

The major part of Habermas's text is concerned with these three principal modern approaches to *verstehende* sociology: phenomenological (Schutz), linguistic (Winch) and hermeneutic (Gadamer). Each of these approaches goes beyond or transcends the previous one(s). In the phenomenological approach to the constitution of meaning in everyday life, 'Language has not yet been understood as the web to whose threads the subjects hang and through which they develop into subjects in the first place.'[28] Similarly, Winch's linguistic approach neglects the Gadamerian requirement to mediate between alternative frameworks. Winch seems to envisage that the linguistic analyst, 'from his free-floating position, can slip into the grammar of any language game without himself being bound by the dogmatism of his own language game, which would be obligatory for linguistic analysis as such'.[29]

The phenomenological and linguistic variants of *verstehende* sociology are often loosely described as 'hermeneutics', and they certainly seem at first sight to correspond to the requirements of a hermeneutically orientated approach to the social world. They are, however, vulnerable to a broadly based hermeneutic critique which argues, in essence, that their conception of meaning is too restricted and that they do not do justice to the hermeneutic basis of social theory.

Symbolic interactionalism, for example, focuses, as the term implies, on interaction; structural aspects of social life are overlooked. Conversely, in the 'phenomenological' tradition, the focus is on cognitive phenomena, the relation between different typifications, such as that the whole enterprise comes to resemble a sociology of knowledge and, in Peter Berger and Thomas Luckmann's *Social Construction of Reality* (1967), is explicitly presented as such. The related approach recommended by Wittgenstein and Winch brings out more sharply one of the problems which arise here: a language-game with its associated view of the world is not a cab which one can get in and out of at will. The hermeneutic process is not the replacement of the interpreter's 'horizon' by that of the object of study, but a dialogical process in which the two horizons are fused together.

This upshot of the hermeneutic critique of *verstehende* sociology is that it must broaden its concept of meaning and recognize the importance of interactive frameworks of meaning. In other words, hermeneutic theorists object to an exclusively subject–object conception of science. But even a broadened hermeneutic approach is not enough on its own. 'Hermeneutic consciousness remains incomplete as long as it does not include a reflection upon the limits of hermeneutic understanding.'[30] These limits are of two related kinds. First, there is the general problem of the 'linguistic idealism' built into hermeneutics, which neglects the fact that language is not just a means of communication which mediates our experience of the world, but is 'also a medium of domination and social power'.[31] 'Sociology may therefore not be reduced to interpretive sociology.'[32] This limit to hermeneutic interpretation manifests itself at a more specific level in relation to what Habermas calls 'systematically distorted communication', exemplified in the psychoanalytic concept of repressed motives. 'In deciphering repressed intentions as unconscious motives, linguistic analysis transcends the dimension of subjectively intended meaning and cultural tradition.'[33]

Habermas believes that this specific problem of distortion can and must be generalized into an awareness of the dependence of language and language-use on broader social processes. 'Hermeneutic experience, encountering this dependence of symbolic context on actual (*faktisch*) relations, becomes a critique of ideology.'[34] He had already claimed that a revival of the public sphere, and a more satisfactory relationship between science and politics, required the organization of social communication in a way approximating to an unconstrained dialogue. He now points to the need to remove internal constraints in that dialogue, in a way which looks forward to what Albrecht Wellmer has called his 'linguistic turn'.[35] But Habermas at this stage is also looking backwards to the formulations of *Theory and Practice*, in his assertion that 'the practical connection between understanding and the initial hermeneutic situation of the interpreter requires a hypothetical anticipation of a philosophy of history with practical intent.'[36]

Knowledge and Human Interests

So far in this chapter I have examined Habermas's anxieties about the way in which scientism undermines the prospects of rational politics in modern societies, and his attempt to demonstrate that the social sciences require a non-scientistic methodology. It should now be easier to see why he felt the need to develop the systematic critique of positivism which he offers in *Knowledge and Human Interests*.[37] It is less clear why he wrote the book in a historical form, though after the publication of *The Theory of Communicative Action* one begins to suspect that this is simply Habermas's preferred mode of operation.[38] There are also, however, more systematic reasons for starting, as he does, with Kant and Hegel. As he puts it in the 1982 preface to *On the Logic of the Social Sciences*, his 'appropriation' of hermeneutics and linguistic analysis had convinced him 'that critical social theory had to break free from the conceptual apparatus of the philosophy of consciousness (*Bewusstseinsphilosophie*) flowing from Kant and Hegel'.[39] Nevertheless, he had made his own way into critical theory through the philosophical tradition[40] and drawn a parallel between critical theory's critique of positivism and Marx's critique of idealism.[41]

Moreover, the positivist reduction of epistemology or the theory of knowledge to methodology or the theory of science means that 'it generally has regressed beyond the level of reflection represented by Kant's philosophy'.[42] 'Retreading this path from a perspective that looks back toward the point of departure may help to recover the forgotten experience of reflection. That we disavow reflection is positivism.'[43]

The theory of 'cognitive' or 'knowledge-guiding' interests is set out in Habermas's Frankfurt inaugural lecture of 1965, printed as an appendix to the English-language edition of *Knowledge and Human Interests*. The underlying structure is again the dichotomy between work and interaction, augmented with the third basic action-form which Habermas had already invoked: power or domination. Thus the natural sciences or, more broadly, the 'empirical-analytical sciences' are governed by a 'technical' interest in the prediction and control of objectified processes: 'the facts relevant to the empirical sciences are first constituted through an a priori organization of experience in the behavioural system of instrumental action.'[44] The historical-hermeneutic sciences are governed by a 'practical' interest in intersubjective understanding. Finally, critical sciences, such as psychoanalysis and the critique of ideology, are oriented to emancipation from 'ideologically frozen relations of dependence that can in principle be transformed.'[45]

Thus 'Orientation toward technical control, toward mutual understanding in the conduct of life, and toward emancipation from seemingly 'natural' constraint establish the specific viewpoints from which we can apprehend reality as such in any way whatsoever.'[46] These interests must not be confused with contingent and partial influences (Stalinism and Lysenko, the Nazis and 'German physics', and so on) against which science, according to Habermas, should be vigilant; they are 'fundamental interests to which it owes not only its impetus but the *conditions of possible objectivity* themselves'.[47] To be aware of the conditions of objectivity, and indeed of the constitution of objects in the foundation of scientific concepts, is to go beyond the objectivism which Habermas identifies, not just in the natural sciences but also in historicist hermeneutics, where it 'conceals the complex of historical influences in which historical consciousness itself stands.'[48] The term 'objectivism' is taken from Husserl,[49] but objectivism cannot be overcome, as Husserl thought, by bridging the gap between the sciences and everyday consciousness with a philosophy which shows that the former are grounded in the intentional acts of the latter. Instead, epistemology must become social theory. 'Philosophy remains true to its classic tradition by renouncing it.'[50]

In place of philosophy as traditionally conceived, Habermas offers a theory which spans philosophy and philosophical anthropology.[51]

> the interests constitutive of knowledge are linked to the functions of an ego that adapts itself to its external conditions through learning processes, is initiated into the communication system of a life-world by means of self-formative processes, and constructs an identity in the conflict between instinctual aims and social constraints. In turn these achievements become part of the productive forces accumulated by a society, the cultural tradition through which a society interprets itself, and the legitimations that a society accepts or criticizes . . . knowledge-constructive interests take form in the medium of work, language and power.[52]

To anticipate a theme which I shall address a little later in the chapter, it should already be clear that the status of the emancipatory interest is set rather differently from the other two, for at least two reasons. First, what corresponds to the work/interaction distinction is an almost exhaustive division between the sciences; in other words, almost all the sciences we have fall into one or the other category in Habermas's model. Emancipatory theory, by contrast, seems more like an empty box containing promissory notes on behalf of psychoanalysis and Marxism – neither of them, to put it mildly, solidly established as sciences.

The second peculiarity about the emancipatory interest is that it is not grounded *in* power, either in the general sense of a capacity to transform the natural and social world[53] or in a Nietzschean conception of life as basically consisting in a struggle for power. The emancipatory interest is directed *against* power in the sense of unjustified domination – establishing a court before which power has to justify itself, if it can.

It might seem, then, that the emancipatory interest is a little insubstantial. Habermas grounds it in the lecture in a passage which anticipates the greater weight placed upon language and then upon communication in general in his later work.

> The human interest in autonomy and responsibility is not mere fancy, for it can be apprehended a priori. What raises us out of nature

is the only thing whose nature we can know: language. Through its structure, autonomy and responsibility are posited for us. Our first sentence expresses unequivocally the intention of a universal and unconstrained consensus.[54]

While Habermas does not discuss, in *Knowledge and Human Interests*, 'the objective context in which the development of the philosophy from Hegel to Nietzsche took place',[55] he emphasizes that the development of science and technology is reflected in the way that the relative positions of philosophy and science have been reversed. Whereas philosophy previously marked out the legitimate place of science within knowledge as a whole,

> the philosophy of science that has emerged since the mid-nineteenth century as the heir of the theory of knowledge is methodology pursued with a scientistic self-understanding of the sciences. 'Scientism' means science's belief in itself: that is the conviction that we can no longer understand science as one form of possible knowledge, but rather must identify knowledge with science.[56]

But the move in philosophical thought from epistemology to methodology cannot simply be reversed, but instead must be reconstructed to create a more adequate basis for understanding the present system of the sciences.

> a future systematic investigation of the basis in interests of scientific knowledge cannot abstractly restore epistemology. Instead it can only return to a dimension that was first opened up by Hegel through the radical self-critique of epistemology and then once again obstructed.[57]

The underlying plot of this story is a fairly simple one. Hegel points out, against Kant, that an investigation of the faculty of knowledge cannot operate in isolation from the knowledge we already have, and thus from the general progress of the human mind in its practical activity. Hegel, however, abandoned this approach, found in his early works and taken up by Marx, for a speculative concept of philosophical science which real science 'had to unmask . . . as bare fiction. It was this that served as the foundation-stone of positivism. Only Marx could have contested its victory.'[58]

Marx naturalizes knowledge as part of general human activity or practice. But Marx's double reduction, of practice to work rather than work plus interaction, and hence of 'natural science' and 'the science of man' to a single science, breaks the connection between the critique of knowledge and social criticism. 'By equating critique with natural science, he disavowed it. Materialist scientism only reconfirms what absolute idealism had already accomplished: the elimination of epistemology in favour of unchained universal "scientific knowledge" – but this time of scientific materialism instead of absolute knowledge.'[59]

This is, of course, more a matter of Marx's self-understanding, his largely implicit philosophy of science, than his substantive work. At the former level, however, Marx converges with Comte's positivist conception of a natural science of society, social physics or sociology. In Comtean or Machian positivism, 'Objectivism . . . limits access to reality to the dimension established by the scientific system of reference through the methodical objectification of reality.'[60]

What is needed, then, is some systematic reflection on the production process of science as a human life-activity. The American pragmatist C. S. Peirce did this for the natural sciences; the German philosopher-historian Wilhelm Dilthey did it for the human sciences. For both, in different ways, the concept of life plays a key role. For Peirce, 'the wonderful success of modern science' is grounded in 'the concrete life of the men who are working to find out the truth'.[61] Similarly, for Dilthey, life interprets itself: 'The human sciences are all founded in lived experience, in the expressions of these experiences, and in the understanding of these expressions.'[62] Peirce's pragmatism is transcendental. In 'the process of inquiry' we constitute reality as established scientific facts.[63] Thus Peirce goes beyond an 'objectivist attitude',[64] but he does not pay sufficient attention to the difference between the scientific community, operating in terms of symbolic action, and the material world which it studies 'from the point of view of possible technical control'.[65] In purging metaphysics from the human mind, Peirce ends up by assimilating beliefs to other processes in the external world, in a monological conception of human learning (children touching stoves and so forth), and neglecting the 'communicative action' of the community of scientists.[66]

In Dilthey's account of the human sciences, by contrast, this context of communication plays a central part. Understanding takes place within a shared framework of ways of life, and builds on this.[67] Thus Dilthey brings out, for Habermas, the way in which 'In its very structure hermeneutic understanding is designed to guarantee, within cultural traditions, the possible action-orientated self-understanding of individuals and groups as well as reciprocal understanding between different individuals and groups.'[68] But Dilthey is too concerned with establishing the objectivity of the human sciences, which he presents, like Max Weber, as a permanent demand on the self-discipline of the researchers who 'must set themselves this aim ever more consciously and critically'.[69]

Thus, like Peirce, he remains affected by an objectivism which blocks self-reflection, defined as a process 'in which the interpreter reflects on the object and himself at the same time as movements of an objective structure that likewise encompasses both and makes them possible.'[70] We therefore need to go beyond Dilthey to Gadamer's philosophical hermeneutics,[71] and further still to an examination of 'the interlocking of empirical-analytic procedures with hermeneutics' in what Dilthey called the 'independently constituted' cultural sciences: linguistics, economics, and so on. These sciences are oriented to providing general theories *and* tied to the understanding of specific historical processes. Dilthey's attempts to ground them in unrealistic theories of 'life' are unconvincing. Habermas suggests that an adequate model of this type of theory can be found in psychoanalysis.

In both empirical-analytic and hermeneutic science, we are dealing with 'methodological rules for the organization of processes of inquiry.'[72] In a formulation which he later comes to recognize as problematical, Habermas calls these rules 'quasi-transcendental':

> They have a transcendental function but arise from actual structures of human life: from structures of a species that reproduces its life both through learning processes of socially organized labor and processes of mutual understanding in interactions mediated in ordinary language.[73]

Thus, although Peirce and Dilthey 'discovered the roots in interest of scientific knowledge', they did not take the further step of locating these interests 'within the conceptions of a history of the species comprehended as a self-formative process'.[74] The reflective understanding of this process is governed by a third cognitive interest, in emancipation. 'In self-reflection, knowledge for the sake of knowledge comes to coexist with the interest in autonomy and responsibility (*Mündigkeit*).'[75] Habermas traces this concept of an 'interest in reason' through Kant and Fichte, ending with an unorthodox but deeply Hegelian formulation in which it is 'Reason's interest in emancipation, which . . . aims at realizing (favourable) conditions of symbolic interaction and instrumental action; and, to this extent . . . assumes the restricted form of the practical and technical cognitive interests.'[76]

Self-reflection takes on an at least putatively scientific form in Freudian theory. Freud's 'depth hermeneutics' deals not only with misunderstandings but with self-deception.[77] Psychoanalysis, the 'talking cure', as Freud's patient Anna O. called it, is centrally oriented around self-reflection under the guidance of the analyst. Moreover, the success of this self-reflection defines the success of the analysis: 'the interpretation of a case is corroborated only by the successful continuation of a self-formative process, that is by the completion of self-reflection, and not in any unmistakable way by what the patient says or how he behaves.'[78] Finally, Habermas suggests that psychoanalysis removes quasi-natural causal disturbances of behaviour by bringing the patient to understand their origins and thereby removing, or at least weakening, their causal force. In methodological terms, it combines hermeneutic understanding and causal explanation; understanding becomes explanatory and also causally efficacious in removing the pathology.[79] Psychoanalysis is thus an 'example' of a critical science which directly combines knowledge and interest.[80]

Second thoughts

It should be clear from the above exposition that *Knowledge and Human Interests* is an enormously ambitious and challenging book, and it inspired a good deal of critical discussion.[81] Habermas has clarified his position from time to time in interviews, and more fully in his 1971 preface to *Theory and Practice*, in the 'Postscript to *Knowledge and Human Interest*', in his 'Reply to my critics'[82] and in the 'Fragment' on 'Objectivism in the social sciences.'[83]

He has also developed further some of the theories of the book, particularly in relation to hermeneutics, communication and truth. And although he now believes that 'the attempt to ground critical social theory by way of the theory of knowledge, while it did not lead astray, was indeed a roundabout way',[84] his later 'reconstructive' theory of communicative action is clearly related to the earlier project, despite differences in strategy and focus.

Habermas's qualifications and reformulations take three main directions. First, he recognizes the force of the paradox noted by Thomas McCarthy, that 'nature' cannot be both transcendentally constituted and 'the ground of the constituting subject'.[85]

Habermas's implicit response, which fits in with a broader shift of emphasis in his thought, is to scale down his epistemological claims and to put more weight on a unified relation of cognition and action.

> With regard to the constitution of the world of experience, we distinguish between two object-domains (things, events; persons, expressions), to which correspond different modes of experience (sensory, communicative), two different forms of empirical language (physical and intentional language), and two types of action (instrumental, communicative).[86]

Habermas continues occasionally to refer to the cognitive-interests model, but the emphasis seems now to be somewhat different and more clearly linked to practical issues in the use of language and the relation between 'scientific object-domains' and 'objectivations which we find pre-given in ordinary life' (*Lebenspraxis*).[87]

The second revision which Habermas introduces is to distinguish more sharply between the context of discovery and the context of justification. Despite the continuity just noted between everyday life and science, the latter involves a step back from action to discourse and the discursive testing of hypothetical claims to validity.[88] Thirdly, Habermas introduces an important differentiation into his discussion of reflection and emancipation, which clears the way for a broadening of the original tripartite division of the sciences to accommodate the 'reconstructive' theories of which his own theory of communicative action is one. As we have seen, he claimed in 1965 that critical science operates on the terrain of self-reflection, which 'releases the subject from dependence on hypostatized powers'.[89] After completing *Knowledge and Human Interests*, he realized that the term 'reflection' is traditionally used to refer both to a subject's reflection on what makes it possible for him or her to perform certain actions and to a more critical insight into the distortions built into these and other processes.[90]

The first of these processes Habermas now calls rational reconstruction, where what is reconstructed is the pre-theoretical knowledge (knowing how, in Gilbert Ryle's sense) of actors. Reconstructions, such as Noam Chomsky's linguistic theory, do not necessarily affect our practice. 'By learning logic or linguistics I acquire theoretical knowledge, but in general I do not thereby change my previous practice of reasoning or speaking.' As for reflection in the second sense, Habermas reformulates in a somewhat more cautious way the analogies drawn between psychoanalysis and collective processes of political enlightenment.[91] The latter must in turn be distinguished from 'the organization of action'.[92]

One of the elements of Habermas's theory which has attracted the most sceptical response is in fact his use of psychoanalysis as a model of a critical science. This was in part a sheer misunderstanding, arising from the juxtaposition of psychoanalysis and the critique of ideology; it seemed as if critical social theorists were being cast as social psychoanalysts in a therapeutic role *vis-à-vis* their societies. This was certainly not Habermas's intention. As the text makes fairly clear, and as he had repeatedly stressed since its publication, he was comparing relatively abstract conceptual and methodological features of the two bodies of theory. The suggestion that it was possible to identify 'systematically distorted communication' in both spheres did not mean that the mechanisms were structurally identical. And, as he put it in a recent interview, one should certainly not represent 'the addressees of critical theory, still less society itself, as a macro-subject whose eyes the theorist aims to open; in a process of enlightenment there are only participants.'[93] Nor, of course, as Russell Keat points out in his excellent book on the subject, was Habermas giving any special weight to personal psychological transformation as a political project.[94]

Bearing these distinctions in mind takes some of the sting out of the criticisms which point to the authoritarian character of psychoanalytic treatment. It remains the case, however, that Habermas offers a somewhat idealized picture of the analytic situation itself, stressing the aspects of self-reflection and enlightenment.[95] More interestingly, in relation to Habermas's theory as a whole, critics agree that he greatly overplays the theme of emancipation, where this is conceived as leaving behind the sources of distortion and, almost, the unconscious itself.[96] Finally, Habermas's account of the criteria of the validity of 'general interpretations', which stresses the rational acceptance of the interpretation by the patient him/herself, tends, as Keat shows, to run into difficult problems to do with self-fulfilling predictions.[97] Despite attempts by Brian Fay and others to defend this model,[98] it can surely not be retained in its original formulation, but at best as a reminder of an aspect of the evaluation of theories in this domain. Habermas's increasingly strong differentiation between context of discovery and context of justification seems to recognize this, though the consensus theory of truth within which he would probably now reinterpret these issues raises its own problems.

I should now like to sketch out a further line of criticism to which Habermas has not yet provided a systematic response. This concerns in particular the technical-instrumental interest ascribed to empirical science, though its ramifications go further. Habermas's characterization of empirical-analytical science as orientated to the prediction and control of objectified processes is firmly based on a positivist account of natural science, in which, as Auguste Comte put it, knowledge leads to prediction and hence to power. As various commentators have shown, this conception must be relativized in the light of the devastating critiques levelled at this positivist model.

The history of logical positivism and of what came to be called the 'standard view' in the philosophy of science is, like that of state socialist planning, in large part the history of attempts to mitigate its more obvious problems.[99] Habermas's position in the 1960s is clearly marked by the 'positivism dispute' in German sociology, in which Popper and his German followers were still trying to hold the line with a variant of the standard view which was clearly demarcated from hermeneutics, critical theory and everyday life. Since that time, and notably under the influence of Thomas Kuhn's *Structure of Scientific Revolutions*, the gradual weakening of the deductivist model of science has been complemented by a growing awareness of the role of interpretation and practical choice in the work of scientists. Once we abandon the initially tight connection between explanation and prediction, Habermas's thesis about the intrinsic link between explanation, prediction and control ceases to be a philosophical claim about the meaning of valid statements in empirical science, and becomes a sociological claim about the ways in which, and the purposes according to which, science is practised in the modern world.[100]

Positivism has an inbuilt tendency to mutate into more and more permissive forms of conventionalism which in turn invite the development of rationalist or realist alternatives in order to salvage a concept of scientific truth. Rationalism and certain versions of realism stress the necessary truth of true scientific theories, while for a more ontologically oriented, and in my view more defensible, version of realism science aims to describe the natures and causal powers of things which exist independently of our descriptions of them.[101] If realism is a *possible* theory of science, let alone a better one than the various alternatives, it becomes less easy for Habermas to establish a tight connection between the empirical claim that science and technology involve the domination of nature and the 'quasi-transcendental' claim that this orientation is what establishes the meaning of scientific statements about the natural world. If realism is a better theory of science, then the cognitive-interest model is considerably reduced in its scope.[102]

Habermas has not had a great deal to say about this issue, beyond pointing out the incompatibility of the two positions; 'any transcendental approach, in the last analysis, precludes that there can be any such thing as truthfulness to reality in the sense postulated by scientific realism.'[103] On the other hand, Habermas's quasi-transcendentalism seems to be getting less and less transcendental. He is also prone to make very strong realist claims for reconstructive sciences: whereas theoretical descriptions in empirical science may be interpreted in a realist way, reconstructions *must* be.

> Rational reconstructions . . . can reproduce the pre-theoretical knowledge that they explicate only in an essentialist sense; if they are true, they have to correspond precisely to the rules that are operatively effective in the object domain – that is, to the rules that actually determine the production of surface structures.[104]

What Habermas is doing here is to reverse the more familiar situation, in which a realist interpretation is accepted for the natural sciences but doubts are expressed about the possibility of its extension to the human and social sciences. This is based on, among other reasons, the greater apparent convergence of knowledge in the natural sciences, and the fact that a realism about natural-scientific theories (i.e. crudely that true theories describe how things actually work) is generally supported by a realism about the entities postulated by the theory (molecules, viruses, etc.).[105] In the domain of the social sciences, as I have argued elsewhere, these identifications are necessarily more tentative. While this does not mean that we must abandon the project of a realist interpretation of social science, it does suggest that it is unwise to tie oneself to particular and increasingly contentious examples, such as Chomskian linguistics, as firmly as Habermas has tended to do.

Habermas's early work in retrospect

If Habermas had given up writing at the end of the 1960s, he would already have provided a very substantial and challenging body of philosophical and sociological work. The issues he had tackled, such as the nature of modern democracy, the 'scientization' of politics and other spheres of life, the critique of positivism and the outline of an alternative philosophy of science and alternative methodological orientations for the social sciences, and, finally, the reformulation of the Marxian critique of capitalism and ideology in these new theoretical and practical conditions, were central to contemporary concerns. *Knowledge and Human Interests* is undoubtedly the crowning achievement, but while its critical part stands on its own, its positive implications amount to an enormous promissory note to fill out, some time, just what a critical social science would look like. One organizing metaphor which had been important seemed now to have been abandoned, that of the (empirically falsifiable) philosophy of history with a practical purpose.[106] The possibility of using the critical reflection on language and communication as an alternative foundation is anticipated here and there in the early work, but is nowhere spelled out.

A fixed point remains, however: Habermas's insistence on the interplay of philosophical and empirical considerations, the role of philosophy 'in communication with the sciences and effective at large'[107] or as what he later called 'placeholder and interpreter'.[108] Finally, the somewhat diffuse anxiety about 'technology', which Habermas first acquired from Heidegger and from the general postwar ambiance, has become a more focused concern with scientism. Although, as we saw, he did not discuss the 'objective context' of the development of philosophy from Hegel to Nietzsche,[109] he says enough about the changing role of scientific reasoning in modern culture to make it clear that this is a likely future theme. In 1971 Habermas moved to the Starnberg research institute, and this also marks a break in his intellectual development.

3

Communication and Discourse Ethics

Habermas's work took an important new direction in the 1970s, leading up to the publication in 1981 of *The Theory of Communicative Action*. His output in this period can be briefly summarized as follows: papers on the theory of language, communication and truth, a substantial polemic with the system theorist Niklas Luhmann, an important book on the 'crisis of legitimation' in late capitalist societies and work on the evolution of moral norms, feeding into a 'reconstruction' of historical materialism. Underlying all this was a fundamental reorientation away from classical social and political philosophy (*Theory and Practice*) and epistemological questions (*Knowledge and Human Interests*) towards a sharper focus on language and communicative action. Habermas's version of critical theory is no longer a philosophy of history with a practical purpose; it finds its starting point in a theory of communicative competence.[1]

Not that Habermas suddenly discovered the theme of communication. As we have seen, it was a substantive preoccupation in the *Structural Transformation of the Public Sphere* and in his essays on theory and practice and science and technology, and a central theoretical element in his critical appropriation of Marxism and hermeneutics. He was already claiming in 1965 that in the structure of language 'autonomy and responsibility are posited for us. Our first sentence expresses unequivocally the intention of universal and unconstrained consensus.'[2]

This theme begins to come to the fore in the essay discussed in the previous chapter which restricted 'hermeneutics' claim to universality'[3] by reference to systematically distorted communication. In that essay, he also contrasts hermeneutic reflection with the systematic reconstruction of linguistic competence, exemplified by Noam Chomsky's theory of language.[4] Hermeneutic understanding, he insists, can 'lead to the critical ascertainment of truth only to the extent to which it follows the regulative principle: to try to establish universal agreement within the framework of an unlimited community of interpreters.'[5]

Habermas developed these ideas in his essays on communicative competence[6] and theories of truth[7] and in his 1970–1 Christian Gauss Lectures at Princeton on the grounding of sociology in a theory of language.[8] The last of these texts, which relates these themes to the context of sociological theory, is of particular interest. Although Habermas, as we have seen, has now abandoned the idea of giving a linguistic foundation to social theory, this 'trial run' at the theory of communicative action or, as he called it at this time, a 'communication theory of society',[9] brings out the relevance of what might otherwise seem rather pedantic discussions of language. This phase of his work is rounded off by a somewhat later article, 'What is universal pragmatics?'[10]

As we have seen, Habermas was being pushed from a variety of directions towards a focus on intersubjectivity and mutual understanding. At the most empirical end, there was his practical concern with the possibility of rational moral and political discourse in the public sphere of modern societies. At a more methodological level, the analysis of intersubjective communication in *Knowledge and Human Interests*, and the notion of emancipation as crucially involving the demolition of systematic obstacles to understanding, had drawn rather large theoretical cheques which needed to be covered. And, at the level of fundamental theoretical strategy, the difficulty of satisfactorily representing critical theory in terms of the philosophy of history and what he has come to call the 'philosophy of the subject' may have sharpened Habermas's sense of the need for an alternative foundation. The philosophy of the subject does not offer an adequate account of communicative experience: in Richard Bernstein's phrase, it 'obscures and even blocks the way to grasping the intrinsic intersubjective and dialogical character of communicative action.'[11] Habermas therefore began to pursue a strategy of generalizing some relatively new analyses of communication into a more holistic and historical theory.

At this stage in his work, Habermas thought in terms of broadening Chomsky's theory of linguistic competence into a theory of communicative competence, a universal pragmatics which would 'allow one to find and reconstruct the systems of rules according to which we produce complexes of interaction, i.e. the symbolic reality of society itself'.[12] Universal pragmatics is distinguished from linguistics by the fact that it studies utterances rather than sentences, and from sociolinguistics by the fact that the utterances it studies are not tied to specific and variable contexts: 'The task of universal pragmatics is to identify and reconstruct universal conditions of possible understanding (*Verständigung*). . . . I take the type of action aimed at reaching understanding to be fundamental.'[13]

Acts of linguistic communication,[14] Habermas argues, presuppose four validity-claims: that what we say is comprehensible, that it is true, that it is right, i.e. that there is a normative basis for the utterance, and that it is a sincere (*wahrhaftig*) expression of the speaker's feelings. The 'background consensus' between speaker and hearer includes the fact that they implicitly make these claims and could if necessary justify them. Thus we can ask a speaker 'What do you mean?', 'Is what you say true?', 'Are you entitled to say that?' and 'Do you really mean it?' In other words, at the back of every act of communication is the implication that we could reach a consensus on the validity of these claims. Finally Habermas claims that we can only distinguish, as a matter of principle, between a genuine and a false consensus if we presuppose the possibility of an unconstrained dialogue to which all speakers have equal access and in which only the 'force of the better argument prevails'. This is what he calls the 'ideal speech situation'. And this in turn presupposes the possibility of a form of social life in which communication would take place in this way.[15] Of course, Habermas admits, actual contexts of argumentation do not often correspond to the ideal speech situation. Yet it is more than just a fiction, or a regulative idea in Kant's sense of the term, since we do in fact have to assume its possibility.

> So far as we accomplish speech acts at all, we stand under the curious imperatives of that power which, with the honourable title of 'reason', I aim to ground in the structure of possible speech. In this sense I think it is meaningful to speak of an immanent reference to truth in the life-process of society.[16]

I shall not discuss Habermas's arguments in detail here, but it is important to note that his concept of validity-claims covers both the domain of factual truth and that of moral or expressive statements. It is here that Habermas's consensus theory of truth becomes particularly important. Truth, as we have seen, Habermas analyses as a 'validity-claim' – indeed the paradigmatic one. The discursive redemption or cashing (*Einlösung*) of truth-claims cannot, Habermas argues, be carried out by a direct comparison of utterances with reality, as postulated by correspondence theories of truth. Propositions are not like pictures, which can be more or less like what they represent; 'truth is not a comparative relation.' The alleged correspondence between true statements and reality can only be expressed in statements. 'Ontological theories of truth attempt in vain to break out of the linguistic (*sprachlogisch*) domain which is the only place where the validity claims of speech acts can be clarified.'[17]

Truth must instead be defined in terms of a projected consensus:

> I am entitled to ascribe a predicate to an object if and only if any other person who could enter a discussion with me would ascribe the same predicate to the same object. . . . The condition for the truth of statements is the potential agreement of everyone else.[18]

This may seem a roundabout account of truth compared to one – shared by common sense, Tarski's 'semantic' theory of truth (which Habermas rejects as circular) and philosophical realism – that what makes 'Habermas is in Frankfurt' true is that Habermas is in Frankfurt rather than, say, New York. But, whatever the problems of this theory, it is easy to see why it appeals to Habermas: first, it embodies, like the ideal speech situation, a forward reference to an intersubjective consensus, and perhaps to a rational form of life. Second, whereas correspondence theories of truth cannot easily be extended to cover the domains of ethical and aesthetic judgements, such as 'murder is wrong' or 'château-bottled wine usually tastes nicer than *ordinaire*', it is not impossible to imagine a rationally founded consensus on such judgements. Although the validity of norms or the sincerity (*Wahrhaftigkeit*) of expressions of subjective feelings must not be confused with propositional truth, we do not do justice to the meaning of normative validity if we simply say that truth and falsity are not relevant to ethical statements.

> When I state that one norm should be preferred to another, I aim precisely to exclude the aspect of arbitrariness: rightness and truth come together in that both claims can only be vindicated discursively, by way of argumentation and a rational consensus.[19]

Habermas argues that this model of discursive validation does not apply to all the validity-claims raised by speech acts. Understandability, in particular, is not simply raised as a claim which could be satisfied; it has to be satisfied if in fact the communication is to count as successful. Secondly, the theory of truth based on the pursuit of consensus applies only to claims to truth and rightness.

> Claims to sincerity (*Wahrhaftigkeit*) can only be validated in actions. Neither interrogations nor analytic dialogues between doctor and patient can count as discourses in the sense of a cooperative search for truth.[20]

Discourses are themselves of various types: hermeneutic discourses concern questions of interpretation; theoretical-empirical discourses concern 'the validity of empirical claims and explanations', and practical discourses concern the application of methodological or other standards.[21]

These forms of discourse are distinguished from those of 'aesthetic' or 'therapeutic' critique. In therapy, sincerity or insincerity are not *grounded* but *revealed* by consistency or inconsistency with action.[22] And aesthetic judgements do not so much imply the direct grounding of standards of value as the bringing of objects into relation with those standards.

> Above all, however, the type of validity claim attached to cultural values does not transcend local boundaries in the same way as truth and rightness claims. Cultural values do not count as universal; they are, as the name indicates, located within the horizon or lifeworld of a specific group or culture. And values can be made plausible only in the context of a particular form of life.[23]

This passage raises some problematic issues in Habermas's model. Few people would question his analysis of aesthetic judgements, but that of moral-practical ones is more contentious. In the positivist tradition, or more broadly for any ethical subjectivist position, practical discourse is constrained only at best by requirements of consistency and practicability. Habermas's position here is somewhat equivocal. He is 'inclined . . . to a cognitivist position', but since he also upholds a consensus theory of truth it is not quite clear what he means here by 'cognitivist'. For the time being, he relies on a reference to the everyday participant's position: 'No-one would enter into moral argumentation if he did not start from the strong presumption that a grounded consensus could in principle be achieved among those involved.'[24]

Running through his essays of the 1970s is a line of development in Habermas's thought from communicative competence to a broader concept of interactional competence which in turn develops into a theory of communicative action. Before leaving the model of communicative competence, however, we need to examine one further aspect emerging from it: a new account of systematically distorted communication or the 'pathology of communication'.[25] This is a matter not just of the intrusion of causal obstacles to understanding, expressed in psychoanalysis as privatized language-use or de-symbolization, but of 'the lack of interactive competences'.[26]

The development of cognitive competence can be measured in terms of 'clearly decidable problems, i.e. problems to which there are true solutions'. Moral judgement can also at a pinch be represented in terms of a logic of development, though less securely than in the former case of cognitive judgements which are underwritten by science. But interactive competence does not just have 'to resolve problems of knowledge and moral insight at an adequate level, but rather to preserve processes of mutual understanding even in conflict situations, without breaking off communication or preserving it only as an illusion'. As in his discussion of psychoanalysis, Habermas sets the condition of 'conscious conflict resolution' (*Verarbeitung*) in relation to the normality conditions of linguistic communication: 'conscious conflict resolution means conflict resolution under conditions of undistorted communication'.[27]

Wherever speech is separated out from immediate contexts of action it is subject to external and internal organization. The term 'external organization' refers to the ordering of discussion in time and space, who can participate, in what order, and so on; 'internal organization' denotes the 'universal-pragmatic regulation of speech act sequences' according to the principles of understandability, truth, rightness and sincerity.

> I see the key to the pathogenesis of linguistic communication . . . in particular overloads of the external organization of the discussion, which must be displaced (*abgewältzt*) onto the internal organization of the discussion and lead to a systematic distortion.[28]

What gives rise to systematic distortion is not the mere violation of one of the universal pragmatic principles, for example in telling a lie,[29] but when the lie serves to conceal a conflict which 'smoulders on' beneath the cover of an apparent consensus. Habermas illustrates the resultant pseudo-communication with reference to the literature on 'schizogenic' families, whose members' failures of identity management and resulting identity conflicts lead to distortions of communication. Though he does not pursue the idea in this text, there is the possibility here of a linguistically based theory of ideology which contrasts interestingly with that offered in *The Theory of Communicative Action*.[30]

Universal pragmatics

Habermas's work of this period is a changing structure of diverse elements. Some of these are presented in *The Theory of Communicative Action*, others are superseded in his later work, while further themes which he has not recently addressed seem likely to recur in subsequent writings.[31] This dynamic aspect makes judgement difficult, but this is a good point at which to attempt a provisional assessment of Habermas's universal pragmatics.

Assuming, as I think we must, that Habermas and his critics are right about the unviability of the original cognitive-interest model, we must consider how successful is its successor. The situation is complicated by the fact that Habermas is offering a moving target, in the sense that he starts with the idea of a linguistic foundation for social theory and gradually abandons it. There was certainly something unrealistic about the idea of a 'generative grammar' of social action, if that was ever what Habermas had in mind. What remains to be seen is whether critical theory, in giving up the idea of a metatheoretical foundation, is able to hold together the two poles of social theory and moral philosophy. The shift to learning theory which is evident in Habermas's work of this period creates problems, as I shall suggest in the next chapter, when it is extended into an evolutionary theory of social development. To put it crudely: children, and to some extent adults, do learn, but societies do not, except in a highly metaphorical sense – as Habermas himself recognizes.

I shall confine myself here to the specific claims which Habermas makes for universal pragmatics. Even here, perhaps, one can see the tension between a normative reading of the four validity-claims and of the ideal speech situation and the notion that they are in some sense latent in actual speech. This suggests perhaps that we should not worry too much about the precise specification of the model, since its incorporation into actual contexts of discussion will necessarily involve a fairly rough translation. This also defuses vulgar objections to the ideal speech situation which understand it as an (unrealizable) concrete fantasy. A more specific set of problems arise, however, with Habermas's concept of truth, which seems too roundabout to be defensible on its own. Habermas seems to concede this: 'The criteria of truth lie at a different level than the idea of redeeming validity-claims which is expounded in terms of the theory of discourse.'[32] The concept of validity-claims is what counts: it is crucial for Habermas because it enables him to defend the idea that there are rational criteria for ethical, if not aesthetic judgements, against a positivism which restricts truth to the domain of empirical fact. Before turning to the discussion of the truth of 'practical' judgements in *Legitimation Crisis*, I shall examine some of the themes in the philosophy and sociology of ethics, and of cognitive and social development, which lead on from Habermas's discussion of learning theory in the texts considered in this chapter.

It is clear enough that Habermas never intended the ideal speech situation to be understood as a concrete utopia which would turn the world into a gigantic seminar. He has sometimes compared it to what Kant called a transcendental illusion, involving the extension of the categories of the understanding beyond the limits of experience, but with the difference that this illusion is also 'a constitutive condition of the possibility of speech'.[33] But the terminology of preconditions is notoriously slippery, and Habermas has repeatedly slid between different formulations.[34] There is, however, a fairly clear movement in his thinking towards stressing the virtual and ideal aspects; whatever 'our first sentence' commits us to cannot, it seems, be spelled out very precisely, and the constraint is less a strictly logical one than that identified in the notion of 'performative contradiction'.[35] The emphasis therefore shifts, rightly in my view, from a fruitless search for precise entailments and commitments to a broader account of communicative action in general, and moral reasoning in particular.[36]

Before moving on to the latter issue, it may be helpful to look at the further development of these ideas in *The Theory of Communicative Action*. One of the central elements of Habermas's theory is the distinction between the genuinely communicative use of language to attain common goals, which Habermas takes to be the primary case of language-use and 'the inherent telos of human speech',[37] and strategic or success-oriented speech, parasitic on the former, which simulates a communicative orientation in order to achieve an ulterior purpose.

Habermas initially believed that he could show this in terms of J. L. Austin's distinction between locutionary, illocutionary and perlocutionary speech acts.[38] A locutionary act involves saying something, an illocutionary act does something in the act of saying something, and a perlocutionary act produces a certain effect via doing-something-by-saying-something. Thus if I say 'Good morning' (locutionary) I am uttering a greeting (illocutionary) and thereby showing how polite I am. By saying 'I promise to return the book' (locutionary) I am issuing a promise (illocutionary) and offering reassurance to a possibly suspicious lender.

What Habermas wanted to claim is that perlocutionary effects, intended but not made explicit, are a sign of strategic action, as opposed to communicative action. Perlocutionary acts are parasitic on illocutionary acts, not just in the trivial sense noted by Austin, but in the sense that 'while speech acts can . . . be employed strategically, they have a constitutive meaning only for communicative action'. The latter is distinguished from strategic action by the fact that '*all* participants pursue their illocutionary aims without reservation'[39] 'in order to arrive at an agreement that will provide the basis for a consensual coordination of individually pursued plans of action'. Thus in the example given above, if my intention is to offer reassurance I should do so explicitly, saying, for example, 'I can see that you are wondering if I will return your book, and I assure you that I will', raising a validity-claim of sincerity (and also making a factual prediction about the future) about which we can reach a provisional agreement.

Habermas goes on to offer examples of speech acts and affirmative responses:

1   I (hereby) promise you that I shall come tomorrow.
1a   Yes, I shall depend on it.
2   You are requested to stop smoking.
2a   Yes, I shall comply.
3   I confess to you that I find your actions loathsome.
3a   Yes, I believe you do.
4   I can predict (to you) that the vacation will be spoiled by rain.
4a   Yes, we'll have to take that into account.

Accepting Habermas's reminder that formal pragmatics is concerned only with standard speech acts[40] – and passing over the curiously unsatisfactory pair 3 and 3a – it remains deeply implausible that one could establish such a sharp separation as Habermas wants between illocutionary and perlocutionary effects. In response to criticisms by Jeffrey Alexander and others, Habermas weakens the connection between the formal distinction between illocution and perlocution and

> the action-theoretic distinction between strategically and non-strategically intended perlocutionary effects. . . . I term those effects strategically intended which come about only if they are not declared or if they are caused by defective speech acts that merely pretend to be valid . . . one can no longer consider all perlocutions to be latent-strategic action.[11]

With these qualifications and precisions which Habermas has added, the emphasis shifts back, as I think it should, to the broader issue of how, if at all, one can distinguish communicative and strategic action; I shall return to this later when discussing the more substantial objections made to Habermas's theory. There remains one more formal aspect of Austin's analysis which Habermas develops in his own model: the distinction between types of illocutionary act. As Habermas shows with the homely example of a professor asking a seminar participant to fetch a glass of water, even a simple request, understood not as a mere demand but 'as a speech act carried out in an attitude oriented to understanding' raises claims to normative rightness, subjective sincerity and factual practicability which may be questioned. The addressee of the request may reject it as illegitimate ('I'm not your servant'), insincere ('You don't really want one') or mistaken as to its existential preconditions (availability of a source of water).

Speech acts can, however, be classified according to the illocutionary effect which is primarily intended by the speaker: Habermas distinguishes between constative (assertoric), expressive (experiential) and regulative (imperatives, intentional sentences, e.g. premises) speech acts and sentence forms.[42] Corresponding to these are what Habermas calls world-attitudes: an objectivating, neutral attitude to facts in the world, an expressive attitude to the speaker's own subjective world, and a norm-conformative attitude to legitimate expectations.[43] Finally, Habermas notes that regulative and expressive speech acts are 'constitutive for' normatively regulated and dramaturgical action, and suggests 'conversation', in a broad sense which includes argumentation, as the form of communicative action in which constative speech acts play the greatest part.[44] Habermas thus arrives at a typology of 'linguistically mediated interaction' in which normatively regulated and dramaturgical action appear, along with conversation, as 'three pure types – or better, limit cases, of communicative action'.[45] (See figure 1.)

Finally, Habermas considers the use of this formal-pragmatic reconstruction for a sociological theory of action. First, he indicates the ways in which one can relax the methodological restrictions of formal pragmatics – its focus on isolated, standard speech acts. We must, he claims, include a reference to a performative attitude which includes the objectivating, norm-conformative and expressive attitudes with their respective reference to the objective, social and subjective worlds.[46] Participants in communication relate to all of these worlds simultaneously. They also draw on background knowledge drawn from the lifeworld, and analysis must follow them in this.

Second, he claims, empirical pragmatics needs formal pragmatics to clarify the content, and in particular the rational basis of everyday speech, to distinguish literal and ironic or playful usage and to identify, for example, systematically distorted communication, which Habermas differentiates from conscious deception or manipulation as forms of concealed strategic action.[47] Formal pragmatics bring out the 'different sorts of knowledge' embodied in social action: the effectiveness of teleological actions, the truth of constative speech acts and theories, the rightness of normatively regulated speech acts and of the norms themselves, and the truthfulness or sincerity of dramaturgical actions and the value standards embodied in works of art.[48]

Habermas's extremely bold and suggestive line of analysis cannot, in the end, be upheld in its original strict formulations, but its mutations into a broader context are in my view even more creative and important. Habermas's analysis of language was developed in direct relation to his formulation, with Apel, of a 'discourse ethics'. As Seyla Benhabib has shown, this connection now looks a good deal weaker, but it remains significant:

> Whereas formerly Habermas asked whether the conditions of an ideal speech situation *entailed* the acceptance of certain ethical norms, he is now asking whether all subjects capable of speech and action, in that they act communicatively, do not also dispose of a certain moral know-how which involves recognizing a certain moral principle which they can deny at the risk of a *performative contradiction* only.[49]

Formal-pragmatic features / Types of action	Characteristic speech acts	Functions of speech	Action orientations	Basic attitudes	Validity-claims	World relations
Strategic action	Perlocutions Imperatives	Influencing one's opposite number	Oriented to success	Objectivating	(Effectiveness)	Objective world
Conversation	Constatives	Representation of states of affairs	Oriented to reaching understanding	Objectivating	Truth	Objective world
Normatively regulated action	Regulatives	Establishment of interpersonal relations	Oriented to reaching understanding	Norm-conformative	Rightness	Social world
Dramaturgical action	Expressives	Self-representation	Oriented to reaching understanding	Expressive	Truthfulness	Subjective world

Figure 1 Pure types of linguistically mediated interaction

Source: The Theory of Communicative Action, vol. 1.

Moral competence and discourse ethics

It is possible to draw a rough division between Habermas's evolutionary theorizing, discussed at more length in the next chapter,
and his communication-theoretic approach, but the various themes
are all intimately interrelated. Even in its static form, universal
pragmatics has developmental concepts bound up with it. As we
have seen, it is a mistake to read the anticipation of the ideal speech
situation as pointing towards a concrete utopia of pure communicative action untainted by domination. But the concept of discourse
undoubtedly contains a short-run teleological process in which we
strive to justify assumptions and redeem validity-claims, and the
same is true of the overcoming of systematic distortions to communication in Habermas's model of psychoanalysis. And although
discourse is not set up as an evolutionarily higher level than communicative action, but rather as an adjunct to it, to which we have
recourse when necessary, it is clear that the ability to enter the
sphere of discourse presupposes certain cognitive capacities (e.g.
metacommunication); and the willingness to do so, rather than just
dogmatically repeat one's assertions, appears as a kind of moral
requirement.

As soon as we treat communicative competence as something
that has to be acquired, it begins to look as if we have to deal with
cognitive and moral learning processes at both the individual and
the social level, since the individual capacities presuppose a social
context, including a necessarily public language, for their exercise.
I shall begin with the individual level, which Habermas discusses
in the essays on role competence and interactional competence
already mentioned, a long article on 'Moral development and ego
identity',[50] and two more recent ones on 'Discourse ethics' and
'Moral development and communicative action'.[51]

Corresponding to the validity-claims in Habermas's universal
pragmatics are the domains of reality to which they refer.[52] We must
postulate, in addition to the 'objective' world, a normative world of
legitimate social relations and a subjective world of feelings and
attitudes. Truth relates to external nature, rightness to society,[53]
truthfulness or sincerity to inner nature, and comprehensibility to
language. Accordingly, the self develops cognitive, linguistic and
interactive capacities. What about the 'inner nature' of the self? Ego
development involves not just the awareness of inner self but also
'integration into universal structures of cognition, speech and inter-

action', along with the further process of the development of affects and motivations.[54] Interactive competence is central both to ego identity and to moral consciousness, liberating the adolescent, as McCarthy puts it, 'not only from the egocentrism of early childhood but from the sociocentrism of tradition-bound role behaviour as well'.[55] The connection with moral consciousness is established by 'Habermas' thesis that "moral consciousness" is at bottom only the ability to employ interactive competence for a conscious regulation of morally relevant conflicts'.[56] Thus the psychologist Lawrence Kohlberg's stages of moral development can be mapped onto, and derived from, Habermas's stages of the development of role competence.[57]

I shall not attempt to summarize here the detailed arguments made by Habermas and Kohlberg for their respective models; the general line of development should be intuitively clear from table 1.[58] Two major and, as it turns out, related questions arise, however, from this programme. First, assuming that the stages of moral consciousness can be empirically specified and documented,[59] it does not follow that each is superior to the previous one. Habermas is attracted by Kohlberg's idea of a complementary relationship between the psychological claim that 'individuals prefer the highest stage of reasoning they comprehend, a claim supported by research', and the 'philosophical claim that a later stage is "objectively" preferable or more adequate by certain moral criteria';[60] this view of the interrelationship between philosophy and science is one which Habermas has advanced at various times.[61] But he concedes that, even if empirical psychology restricts the choice of acceptable moral theories to those which are consistent with the psychological evidence, the choice between competing ethics 'has to be settled with another kind of argument'.[62]

The problem can be avoided, Habermas suggests, by dropping the idea of successive stages of post-conventional morality. Taking up a suggestion made by McCarthy, Habermas agrees that we should treat the moral reasoning of post-conventional subjects as on a level with the metatheoretical disagreements of moral philosophers: the oppositions between utilitarianism, contract theory, and so on. Unless you are Hegel, it is inappropriate to order these theories into a developmental sequence. This strategic withdrawal does not, however, resolve all the problems of the Kohlberg model; indeed the even greater weight now placed on the transition from conventional to post-conventional moral reasoning makes Kohlberg's discovery of an intermediate stage ($4\frac{1}{2}$) somewhat em-

Table 1

Levels of interaction	Actions	Motivations	Actors	Reciprocity requirement	Stages of moral consciousness	Idea of the good and just life	Domain of validity
1	Concrete actions and consequences of action	Generalized pleasure/pain	Natural identity	Incomplete	1 Punishment/obedience orientation	Maximization of pleasure/avoidance of pain through obedience	Natural and social environment (undifferentiated)
				Complete	2 Instrumental hedonism	Maximization of pleasure/avoidance of pain through exchange of equivalents	
2	Roles	Culturally interpreted needs	Role identity	Incomplete	3 Good-boy/nice-girl orientation	Concrete morality of primary groups	Group of primary reference persons

	Systems of norms / (Concrete duties)	Ego identity	Orientation	Concrete morality of secondary groups	Members of the political community
3	Principles	Complete			
	Universalized pleasure/pain (utility)		4 Law-and-order orientation		
	Universalized duties		5 Social-contractual legalism	Civil liberties, public welfare	All fellow citizens
			6 Universal ethical principle orientation	Moral freedom	All humans as private persons
	Universalized need interpretations		7 Communicative ethics	Moral and political freedom	All as members of a fictive world society

Source: Thomas McCarthy, *The Critical Theory of Jürgen Habermas.*

barrassing. These 'relativistic value-sceptics', typically adolescents, recognize that different societies impose different moral obligations but see differences, and the obligations themselves, as basically arbitrary. Now it may be possible to explain the relative persistence of this stage in terms of a transitional stage between conventional and post-conventional thinking, and Habermas briefly outlines such an argument. A major tradition of Western thinking about morality, marked by such names as Marx, Weber and Karl Popper, defends something like this position.[63]

A further problem arises however with the discovery that not only may half the US population fail to reach Kohlberg's post-conventional level 3 (stages 5 and 6 in Table 1) but that women's judgements, in particular, often put them in stage 3 when other evidence suggests 'greater moral maturity'.[64] Although Habermas, as we shall see, believes that he can handle such problems in his model of a discourse ethics, it is clear that this will have to be justified by something more than a developmental model; the status of the discourse ethic is therefore the second major issue to be addressed. And at the back of all this is the broader question, which becomes even more pointed when Habermas moves on to questions of social evolution, of whether he can justify in universalistic terms a conception of moral reasoning which not only may be class and gender biased but presupposes the specific historical values of European modernity.[65]

In his most recent attempt to ground a discourse ethic, which he sees as one of the reconstructive sciences,[66] Habermas notes that it 'stands and falls with two assumptions, that (a) normative validity claims have a cognitive meaning and can be treated like truth claims, and that (b) the grounding of norms and prescriptions demands the carrying-through of an actual dialogue and in the last instance is not possible monologically, in the form of an argumentation process hypothetically run through in the mind.'[67]

Habermas starts from a principle of universalization related to, but also importantly different from, that of Kant. As McCarthy puts it, 'The emphasis shifts from what each can will without contradiction to be a universal law to what all can will in agreement to be a universal norm.'[68] This discourse ethic is, Habermas concedes, necessarily somewhat formal. 'It specifies no orientation as to content, but rather a procedure: practical discourse.'[69] It draws a sharp distinction between questions of justice and questions of the 'good life', the latter can only be addressed 'within the unproblematic horizon of a historically concrete form of life or the individual conduct of life'.[70] On the other hand, a universalistic morality can bridge the division between morality and law: 'the dichotomy between in-group and out-group morality disappears, the opposition between morally and legally regulated areas is relativized, and the validity of all norms is tied to discursive will-formation'.[71] And if Habermas's model is necessarily somewhat abstract it avoids, perhaps, the 'moral rigorism', as he puts it,[72] of Kantian and Kohlbergian theory. Habermas concedes that moral judgement requires to be complemented by 'sensitivity to context and skill (*Klugheit*) on the one side, and autonomous self-determination on the other'.[73] His model of discourse, he claims with some plausibility, is more open to such mediation than that of the monological moral reasoner implied by Kant and Kohlberg; on the other hand, it is clear that Habermas does not take us far in this direction.[74]

Habermas has continued to work through issues of this kind; situating his discourse ethic in relation to Hegel's critique of the abstractions of Kant's moral theory and related approaches to moral and political questions. Hegel rejects both 'the abstract universalism of justice' and any particular concrete account of justice and morality. 'Discourse ethics takes up this basic intention of Hegel so as to redeem it by Kantian means.'[75] In other words, the choice should not be one between, on the one hand, a universalistic ethical theory which necessarily abstracts from all content and, on the other, a concrete but inevitably parochial theory which simply underwrites some local set of moral judgements. Even a universalistic principle, such as Habermas's (or for that matter Kant's), has to be shown to do more than just 'reflect the prejudices of a contemporary adult white male Central European of bourgeois education'.[76]

Habermas makes two related claims for his discourse ethic. First, he maintains that it expresses our moral intuitions, at least as these bear on the process of discursive justification of norms.[77] Secondly, this focus on normative consensus as opposed to abstract universalizability means that a discourse ethic, unlike Kant's, can go beyond a pure concept of justice to include 'those structural aspects of the "good life" which can be separated from the concrete totality of particular forms of life in terms of universal principles (*Gesichtspunkte*) of all communicative socialization.'[78]

Thus even a moral philosophy which confines itself, rightly, to justifying and elucidating the 'moral point of view', rather than preempting the concrete moral decisions of social actors, includes a kind of vision of the good life as one which embodies these forms of moral-political reasoning:

every universalistic morality is dependent on accommodating forms of life. It requires a certain correspondence with practices of socialization and education which endow the adolescent with strongly internalized controls of conscience and demand relatively abstract ego identities. A universalistic morality also requires a certain correspondence with political and social institutions in which post-conventional representations of law and morality are already incorporated.[79]

As it happens, Habermas goes on, 'Western' societies have over the past two or three centuries approximated to these principles; indeed this is what made possible the development of moral universalism by Rousseau and Kant.

Habermas's and Apel's discourse ethics has attracted very substantial discussion. Their position falls squarely on the battle-lines between those who uphold an essentially Kantian notion of universalizability, such as R. M. Hare and, in a related application to social justice, John Rawls, and the 'contextualists' or 'communitarians' who stress the embeddedness of moral principles in cultures and ways of life, where these are themselves seen as objects as well as sources of moral value. Habermas, while committed to a basically deontological approach – that is, one cast in terms of what is *right* – is sensitive to these contextualist objections. As he puts it in his discussion of the American pragmatist philosopher G. H. Mead, 'The critique of ethical formalism takes exception, first of all, to the fact that preoccupation with questions of the validity of moral norms misleads us into ignoring the intrinsic value of cultural life-forms and life-styles'.[80] We cannot judge the relative success of whole ways of life as we can judge a specific norm or perhaps an institutional system. Similarly for individuals, 'the answer to the question, who does one want to be, cannot be rational in the way that a moral decision can.'[81]

Nor, of course, is communication theory's version of the principle of universalizability an orthodox Kantian one. As Seyla Benhabib puts it,

Instead of asking what an individual moral agent could or would will, without contradiction, to be a universal maxim for all, one asks: what norms or institutions would the members of an ideal or real communication community agree to as representing their common interests after engaging in a special kind of argumentation or conversation? The procedural model of an argumentative praxis replaces the silent thought-experiment enjoined by the Kantian universalizability test.[82]

This principle is open between the two positions and therefore unlikely to satisfy either side. The community might agree on a ruthlessly consistent application of the set of formal principles favoured by the Kantian, but the Kantian would worry that they might have chosen differently; they might have rejected what Marx called the 'narrow horizon of bourgeois right' in favour of a more informal approach to the furtherance of good behaviour and good institutions.[83] And of course, if it is *we* who are simulating the running of the ideal speech situation, the thought-experiment becomes almost as artificial as the Kantian one.

Habermas's principle may seem, then, too indeterminate to do the work it is intended to do; it begins to look like not much more than a regulative principle for our moral judgements, i.e. that we bear in mind what we think an ideal communication community *would* say.[84] Unless we can develop a formal system of principles with some confidence that it would indeed be followed by an ideal communication community, we are, after all, pushed into the further question of what sort of community, with what sort of institutions, is in practice most likely to approximate the features of an ideal communication community.[85] Habermas, as we have seen, is happy enough to say that it is only under certain social and cultural conditions, such as those of Western modernity in its better moments, that an approach to moral-practical questions of the kind he advocates is likely to get a fair chance – thus pushing the emphasis, once again, onto a broadly conceived social theory of modernity and the constitutional democratic state.[86]

4

Social Evolution and Legitimation

Social evolution

Evolutionism is an extremely contested topic in twentieth-century social theory.[1] Whether or not evolutionary theory is desirable or possible, Habermas's version, with its characteristic combination of ambition and caution, is one of the most original and challenging. Habermas had strong reasons for extending the developmental model which we encountered in his discourse ethic from the individual to the social level. First, his models were explicitly conceived as theoretical 'reconstructions' of human capacities and designed to serve as a foundation for a social theory.[2] Second, we have repeatedly encountered passages in which Habermas's accounts of the development of *individual* competences presuppose developing social contexts or 'forms of life'. Third, he retains strong links with two broad families of evolutionary theory: the philosophy of history[3] and historical materialism.[4]

It is not at all easy to sort out the many variants of evolutionary theory in the social sciences. Piet Strydom, who is sympathetic to evolutionary theory, complains, in his useful discussion of Habermas's theory of evolution, that critics such as Alain Touraine and Anthony Giddens were wrong to 'take the inflated claims of evolutionists at face value'.[5] This is rather discouraging, in its implication that, besides all the manifest ambiguities we encounter in evolutionary theories, we must also somehow read between the lines. There is, however, a fairly clear distinction between theories which emphasize the Darwinian theme of the adaptation of systems to their environments and those based on a notion of development – what Giddens has called an 'unfolding' model.

Habermas's version is closer to the latter but without the determinism which often accompanies it. While he sees 'system problems' as giving rise to learning processes, his interest is directed to the retrospective reconstruction of the developmental logic of these learning processes – a linear sequence transferable from Piaget's and Kohlberg's models of individual development to the analysis of forms of society or world-views. Evolution in this usage is 'the realization of an ordered sequence of structural possibilities'.[6] This logic of development is distinguished from 'developmental mechanisms or dynamics of how and why developments actually come about'[7] and the contingent processes of real history. Whereas supporters of evolutionary theory, such as Michael Schmidt[8] and, in a different way, Piet Strydom, want to eradicate or, in Strydom's case, restrict the developmental logic model, more sympathetic critics such as Axel Honneth and Hans Joas see Habermas's version as relatively unproblematic.[9]

Habermas's arguments are organized around two basic claims: first, that the development of human society can be represented or reconstructed as a learning process; second, that historical materialism is, or can be reconstructed as, the best available theory of this process. The first claim purports to justify a theory of social evolution, the second a historical materialist one. He begins with his analysis of communicative competence. There is a parallel between individual and social development, between 'the reproduction of society and the socialization of its members'.[10]

Referring to the work/interaction distinction, Habermas argues that historical materialism focuses too narrowly on the first of these:

> learning processes also take place in the dimension of moral insight, practical knowledge, communicative action, and the consensual regulation of action conflicts – learning processes that are deposited in more mature forms of social integration, in new productive relations, and that in turn first make possible the introduction of new productive forces.[11]

Marxism is, however, right to insist on the primacy of production; 'culture remains a superstructural phenomenon'.[12]

Habermas sees himself as 'reconstructing' historical materialism in the sense of 'taking a theory apart and putting it back together

again in a new form in order to attain more fully the goal it has set
for itself'.[13] 'Marx', he argues, 'already understood historical materialism as a comprehensive theory of social evolution'[14] and was right
to do so. On the other hand, the very tight connection Marx establishes between social labour and the history of the species, viewed
as a sequence of modes of production, is problematic, he maintains,
in two respects. First, what Engels called 'the part played by labour
in the transition from ape to man' is overstated; the development of
family structures was arguably just as important.[15] Secondly, the
rigid sequence of modes of production takes over too much from
the philosophy of history: 'the unilinear, necessary, uninterrupted,
and progressive development of a macro subject'.[16]

Habermas offers, first, a 'weaker version' of all these elements.
'Historical materialism does not need to assume a species-subject
that undergoes evolution. The bearers of evolution are rather societies and the acting subjects integrated into them; social evolution can be discerned in those structures that are replaced by more
comprehensive structures in accord with a pattern that is to be
rationally reconstructed.'[17] Second, one should separate this pattern
'from the processes through which the empirical substances develop'; the latter are not necessarily unilinear or irreversible. Third,
teleology cannot be imputed to history, either in traditional or in
modern, neo-evolutionary forms – the latter based on the problematic concept of complexity. Here Marx's original model is preferable: 'Marx judged social development not by increases in
complexity but by the stage of development of productive forces
and by the maturity of the forms of social intercourse.'[18]

Habermas's next step is to examine two central elements of historical materialism: the base–superstructure distinction and the
dialectic of forces and relations of production. Against economistic
reductionism he argues, following Kautsky, that the thesis of the
primacy of base over superstructure should be understood, not in
onotological terms, but in relation to 'the leading role that the
economic structure assumes in social evolution'.[19] This rather unu-
sual interpretation makes the issue similar to that of the crises
caused by a mismatch between forces and relations of production.
But, even when this relation is interpreted in a sophisticated structuralist manner, it does not explain the attainment of new forms of
social integration; this, Habermas suggests, can only be explained
by advances at the level of communicative action which 'follow
their own logic'.[20]

Thus, rather than pursue the classification of modes of production in an attempt to make it more concrete, Habermas proposes 'the search for highly abstract principles of social organization ... which institutionalize new levels of societal learning'.[21] Such principles are embodied in moral and legal systems, grounded in socially shared world-views.[22] If there is an evolutionary progress at this level, it is, unlike natural evolution, transmitted through cultural traditions. It also secures, in a non-arbitrary manner, the concept of progress in historical materialism.[23]

Habermas suggests that such a reformulation is both historically more accurate[24] and intuitively more relevant to our contemporary situation:

> we cannot find in the logic of the rise of system problems the logic that the social system will follow if it responds to . . . an evolutionary challenge. If a socialist organization of society were the adequate response to crisis-ridden developments in capitalist society, it could not be deduced from any determination of the form of the reproductive process, but would have to be explained in terms of processes of democratization.[25]

The form of Habermas's two essays on the reconstruction of historical materialism is reminiscent of some passages in *The German Ideology*: fascinating sketches of slices of world history interspersed with bold theoretical models. The contents and flavour are, of course, very different, given the central place Habermas accords to theories of cognitive development and system evolution. Yet he is concerned to stress that he has not moved so far away from the central themes of historical materialism. Although, for example, 'the investigation of the capitalist accumulation process, on which Marx concentrated above all, hardly plays a role', Habermas's theory remains, he claims, historical and materialist: materialist in its focus on crises of production and reproduction, and historically oriented in its attention to the 'contingent circumstances' which give rise to evolutionary changes.[26]

Any assessment of such a theory-sketch has to be provisional; perhaps the most important point to make is that Habermas has provided a research programme or a scale model of historical materialism rather than the thing itself. Although he has addressed in *theoretical* terms the way in which his evolutionary theory links up with conventional historiography,[27] and occasionally provided examples of possible substantive connections, there is not so far much history in the reconstruction.[28] More worryingly, such an approach seems to entail an opportunistic attitude to the historical past and to the experiences and perceptions of historical actors, gutting this material in order to isolate the formal structures of consciousness and action to be assigned to a sequential model.[29] Habermas equivocates between an evolutionary system model of societal learning in relation to system problems and a more concrete account in which social movements and other social actors are 'the empirical bearers of advances in moral and practical understanding',[30] responding not to system problems but to experiences, notably of injustice. Habermas is in danger of neglecting the real learning processes in history in a Hegelian jump to a level of abstraction which explains less rather than more.

A more serious problem still concerns the postulate of upward development. As Habermas admits, his work tends to be focused very much on the First World, and although his evolutionism does not preclude the hermeneutic understanding of other cultures it may not be the most favourable horizon from which to attempt such an understanding. Critics of Marxism who have objected precisely to its evolutionism will not be impressed to see this element preserved, and even embellished, in Habermas's reconstruction.[31]

Habermas has recognized the force of these objections, though without yet fully integrating them into the structure of his thinking. He may have been influenced by the failure of his Starnberg colleagues, documented in a book published in the same year as *The Theory of Communicative Action*, to get anything useful out of a Piagetian analysis of the law.[32] He has certainly paid close attention to the work of Klaus Eder, who worked closely with him on the evolution of social structures and world-views but has since, as we have seen, come to focus on collective learning processes on the part of real historical individuals and groups, and to abandon the idea of an automatic link between these learning processes and social evolution.[33] It seems unlikely that Habermas would want to go this far, but he is clearly sensitive to the problems of the ontogenetic model.

He is also increasingly conscious of the possibility of *mutual* learning among cultures, between 'us' and 'them',[34] and he takes an extremely strong position against the disruption of 'alien' ways of life, such as those in India at the time of the British invasions and perhaps in the American South.[35] For all this, however, he insists on the distinctiveness of the differentiation achieved in European modernity. Drawing on the debates on the boundaries of philosophy and social anthropology, he argues that there *are* something like universal (*allgemein*) standards of rationality[36] and that human beings can only adopt these standards if their world-views are sufficiently differentiated. This means that these world-views must differentiate, as mythical thought does not, between technical success and moral legitimacy, or more broadly between nature and culture.[37] But this 'decentred' understanding of the world also implies the recognition that one's own world-view is one among others.

In terms of the developmental logic of Habermas's own work, we can see in these texts the consolidation of the conception of reconstructive science and its relationship to critique which comes into its own in the *Theory of Communicative Action*. The theory of social evolution is just that, a theory to be tested in a discursive attitude, and not a philosophy of history. As such, it may, as McCarthy puts it, appear 'to exclude precisely the practical and hermeneutic dimension that made critical theory methodologically distinct from traditional theory'.[38] In fact, however, it is better understood as a tentative theoretical deepening of the basis for a critique of contemporary social reality which requires 'a critical, historical account of how we came to be what we are'.[39] This is illustrated by Habermas's *Legitimation Crisis*, published in 1973.

Legitimation

Habermas's book *Legitimation Crisis* (*Legitimationsprobleme im Spätkapitalismus*) is one of his best known and most influential, though also one of the most problematic. It is a preparatory and tentative work, as indicated by Habermas's expression in the Preface of his concern 'that the clarification of very general structures of hypotheses not be confused with empirical results'.[40] The themes of the book have been carried further by a number of other writers, notably Claus Offe[41] and Johannes Berger,[42] and many of them recur in a different form in *The Theory of Communicative Action*. I shall concentrate here on the connections between this book and the rest of Habermas's work: in particular, the 'reconstruction' of historical materialism and the discourse ethic discussed in chapter 3. These themes very roughly correspond to the first and third parts respectively of *Legitimation Crisis*, while the second part deals specifically with 'Crsis tendencies in advanced capitalism'. The connection between them is essentially grounded in the relation Habermas posits between social and system integration, and the former's basis in (counterfactually presupposed) redeemable validity-claims. The legitimacy of a political order, what makes it deserving of respect rather than mere compliance, is of course one of the most pervasive themes in the history of political theory. This normative discussion has been to some extent undercut in the twentieth century by social theorists such as Max Weber who use the term in a descriptive sense, such that a regime is legitimate if it is considered to be so by the populace.[43] Habermas shares with Weber, however, an emphasis on the factual importance of legitimation processes, and grounds his argument in an analysis of capitalist crisis which picks up some of the themes of *Theory and Practice*.

Habermas begins with the reference to 'late capitalism' in the original title of the book. 'To use the expression "late capitalism" is to put forward the hypothesis that, even in state-regulated capitalism, social developments involve "contradictions" or crises.'[44] In modern social theory, the term crisis involves a disturbance of both system and social integration: 'only when members of a society experience structural alterations as critical for continued existence and feel their social identity threatened can we speak of crises.' Social integration refers to the socialization or, better, sociation (*Vergesellschaftung*) of acting subjects in symbolically structured lifeworlds; system integration to 'the specific steering performances of a self-regulated system'.[45] Echoing his critique of Niklas Luhmann, Habermas insists that, whereas system theory reduces the former to the latter, an adequate theory must deal with the interconnection of both.[46]

More concretely, Habermas describes 'three universal properties of social systems'. Their 'exchange' with their environments involves both production and socialization, linked, it seems, to factual and normative statements respectively. Second, 'Change in the goal values of social systems is a function of the state of the forces of production and of the degree of system autonomy; but the variation of goal values is limited by a logic of development of world-views on which the imperatives of system integration have no influence.' In other words, the increasingly secular, rationalized, universalistic and reflexive character of belief systems is not a simple result of changes in the mode of production on other system properties. Third, learning in both dimensions, production and socialization, 'determines the level of development of a society'.[47]

Habermas distinguishes four types of social formation, their basic organizational principles and the types of crisis to which they

are prone. In 'primitive' societies, based on age and sex roles institutionalized in kinship, change comes mostly from demographic
pressure, ecological effects or inter-ethnic processes such as exchange and war. 'Traditional' social formations like the European
anciens régimes are based on political class rule and threatened by
crises arising from internal contradictions, generating problems
both of system 'steering' and of the ideological legitimation of an
unstable class structure. In liberal-capitalist social formations,
whose organizational principle is the relationship of wage labour
and capital, the economic and political spheres are 'uncoupled',
and class exploitation and class rule become anonymous and
depoliticized. This in turn means that ideologies in liberal-capitalist
societies take on a universalistic form, appealing to the common
interest embodied in a system that appears to legitimate itself. In
practice, the acquiescence of the proletariat may owe more to tradi-
tionalism, fatalism and repression than to the convincing force of
bourgeois ideologies. 'This does not diminish the socially integrative significance of this new type of ideology in a society that no
longer recognizes political domination in personal form.'[48]

Despite this qualification, expressed in terms very close to those
of Max Weber's discussion of legitimate domination, it is clear that
Habermas, like Weber, assigns crucial importance to the ways in
which social orders are legitimated. Ideology, in other words, is not
simply one means among others by which societies are stabilized; it
enters crucially at the level of social integration into the constitution
of societies seen in some way as reflexive learning systems. This
becomes clear when one looks more closely at the crises characteristic of traditional societies in Habermas's model. In addition to the
'crowding out' or undermining of the *ancien régime* state by the
market economy, and the functional weaknesses of the state machine, Habermas emphasizes the ideological incoherence of traditional societies. 'The contradiction exists between validity claims
of systems of norms and justifications that cannot explicitly permit
exploitation, and a class structure in which privileged appropriation of socially produced wealth is the rule.'[49]

As in more conventional forms of Marxism, however, everything
depends on the mediating links between the abstract contradiction
and empirical social conflicts. For Habermas, 'We can speak of the
"fundamental contradiction" of a social formation when, and only
when, its organizational principle necessitates that individuals and
groups repeatedly confront one another with claims that are, in the
long run, incompatible.'[50] In liberal capitalism, because it is the

economic system that is primarily responsible for social integration, economic crises are also social crises: 'the dialectical contradiction between members of an interaction context comes to pass in terms of structurally insoluble system contradictions or steering problems.'[51] (As Marx put it, rather more snappily, political economy is the anatomy of capitalist society.) The question then arises whether this 'logic of crisis' also applies to advanced or 'organized' capitalism, characterized by oligopolistic corporations and state intervention to support or compensate for market mechanisms.[52] The interventionist welfare state, like the pre-capitalist state, again requires direct legitimation. This is provided by a system of formal representative democracy and a structurally depoliticized sphere, which secures mass loyalty but keeps participation below a level which 'would bring to consciousness the contradiction between administratively socialized production and the continued private appropriation and use of surplus value'.[53]

Compared to the analysis in *Structural Transformation of the Public Sphere*, the context is now more explicitly one of a 'processed and repressed system crisis',[54] in which economic tendencies may be displaced on to the political and sociocultural systems.[55] This continues a process characteristic of the classical bourgeois state, in which economically based class conflicts came to be 'channelled into the political system as an institutionalized struggle over distribution'.[56] When this system is instituted, we have the modern welfare state. Now, however, the economic and political systems are recoupled; the politicians are held responsible for the performance of the economic system. Crises become increasingly, in Claus Offe's phrase, crises of crisis management.

Twenty years on, it is interesting to look back at this book which was written in the aftermath of the events of May 1968, before the first oil price shock and the neo-conservative turn known in West Germany as the *Tendenzwende*. Many early readers of the book, especially in countries like the UK whose economies were already in a very shaky state, questioned the notion that cyclical crises of capitalism could be deflected in the way Habermas suggested, and stuck to more orthodoxly Marxist prognoses of an eventual final crisis.

This has of course not materialized. On the other hand, the more traditional Keynesian methods of economic crisis management have suffered a long period of eclipse. More relevant in this context, the neo-Marxist analysis of the fiscal crisis of the state and the other limitations on the welfare state has been joined by the big batallions of the New Right.[57] Habermas has continued his analysis of the contradictions of the welfare state and social democracy in *The Theory of Communicative Action* and in other writings discussed in the coming chapters.

What stands out most sharply, perhaps, is the instability of the original conceptual relation between legitimation and 'mass loyalty'. While conceding that there are all kinds of loose ends in the book, Habermas has never really responded to the charge that a normative conception of legitimacy is relatively unimportant for the factual stability of real societies. As David Held pointed out, Habermas's theory suffers from 'a problematic emphasis on the centrality of shared norms and values in social integration and on the importance of "internalization" in the genesis of individual identity and social order'.[58] But, as Michael Mann, Anthony Giddens and others have also noted, ideologies are much less systematic than intellectuals, including social theorists, tend to assume.[59] And a normative consensus on the legitimacy of a regime may be less crucial than what critical theory tends to brush aside as a residual category of 'mass loyalty'.

In a related line of criticism, Axel Honneth brings out the complexity of the ideas of natural justice and relatively unarticulated critiques of social injustice which may go along with a pragmatic or fatalistic acceptance of it.[60] The contrast between legitimation and 'mass loyalty' seems much too simple to do justice to this complexity. The long survival, and incredibly rapid collapse, of the state socialist dictatorships in eastern Europe and the USSR are a reminder of the practical difficulties of analyses of this kind.[61]

5

Rational Action and Societal Rationalization

It was clear that Habermas's work of the 1970s required a systematic presentation. In 1981 he produced a massive two-volume work (later followed by a supplementary volume of essays), whose structure somewhat resembles Talcott Parsons's *Structure of Social Action*. Parsons had presented his own action theory via a selective reconstruction of the history of European social theory, and, just as Parsons identified a convergence towards the 'voluntaristic' (in practice, normatively guided) theory of action, so Habermas uncovers the foundations of a theory of communicative action and communicative rationality.

Before looking at *The Theory of Communicative Action* in detail, it is worth bearing in mind, as well as the positive project just mentioned, the alternatives against which Habermas sets it up. These are basically two, one philosophical or metatheoretical, the other sociological or theoretical. Here too the structure of Habermas's critique parallels that of Parsons. Where *The Structure of Social Action* was directed against 'positivism' and 'utilitarianism', Habermas's targets are, first, what he variously describes as transcendental philosophy, the philosophy of consciousness or philosophical fundamentalism on the one hand, and a concept of action on the other hand as an individualistic and goal-centred process. And, just as Parsons had argued that the positivistic-utilitarian theory of action had led social theory astray, so Habermas argues that the twin influences of the philosophy of consciousness and of the individualistic-teleological concept of action have weakened the critique of capitalist modernity since Marx, which for Habermas (and here of course he differs sharply from Parsons) is a far more important project than the development of a watertight action theory.[1]

The Theory of Communicative Action (*Theorie des Kommunikativen Handelns*) is not the sort of book which is easily summarized in a set of numbered themes, but a first attempt might look something like this:

1 The sphere of human activity mapped out by the notions of communicative action, coming to agreement (*Verständigung*), etc. – contrasted with other types of social action.
2 The emergence of communicative action and its role in the evolution of human societies.
3 The development of the concept of communicative action in social theory, including theories about 2.
4 The erosion of the sphere of communicative action and communicative rationality by the market and administrative processes characteristic of the modern world.
5 The critique of 4, thus reformulating in a more adequate form the critique of capitalist modernity since Marx.

These themes are, of course, anticipated in the work discussed in the previous chapter. In *The Theory of Communicative Action* the main emphasis is on 3, but Habermas moves backwards and forwards between 'historical' and 'systematic' issues – the latter presented mainly in 'intermediate reflections'. The following account concentrates on the systematic themes; I discuss the adequacy of Habermas's accounts of other thinkers only when it directly affects his own position.

The book is divided into two volumes, published simultaneously in Germany but with a substantial lag in English. The title of the first volume, *Handlungsrationalität und gesellschafliche Rationalisierung*, is, literally translated, *The Rationality of Action and the Rationalization of Society*; that of the second volume, *Zur Kritik der funktionalistischen Vernunft*, is *Lifeworld and System: A Critique of Functionalist Reason*. My reason for emphasizing the title of volume I is that its main thesis, in a nutshell, is that societal rationalization is not, *pace* Weber, reducible to patterns of action orientations. But nor, as we shall see, is it radically separate from them, as system theory would have it.

Rationality of action

Philosophy and social theory, Habermas argues, converge in a project which one might broadly call the reconstruction of rationality. In modern philosophy, which has abandoned foundationalist metaphysical projects, this convergence towards a theory of rationality stands out more clearly. This sort of philosophy is complementary to the critical self reflection practised by the individual sciences.[2] Sociology has a special relationship to philosophical reflection on rationality. Whereas political science has dropped its links with natural law, and hence with the organization of society as a whole, and economics too has treated the economy as a subsystem in abstraction from questions of social integration, sociology has retained a focus on problems of society as a whole, especially those of modernization and rationalization. And sociology, like social or cultural anthropology, has been concerned with all types of social action, and not only those oriented to 'economic' or 'political' purposes. Sociology confronts issues of rationality at three levels. At the level which Habermas calls empirical or empirical-theoretical, it asks if 'the modernization of society can be described from the standpoint of cultural and societal rationalization' (p. 6). At a theoretical level, sociological action schemes have been mainly oriented to capturing the contrast between community and society (*Gemeinschaft* and *Gesellschaft*) and the rationalization of conduct in that sense. And at a metatheoretical level the understanding of rational action 'became the reference point for understanding all action orientations' (p. 6), and hence the cutting edge of *verstehende* sociology.

Habermas's concept of rationality is defined in terms of the existence of 'good reasons or grounds' (p. 22). This is a cognitivist conception which ties it closely to knowledge or truth,[3] rather than purely procedural considerations, but it also gives primacy to communicative rationality. Unlike the 'cognitive-instrumental' notion of rationality in teleological action, where ideas of the manipulation of, or adaptation to an environment are central, a model of rationality grounded in communication implies an option in favour of 'a wider concept of rationality' oriented to 'argumentative speech' (p. 10).

The validity-claims raised in communicative action relate to what Habermas calls the three 'worlds' to which speakers relate: the objective world of physical things (the cat is on the mat), the subjective world of inner experiences (I dislike that cat) and the social world of roles and norms (you shouldn't kick the cat). More complicated assertions may often involve reference to all three worlds, as when I explain my inappropriate role behaviour by the emotional effects of an event in my childhood (cf. p. 83). But while we relate to all three worlds the recognition that they are distinct is a central aspect of modernity. I can no longer say, for example, that what is true or good is what makes *me* feel good.[4]

These world-relations (*Weltbezüge*) illuminate the four types of action which Habermas now distinguishes. *Teleological* or goal-oriented action involves a decision based on means–ends rationality, given a certain interpretation of a situation. In the variant which he calls *strategic* action the actor takes into account the likely behaviour of other goal-directed actors (p. 85). This utility-maximizing model underlies game theory and decision theory.

Normatively regulated action is that of 'members of a social group who orient their action to common values' and comply with agreed norms, fulfilling agreed behaviour expectations – as in functionalist role theory. *Dramaturgical* action involves the presentation of self examined by Erving Goffman, Rom Harré and others. Finally, *communicative action* is the (verbal or non-verbal) interaction between two or more actors who 'seek to reach an understanding about their action situation and their plans of action in order to coordinate their actions by way of agreement' (p. 86).

At first sight it may seem as if only teleological (including strategic) action is rationally oriented in a strong sense and susceptible of rationalization, but this, Habermas insists, is one of the illusions of modernity (p. 74).[5] In fact, the other types of action involve increasingly complex aspects of rationality. Whereas teleological and strategic action principally involve only relations between the actor and his or her objective world, made up of both human and non-human objects, normatively regulated action also involves the social world of norms. Dramaturgical action involves a further reference by the actor to his or her subjective world of needs and desires, whether this is projected or concealed; this is strategic action playing on the interface between the inner and outer worlds. Finally, in communicative action, the use of language to represent all three worlds and the actor's relation to the world as such is explicitly problematized (p. 94).

> The one-sidedness of the first three concepts of language can be seen in the fact that the corresponding types of communication . . . prove

to be limit cases of communicative action: *first*, the indirect communication of those who have only the realization of their own ends in
view; *second*, the consensual action of those who simply actualize an
already existing normative agreement; and *third*, presentation of self
in relation to an audience. In each case, only one function of language
is thematized: the release of perlocutionary effects, the establishment
of interpersonal relations, and the expression of subjective experiences. By contrast, the communicative model of action, which defines
the traditions of social science connected with Mead's symbolic
interactionism, Wittgenstein's concept of language games, Austin's
theory of speech acts and Gadamer's hermeneutics, takes all the
functions of language equally into consideration. (p. 95)

Habermas stresses that communicative action is not identical with
communication, though it takes place by means of communication:
it 'designates a type of interaction that is *coordinated through* speech
acts and does *not coincide with them*' (p. 101). There remains, however, a certain ambiguity as to whether he is referring to actual types
of action and the relations between them, or to *theories* of action,
such as those listed above, or both.

In understanding the meaning of social actions, the issue of
rationality appears in various ways. In the case of what Max Weber
called subjectively purposive-rational action, we are simply concerned, like the purposively rational actors themselves, with how
far such an action is also objectively rational. Here, our rational
interpretations take the attitude of a participant; 'the interpreter
presupposes a basis for judgement that is shared by all parties,
including the actors' (p. 103). In the case of normatively regulated
action, 'the question of a rational interpretation does not [immedi-
ately] arise, since an observer can ascertain descriptively whether
an action accords with a given norm and whether or not the norm in
turn enjoys social currency' (p. 104). There is, however, the further
issue of whether the norm is also *justified*, and this Habermas describes as rational interpretation. Similarly, in the case of dramaturgical action, 'An interpreter can interpret an action rationally in
such a way that he thereby captures elements of deception or self-
deception' (p. 105).

The concept of rational interpretation may derive from Max
Weber, but it is not particularly precise. For Weber, it is related to
the degree to which our understanding is 'evident', connoting an
intellectual process as opposed to one of imaginative or empathic
re-enactment. Gresham's Law, that bad money drives out good

(because people hoard the 'better' currency), is 'a rationally evident interpretation . . . under the ideal-typical presupposition of purely purposive-rational action'.[6] Clearly Habermas has a much broader notion in mind; rational interpretations characterize not just rational-choice economic models, but cognitivist ethics, psychoanalysis and the Marxist critique of ideology.[7] 'Communicative actions', he claims, 'always require an interpretation that is rational in approach' (p. 106).

This apparently innocuous claim in fact commits Habermas to what he admits is a 'disquieting thesis' that the understanding of communicative actions necessarily involves a rational evaluation of the validity-claims which they raise. Habermas attempts to support this claim with a combination of Gadamer's hermeneutics and the thesis, developed in analytic philosophy of language, that to understand the meaning of a sentence is to understand its truth-conditions, i.e. what has to be the case if it is true. Habermas notes the convergence between the ontological emphasis, by Heidegger and Gadamer, on understanding and coming to agreement (*Verständigung*) as basic aspects of human life and history, and the complementary recognition in the methodology of the social sciences that they have to do with 'symbolically prestructured objects' (p. 108). The social scientist's access to the rules followed by members of a society is through his or her pre-theoretical knowledge of social life as a participant. But this knowledge also makes him or her into a 'virtual participant' in 'the process of communication into which he *entered* only to understand' (p. 112). The social scientist cannot just jump back and forth between the perspectives of participant and observer. 'The interpreter would not have understood what a "reason" is if he did not reconstruct it with its claim to provide grounds, that is, if he did not give it a rational interpretation in Max Weber's sense' (p. 116).

Once again, Habermas emphasizes that a rational as opposed to a descriptive interpretation is an *option* in relation to teleological, normatively regulated or dramaturgical action. We can *choose* whether to take seriously the claims implicitly or explicitly made by actors for the purposive rationality, normative correctness or sincerity of their actions. As soon as we describe behaviour as communicative action, however, we are 'in there' with the participants (p. 119).

If Habermas *has* shown, as he claims, the centrality of 'the rationality problematic' to sociology in terms of both its models of action and the understanding of meaning, there remains the question of societal rationalization and modernization. Sociology *happens* to have developed around this issue, but there is also 'an internal relation between sociology and the theory of rationalization' (p. 137). Since sociology cannot avoid using concepts of rationality, it needs universalistic ones, if it is not to fall into a particular and limited perspective. The model of the raising and grounding of validity-claims 'would have to be shown to be universally valid'.[8]

How might one argue for such a conception? The first way, Habermas suggests, is the formal-pragmatic reconstruction of communicative action – the sort of approach, presumably, which we find in some of the essays in *Communication and the Evolution of Society*. Second, one might assess the empirical usefulness of the model in relation to such varied phenomena as systematically distorted communication, anthropogenesis and developmental psychology; again, Habermas and others have sketched out some possible work in this direction. Given the scale of research that would be required to carry through these approaches systematically, Habermas adopts a third, 'somewhat less demanding' strategy:

> to work up the sociological approaches to a theory of societal rationalization . . . with the systematic aim of laying out the problems that can be solved by means of a theory of rationalization developed in terms of the basic concepts of communicative action. (p. 140)

Habermas's aim, then, is a double one: to demonstrate the theoretical power of the notion of communicative action and to ask 'whether, and if so how, capitalist modernization can be conceived as a process of one-sided rationalization' (p. 140).

Societal rationalization

It is clear that Max Weber will take pride of place in any discussion of societal rationalization. As Habermas puts it, 'Among the classical figures of sociology, Max Weber is the only one who broke with both the premises of the philosophy of history and the basic assumptions of evolutionism and who nonetheless wanted to conceive of the modernization of old-European society as the result of a universal-historical process of rationalization' (p. 143). We have already seen Habermas invoke the precedent of Weber's concept of rational interpretation, but his account of the contrast between mythical and 'modern' thought, the differentiation of spheres of action and validity is deeply indebted to Weber's notions of the disenchantment of the world and the rationalization of action orientations – first in the realm of religion and then in the secular world.

I shall not examine Habermas's account of Weber in detail. Briefly, his criticism of Weber is that when he analyses the rationalization of modern Western society he puts too much emphasis on the narrow aspect of purposive rationality. In other words, it is not that Weber's concept of rationalization is too broad and diffuse, as many critics have complained, but that it is too limited, and exists in an uneasy relationship with the image of a substantively rational society, which for Weber is a lost utopia.

Max Weber views the institutional framework of the capitalist economy and the modern state in a different way from Marx: not as relations of production that fetter the potential for rationalization, but as subsystems of purposive-rational action in which occidental rationalism develops at a societal level (p. 144). It is mainly the capitalist economy and the state, Habermas suggests, that Weber aims to explain in terms of rationalization. But these processes were made possible, as Weber himself showed, by an earlier and more fundamental rationalization process involving two main components: 'the methodical conduct of life, along the lines of a vocational ethic, . . . and the organized measures of formal law. Considered formally, both are based on the same structures of consciousness; posttraditional legal and moral representations' (p. 166). We can distinguish between a broad concept of rationalization spanning action orientations and world-views, and a narrower concept of societal rationalization focusing on the economy and the state (p. 178). For the first rationalization to develop into the second, religious asceticism had to be relocated in the secular world, in the Protestant work ethic, and (although, as Habermas notes, Weber did not deal with this aspect in much detail) modern science had to make possible the overcoming of the separation between theory and experimental practice (p. 214; cf. p. 220).

As we saw in the previous section, Habermas argues that speakers adopt propositional attitudes to three 'worlds': the objective world of entities, the subjective world of mental states and the objective world of social norms. The attainment, in modernity, of what Piaget called a 'decentred' understanding of the objective world, that is one which is neither egocentric, like that of a baby, nor sociocentric, as in magical and mythical thought, involves the differentiation of the social and subjective worlds from the objective world. This process of differentiation, Habermas claims, takes place in, or perhaps against the background of, the lifeworld and is a central process in its rationalization.

Habermas's concept of the lifeworld is less like that in Husserl's phenomenology, where the stress is on its pre-interpreted quality, than the social-phenomenological concept of the everyday, including (but not reducible to) what Alfred Schutz calls the 'stock of knowledge at hand'. But Habermas's concept is also more culturally differentiated than Schutz's: 'the lifeworld also stores the interpretive work of preceding generations.' The world-views embodied in lifeworlds themselves, as we have seen, become decentred as they become more sophisticated: this means that less and less can be taken for granted as unquestioned shared knowledge and practice, and more and more depends on 'the interpretive accomplishments of the participants themselves' and on their 'risky, because rationally motivated agreement'. In other words, the 'rationalization of the lifeworld' involves a shift from 'normatively ascribed agreement' to 'communicatively achieved understanding'.

What Habermas has done, in essence, is to extract from Weber an implicit question which was one of the principal themes of the previous chapter: 'How did the structures of the lifeworld familiar in traditional societies have to change before the cognitive potential that resulted from religious rationalization could be fully exploited at a societal level and embodied in the structurally differentiated orders of life in a society modernized in this way?' (p. 220). If one begins to think in this counterfactual way, the question arises whether the rationalization of consciousness could have given rise to different types of societal modernization from those which actually occurred in Europe 'and, if so, how the selective pattern of capitalist rationalization can be explained' (p. 221).

Weber does of course pose counterfactual questions, but mostly in terms of why autonomous modernization took place only in the West. When he turns from cultural to societal rationalization, his concept of rationality becomes narowed down, excluding wider dimensions of rationality. This leads to a tension between Weber's would-be value-free sociological analysis and his more speculative observations, such as those at the end of *The Protestant Ethic* where he gloomily contemplates a wholly bureaucratized world. 'The repressed problems turn up again in his reflections on the state of our times, where he implicitly relies on standards by which he can assess and criticize a rationality that has shrunken to a totalized purposive rationality' (pp. 221–2).

Habermas is recapitulating, as he notes in a footnote (p. 233), Herbert Marcuse's criticism that Weber's theory allows capitalist instrumental rationality to predominate over any alternative, just as it did in reality. The rationalization of law, along with the Protestant ethic, are the two primary mechanisms of rationalization of action, in both senses of the term: the reflexive reorientation of conduct in moral-practical terms and its purposive-rational co-ordination. But, whereas the Protestant ethic *came to be* secularized, modern law *began* in a secularized form. Weber's error, according to Habermas, is to overemphasize the separation of law from substantive evaluative contexts. Whereas in the case of the Protestant ethic he gives reasons why there can never be an enduring institutionalization of secularized moral-practical structures of consciousness, he reinterprets modern law in such a way that it is detached from that evaluative sphere and can appear from the start as an institutional embodiment of cognitive-instrumental rationality (p. 243; cf. p. 254).

This fits in with what Habermas calls Weber's 'diagnosis of the times', his more speculative (and non-value-free) reflections on the loss of meaning and the loss of freedom characteristic of modernity. The loss of meaning thesis is, Habermas suggests, a variant of Nietzschean nihilism which Weber tends to present in terms of a new polytheism, an unending combat between competing gods, demons or (more literally) value systems. As Habermas puts it, 'reason splits itself up into a plurality of value spheres and destroys its own universality . . . within modern society there is no longer any legitimate order that could guarantee the cultural reproduction of the corresponding value orientations and action dispositions' (p. 247).

Weber's second thesis, in Habermas's reconstruction, is that the spread of systems of purposive-rational action produces the 'iron cage' which he refers to at the end of *The Protestant Ethic*. Habermas takes issue with both theses, and with the 'implication' that Weber sees the second as following from the first. Weber is right to stress the differentiation of value spheres in modernity, but wrong to interpret it as leading to a free-for-all between irreconcilable claims.

The unity of rationality in the multiplicity of value spheres rationalized according to their inner logics is secured precisely at the formal level of the argumentative redemption of validity claims. . . . Weber

did not distinguish adequately between the particular value contents
of cultural traditions and . . . universal standards of value.

Thus, while we cannot of course decide whether, say, German or
French culture is superior, we *can* rationally assess the applicability
of standards of truth, justice and taste (pp. 249ff).

Second, on the loss of freedom thesis, Weber 'plays down the
structural analogies that obtain between moral development and
the rationalization of law [and] . . . considers law primarily as a
sphere which, like the provision of material goods or the struggle
for legitimate power, is open to formal rationalization' (p. 251).
Thus law as a post-traditional mode of regulating social relationships according to principles is part of the first rationalization; law
as a purposive-rational 'parallel case to the embodiment of cognitive-instrumental rationality in the economy and the state administration' (p. 254) is a central part of the second rationalization.

Weber's detailed account of modern private law, emphasizing
the aspects of positivity, legalism and formality, brings out its func-
tionality for capitalist exchange and enterprise. But, even if Weber is
right to stress these aspects of law, they do not explain how it came
to have these properties and functions, nor how the law as a whole
might be said (contra Weber's legal positivism) to require normative justification (p. 262).[9]

The importance of this detailed critique of Weber, which I have
merely outlined here, lies in his pervasive influence on the whole
tradition of Western Marxism, such that a reconstruction in more
adequate terms of the Marxist critique of capitalism also requires a
reformulation of central aspects of Weber's theorizing. In particular,
Habermas suggests, Weber's action theory needs to be expanded to
show, more fully than he did, that purposive rationality is only one
dimension of the rationalization of action. Second, and this is the
principal theme of the second volume of *The Theory of Communicative Action*, an adequate account of the rationalization of law requires us to go beyond the limits of a theory of action in the
direction of system theory.[10]

It is clear, I think, that in *The Theory of Communicative Action*
Weber is playing something like the role that Hegel played for
Marx.[11] Weber, for Habermas, must be not so much stood on his
head (or put back the right way up) as persuaded to stand on two
legs rather than one, to support his theory of modernity with more
systematic and structural analyses than those of the (purposive-
rational) rationalization of action. And, as we have just seen, this

reminder to Weber to use both his legs has two implications: the opening up of the concept of rationalization and the recourse to system theory.

Weber 'parts company with a theory of communicative action' when he defines action in terms of the actor attaching a subjective meaning to it. 'He does not elucidate "meaning" in connection with the model of speech; he does not relate it to the linguistic medium of possible understanding, but to the beliefs and intentions of an acting subject, taken to begin with in isolation' (p. 279). This leads him to his familiar distinction between value-rational, purposive-rational, traditional and affectual action. What Weber should have done instead was to concentrate not on orientations of action but on 'the general structures of the lifeworld to which acting subjects belong' (p. 328).[12]

Habermas ends volume 1 with a discussion of the Weberian continuities in early critical theory. The differentiation of fields of knowledge into discrete spheres such as science, art and moral/legal/political theory, oriented to distinct validity-claims, amounts to a rationalization of the lifeworld: Weber mapped the shift from traditional action (*Gemeinschaftshandeln*) to rationally regulated social action (*Gesellschaftshandeln*). 'But only if we differentiate *Gesellschaftshandeln* into action oriented to reaching understanding and action oriented to success can we conceive the communicative rationalization of everyday action and the formation of subsystems of purposive-rational economic and administrative action as complementary developments' (p. 341).

Thus, at the same time as the decline of traditional consensus puts a greater burden on *Verständigung*, there is a process whereby what Habermas, following Parsons, calls the 'steering media' of money and power and what Weber, more concretely, tends to refer to as the market and administrative power are differentiated out of the lifeworld and legitimated as a whole through the law. At the same time as communicative action in the lifeworld, the pursuit of agreement in language, becomes increasingly a matter of rational argumentation and discursive justification, the mechanisms of market and administrative state power also become more sophisticated and tend to undermine the scope of communicative action and the pursuit of agreement. Marx and Engels, in *The Communist Manifesto* and in their subsequent work, described a central aspect of this process in terms of exploitation in and by the capitalist labour market. Western Marxism, from Lukács to Habermas himself, generalizes this analysis.

Horkheimer and Adorno follow Weber in their diagnoses of a loss of meaning in the modern world produced by the fragmentation of reason,[13] and the loss of freedom produced by the growth of bureaucratic subsystems and captured in Adorno's 'administered world'. Lukács brings together Marx and Weber, reification and rationalization. Just as, for Hobbes, man is a wolf to man, in developed capitalism men and women become commodities for one another, trapped in a nexus of apparently objective and increasingly instrumental relations (p. 359). Horkheimer and Adorno take up Lukács's diagnosis of reification, without of course being able to share his optimistic scenario of its transcendence in proletarian class-consciousness.[14] They take the categories of reified thought or consciousness, which Lukács derived from the commodity form, as fundamental, thus turning away from a social theory to a more abstract anthropological account of the relation between 'man' (exemplified by Odysseus, Kant, Sade, etc.) and 'nature', in which ideas of reconciliation, mimesis, or whatever, can only be metaphors.

The history of early critical theory has been well analysed by Jay, Dubiel, Honneth, Wiggershaus and many other writers. The interesting twist in Habermas's account, apart from his status as the chief legatee of the whole business, is his explanation of its decline into an increasingly pessimistic critique of culture (*Kulturkritik*). Whereas most commentators focus on the critical theorists' increasing disillusionment in the face of the consolidation of post-war Stalinism and consumer capitalism, Habermas claims 'that the programme of early critical theory foundered not on this or that contingent circumstance, but from the exhaustion of the philosophy of consciousness' (p. 386). Running right through Western philosophy, Habermas argues, 'is a common basic model' in which 'the subject relates to objects either to represent them as they are or to produce them as they should be' (p. 387). Horkheimer and Adorno conceive of and criticize this form of subjective reason as instrumental reason. They give a name – mimesis – to what is lost in the application of instrumental reason, but they cannot provide a theory of it. The turn proposed by Habermas, from a model of the individual subject conceptualizing and manipulating objects in the world (including other people) to a model of intersubjective understanding and communicative rationality, permits a reformulation of the reification problematic.

The problem of reification arises less from a purposive rationality that has been absolutized in the service of self-preservation, from an instrumental reason that has gone wild, than from the circumstance that an unleashed functionalist reason of systems maintenance disregards and overrides the claim to reason ingrained in communicative sociation and lets the rationalization of the lifeworld run idle. (pp. 398–9)

As we shall see in the next chapter, Habermas finds in the work of Mead and Durkheim the 'basic concepts in which Weber's theory of rationalization can be taken up and freed from the aporias of the philosophy of consciousness: Mead with his communications-theoretic foundation of sociology, Durkheim with his theory of social solidarity that interrelates social integration and system integration' (p. 399).

6

The Colonization of the Lifeworld

Reconceptualizing the lifeworld

In volume 2 of *The Theory of Communicative Action* (*Lifeworld and System: A Critique of Functionalist Reason*), Habermas notes the parallel critiques of the subject-object model of philosophy and of introspection in the early twentieth century in analytical philosophy of language and psychological theories of behaviour. 'Both renounced direct access to the phenomena of consciousness and replaced intuitive self-knowledge, reflection, or introspection with procedures that did not appeal to intuition. They proposed analyses that started from linguistic expressions or observed behaviour and were open to intersubjective testing.'[1] These two research programmes developed separately, and in increasingly specialized ways, in the course of the century, in analytic philosophy, post-empiricist philosophy of science and speech-act theory. In a parallel though entirely separate development, G. H. Mead examined the phenomena of consciousness in terms of their roots in processes of symbolic interaction.[2]

Mead's account of the development of normatively regulated self–others relations out of linguistically mediated interaction is, however, somewhat compressed, in Habermas's view. Moving from the conventions which underlie symbolically mediated, as opposed to gestural, interaction to the normative conventions which govern human societies, Mead 'traces the development that starts from symbolically mediated interaction only along the path that leads to normatively regulated action, and neglects the path that leads to propositionally differentiated communication in language' (p. 23). This, Habermas suggests, is because Mead's focus is an ontogenetic one on the socialization of the child into an already existing community. He therefore misses the phylogenetic dimension of the origins of human lifeworlds.

> Participants in symbolically mediated interaction can transform themselves, so to speak, from examples of an animal species with an inborn, species-specific environment into members of a collective with a lifeworld only to the degree that a generalized other – we might also say: a collective consciousness or a group identity – has taken shape. (p. 45)

Habermas therefore turns, not surprisingly, to the French sociologist Emile Durkheim's concept of the collective consciousness, as expressed first in religion, in 'primitive' societies, and later in a wider range of cultural forms.[3] This, however, is also too undifferentiated. Durkheim 'rashly subsumes both the communality of normative consensus accomplished through ritual and the intersubjectivity of knowledge established through speech acts under the same concept of collective consciousness' (p. 57). Thus, as Parsons and many others have noted, Durkheim does not adequately distinguish between general cultural values and more specific norms; nor does he show how the former feed into the latter: 'how institutions draw their validity from the religious springs of social solidarity' (p. 57).

This neglect of communicative action in its role as 'a switching station for the energies of social solidarity' is also the source of Durkheim's dualistic conception of human nature as both egoistic and moralized, i.e. socialized. Again this is a familiar criticism of Durkheim, but Habermas relates it interestingly to Durkheim's alleged entrapment in 'the mentalistic conceptualizations of the philosophy of consciousness' (p. 57). Even the states of the collective consciousness, he reminds us, are presented as conscious states of the *individual*. In a section entitled 'The rational structure of the linguistification [*Versprachlichung*] of the sacred', Habermas links these elements into a (somewhat speculative) hypothesis about the historical origins of our sociocultural order. 'The socially integrative and expressive functions that were at first fulfilled by ritual practice pass over to communicative action; the authority of the holy is gradually replaced by the authority of an achieved consensus' (p. 77).

Habermas's argument, which I shall not summarize in detail here, involves combining the insights of Durkheim and Weber into the development of law, religion and morality with a thought-experiment involving the differentiation of a hypothetical 'limit case of a totally integrated society' (p. 87). Thus, to take a particularly striking example from the development of law, 'the development of the contract from a ritual formation into the most important instrument of bourgeois private law suggests the idea of a "linguistification" of a basic religious consensus that has been set communicatively aflow' (p. 82). What Weber called the rationalization of religion is another crucial aspect, involving, among other things, the mediation between religious world-views and the profane knowledge of an increasingly scientific and secular world (pp. 88–9).[4]

What Habermas is doing here, in other words, is reconstructing his claims about the rationalization of the lifeworld and the communicative validation of agreement (cf. pp. 75–6 above) in more concrete terms.

> The universalization of law and morality noted by Durkheim can be explained in its structural aspect by the gradual shifting of problems of justifying and applying norms over to processes of consensus formation in language. Once a community of believers has been secularized into a community of cooperation, only a universalistic morality can retain its obligatory character. And only a formal law based on abstract principles creates a divide between legality and morality such that the domains of action, in which the responsibility for settling disputed questions of applying norms is institutionally lifted from participants, get sharply separated from those in which it is radically demanded of them. (pp. 90ff)[5]

Mead is also relevant for Habermas as the inventor of discourse ethics. Taking up Kant's central claim that principles of moral action must be universalizable, Mead develops the idea of the impartial consideration of all interests, including one's own, in a description of an ideal communication community which could have been written by Habermas himself (pp. 94ff). Like Durkheim, Habermas argues, Mead develops this idea into an account of individual identity (pp. 96–106 and 109–10) and an outline theory of the modern democratic and law-based state (p. 96).

Habermas ends his discussion of Mead with two reservations. The first concerns the conflict which we noted in chapter 3 between moral-legal formalism and the stress on concrete ways of life.

Mead's celebration of formalism leads him to neglect the areas of ethical choice which cannot be formalized (p. 109). Habermas's second reservation is a more familiar one about 'the idealism of Mead's theory of society'.

> The material reproduction of society – securing its physical mainte-
> nance both externally and internally – is blended out of the picture of
> society understood as a communicatively structured lifeworld. The
> neglect of economics, warfare, and the struggle for political power,
> the disregard for dynamics in favor of the logic of societal develop-
> ment, are detrimental, above all, to Mead's reflections on social evol-
> ution. Precisely insofar as social integration has more and more to be
> secured via communicatively achieved consensus, there is a pressing
> question as to the limits of the integrative capacity of action oriented
> to reaching understanding, the limits of the empirical efficacy of
> rational motives. The constraints of reproducing the social system,
> which reach right through the action orientations of sociated indi-
> viduals, remain closed off to an analysis restricted to structures of
> interaction. The rationalization of the lifeworld, which occupies
> Mead's interest, has to be located in a systematic history accessible
> only to functional analysis. (p. 109)

Leaving aside the issue of how valid this is as a criticism of Mead,[6] two issues remain in relation to Habermas's project. First, is he right to draw the conclusion that the analysis of domains outside the lifeworld, and the rationalization of the lifeworld itself, requires a turn to functionalism and system theory?[7] Second, despite Habermas's pact with system theory (or perhaps because of it), does his own theory, at least as developed in this book, remain open to this second charge which he addresses to Mead? I shall return to this later.

Having identified a paradigm change within the theory of action, Habermas now addresses the issue of the relation between action theory and systems theory. Using the example of Durkheim's *Division of Labour*,[8] he argues that in analysing such connections between 'stages of system differentiation and forms of social integration' one must distinguish mechanisms for co-ordinating action that harmonize the action orientations of participants from mechanisms that stabilize non-intended interconnections of actions by way of functionally intermeshing action consequences. In one case, the integration of an action system is established by a normatively secured or communicatively achieved consensus; in the other case, by a non-normative regulation of individual decisions that extends beyond the actors' consciousnesses. This distinction between a social integration of society, which takes effect in action orientations, and a systematic integration, which reaches through and beyond action orientations, calls for a corresponding differentiation in the concept of society itself (p. 117).

Habermas thus proposes 'that we conceive of societies simultaneously as systems and lifeworlds' (p. 118). The lifeworld, as we have seen, appears in interaction as a context of relevance, conceived not in terms of consciousness but as 'a culturally transmitted and linguistically organized stock of interpretive patterns' (p. 124). It is the 'horizon' within which human beings refer to items in the objective, subjective and normative worlds. The Schutzian concept of the lifeworld moves away from that of transcendental phenomenology, but it remains 'culturalistic', emphasizing the knowledge of participants in communication. Habermas therefore wishes to broaden it out into a more everyday concept which also includes 'the solidarities of groups integrated via norms and values and the competences of socialized individuals' (p. 135).

> Under the functional aspect of mutual understanding, communicative action serves to transmit and renew cultural knowledge; under the aspect of coordinating action, it serves social integration and the establishment of solidarity; finally, under the aspect of socialization, communicative action serves the formation of personal identities. The symbolic structures of the lifeworld are reproduced by way of the continuation of valid knowledge, stabilization of group solidarity, and socialization of responsible actors. The process of reproduction connects up new situations with the existing conditions of the lifeworld; it does this in the semantic dimension of meanings or contents (of the cultural tradition), as well as in the dimensions of social space (of socially integrated groups), and historical time (of successive generations). Corresponding to these processes of cultural reproduction, social integration and socialization are the structural components of the lifeworld: culture, society, person. (p. 137)[9]

This conception can be contrasted with the culturalistically abridged concept of the lifeworld in the phenomenological sociology of Schutz or of Berger and Luckmann, which reduces communicative action to processes of interpretation or *Verständigung*, the Durkheimian conception of society emphasizing the aspect of normative integration, and the Meadian tradition which is concerned only with the socialization of individuals and thus 'shrinks down to social psychology' (p. 140).

Habermas goes on to sketch out a more adequate concept of a lifeworld embodying cultural reproduction (continuity of tradition, coherence and rationality of knowledge), social integration (stabilization of group identities, solidarity) and socialization (transmission of generalized competences for action, harmonization of individual biographies with collective forms of life). The corresponding failures take the form of loss of meaning, crises of legitimation and orientation, in the case of cultural reproduction, anomie and the absence of social solidarity in the case of social integration, and psychopathologies (especially those of the ego) in the case of socialization. 'The individual reproduction processes can be evaluated according to standards of the rationality of knowledge, the solidarity of members, and the responsibility of the adult personality' (p. 141).

The idea of the rationalization of the lifeworld thus means that 'the further the structural components of the lifeworld and the processes that contribute to maintaining them get differentiated, the more interaction contexts come under control of rationally motivated mutual understanding, that is, of consensus formation that rests in the end on the authority of the better argument' (p. 145). More concretely, the rationalization process involves processes of structural differentiation towards a hypothetical end state in which cultural traditions are constantly criticized and renewed, political forms are dependent on formal procedures of justification, and personalities are increasingly autonomous. The relation to tradition, institutions and the contents of socialization processes becomes increasingly reflective and critical. (Habermas gives the example of the growth of secular formal education.)

These structures do not of course develop in automatic harmony or without challenge; the conservative counter-Enlightenment blamed the pathologies of post-traditional society (loss of meaning, anomie, alienation) on the rationalization of the lifeworld. Marxism, by contrast, endorses this process of rationalization and explains its pathological accompaniments in terms of 'the conditions of material reproduction' – in other words, processes outside the symbolic reproduction of the lifeworld. Reformulating the thesis of 'The Reconstruction of Historical Materialism', Habermas states that the rationalization of the lifeworld reformulates the conditions of the reproduction of social systems (p. 148). And, if the perspective of Marxism is too limited, so is that of *verstehende* sociology. Positing, as did Mead, a culturalistic lifeworld, it presupposes the autonomy of actors (i.e. the idea that their interactions can be explained by their own intentions and decisions), the independence of culture from all external constraints, and the idea that undistorted communication can always be achieved – in methodological terms, the universality of hermeneutics. To get beyond these three 'fictions' we must 'drop the identification of society with the lifeworld'. Social actions are also co-ordinated by external, 'norm-free' systems such as those of the market. We must therefore distinguish between social and system integration and retain both perspectives. To understand the integration of society only as social integration is to limit one's perspective in the ways described above. Conversely, to see society only as a self-regulating system is to cut off access to the structures of the lifeworld, which themselves are crucial for system maintenance. 'Societies are *systematically stabilized* complexes of action of *socially integrated* groups', and social evolution involves *both* an increase in society's 'steering capacity' *and* the differentiation of culture, society and personality (p. 152).

The uncoupling of system and lifeworld

As these two components of society become differentiated in the way just described, they also become differentiated from one another. As new systems emerge, notably states and market economies, they become increasingly 'detached from the social structures through which social integration takes place'. In other words, 'the lifeworld, which is at first coextensive with a scarcely differentiated social system, gets cut down more and more to one subsystem among others'. Although these systems have to be 'anchored in the lifeworld', their detailed workings are not.

> Members behave toward formally organized action systems, steered via processes of exchange and power, as toward a block of quasi-natural reality; within these media-steered subsystems society congeals into a second nature. Actors have always been able to sheer off from an orientation to mutual understanding, adopt a strategic attitude, and objectify normative contexts into something in the objective world, but in modern societies, economic and bureaucratic spheres emerge in which social relations are regulated only via money and power. (p. 154)

Habermas draws a contrast with a model of a tribal society, which 'reproduces itself as a whole in every interaction' (p. 157).[10]

Thus, for example, the exchange of women in marriage is both social and system integration (p. 163). System differentiation comes in with exchange relations and power relations, with these subsystems then being 'anchored' in the lifeworld by institutional means. As in his earlier writings on this subject, Habermas suggests that this model roughly corresponds to the Marxist model of base and superstructure, in which the base is dominant in relation to social change, and understanding the institutional system as also part of the base (p. 168).

Following the French Marxist anthropologist Maurice Godelier,[11]. Habermas claims that 'In tribal societies, whether stratified or not, the kinship system takes on the role of relations of production' (p. 168). 'Base and superstructure can separate off from one another only when the kinship system breaks down as the basic social structure, thus bursting apart the clamps that held systemic and socially integrative mechanisms tightly together' (p. 169). In traditional societies the state concentrates

> the capacity for action of society as a whole; by contrast, modern societies do without the accumulation of steering functions within a single organization. . . . The capitalist economy can no longer be understood as an institutional order in the sense of the traditional state; it is the medium of exchange that is institutionalized, while the subsystem differentiated out via this medium is, as a whole, a block of more or less norm-free sociality. (p. 171)

Habermas skates over a lot of historical sociology in the few pages just summarized. Without going into detailed questions about the actual organization and 'steering capacity' of traditional states, nor, for the moment, about Habermas's use of the language of system theory, we may perhaps accept the plausibility of his model of institutional differentiation. However inefficient and sclerotic they may have been, *ancien régime* states, or at least courts, were very much the symbolic and practical centres of their societies, in so far as these societies had such a centre. In capitalist societies, by contrast, however mercantilist or state-interventionist, the economic system does tend to operate according to its own principles, and administrative systems, too, tend to be differentiated, and relatively independent of direct state control.[12]

These processes of system differentiation can also be viewed from what Habermas calls 'the internal perspective of the lifeworld involved'. In tribal societies, system differentiation takes the form of marital exchange and 'the accumulation of prestige'; it 'does not yet make itself noticeable by intervening in the structures of the lifeworld' (p. 172). In class-divided societies with a state, the political order is legitimated if at all, *vis-à-vis* the lifeworld, 'through religious worldviews taking on ideological functions'. Thirdly, in modern societies, processes of exchange via media operate by themselves as subsystems, 'detached from normative contexts', and thus 'challenge the assimilative power of the lifeworld'. The social system made up of these subsystems escapes from the intuitive knowledge of everyday communicative practice, and is henceforth accessible only to the counter-intuitive knowledge of the social sciences developed since the eighteenth century (p. 173).

Thus, although it is the differentiation in and rationalization of the lifeworld that makes these processes of system differentiation or 'increase in complexity' possible,[13] they develop at the expense of lifeworlds, which become more and more 'provincial'. 'In a differentiated social system the lifeworld seems to shrink to a subsystem' (p. 173). As Habermas's use of the term 'second nature' implies, the model is that of the paradox running from Hegel through Marx and Engels to Weber and Lukács, in which the development of aspects of a society takes place at the expense of their links with the whole. Modern forms of moral reasoning embody a higher, post-conventional stage of consciousness or communicative rationality, but at the same time they are marginalized by the formalization of market and administrative structures.

In a dense but important section, which anticipates his more recent work discussed in chapter 9 below, Habermas spells out his view of the developmental interrelation between market and legal structures: 'Insofar as actions are coordinated through a delinguistified medium such as money, normatively embedded interactions are turned into success-oriented transactions among private legal subjects.' The legal order of the *Rechtsstaat* comes to be legitimized as a whole. Civil rights and popular sovereignty, together with the jurisprudential principles which underlie the various forms of criminal, civil and public law and 'embody postconventional structures of moral consciousness', form 'the bridges between a de-moralized and externalized legal sphere and a deinstitutionalized and internalized morality' (p. 178).

Thus what Durkheim and Parsons call the generalization of values, 'the tendency for value orientations that are institutionally required of actors to become more and more general and formal in the course of social evolution' (p. 179), is in fact a more paradoxical and contradictory process. 'The development of law and morality, from which value generalization originates, [is] an aspect of the rationalization of the lifeworld', further developing the communicative rationality of argumentation, but it also opens up space for the co-ordination of action by formal steering media (pp. 180–1).

We thus have three interrelated distinctions. That between system and social integration is based on two others, between action oriented to success and action oriented to mutual understanding, and between mechanisms of action co-ordination which develop and formalize mutual understanding (such as trust and rationally justified authority) and mechanisms which replace it, such as money and power.[14]

One might question how far the distinction between system and social integration maps on to, as opposed to just 'presupposing', the first two. Where 'system' versus 'social' integration is simply an analytical distinction, the connection with types of action might be argued to be also analytic, but Habermas, for all his talk of actor and system 'perspectives', clearly understands the media-steered subsystems such as economic or state systems in a more substantial sense. And in these real-world contexts it is clear that even a basically strategic process such as market exchange may include genuinely communicative elements. Just as he had to concede that perlocutionary actions were not of themselves a direct indicator of a strategic orientation, so Habermas, as we shall see in chapter 7, has increasingly differentiated between action orientations and the systems which co-ordinate actions.

A second issue, which Habermas himself raises, is that of the direction of influence from system processes, once established, and the corresponding lifeworld of a given society.

> These structures do, of course, remain linked with everyday communicative practice via basic institutions of civil or public law. We cannot directly infer from the mere fact that system and social integration have been largely uncoupled to linear dependency in one direction or the other. Both are conceivable: the institutions that anchor steering mechanisms such as power and money in the lifeworld could serve as a channel either for the influence of the lifeworld on formally organized domains of action or, conversely, for the influence of the system on communicatively structured contexts of action. In the one case, they function as an institutional framework that subjects system maintenance to the normative restrictions of the lifeworld, in the other, as a base that subordinates the lifeworld to the

systemic constraints of material reproduction and thereby 'mediates' it. (p. 185)

Both of these models can be found in classical social theory. Marxism stresses the destructive impact of systems on lifeworlds, of base on superstructure – a process to be overcome by a transformed, socialist lifeworld. Systems theory, Habermas suggests, in a way inherits the Marxist problematic. It shares the notion that the systemic constraints of system maintenance 'reach right through the symbolic structures of the lifeworld', though without Marx's critical perspective on this process (p. 186). It therefore misses the paradox of rationalization, central to Marx, Weber and critical theory, in which 'The rationalization of the lifeworld makes possible the emergence and growth of subsystems whose independent imperatives turn back destructively upon the lifeworld itself' (p. 186).

Whereas social integration involves the consensual co-ordination of action orientations, system integration means the automatic, or at least 'inconspicuous', co-ordination of the effects of action. Thus system processes may simply operate through action contexts without modifying them. However, 'where system integration intervenes in the very forms of social integration . . . the subjective inconspicuousness of systemic constraints that instrumentalize a communicatively structured lifeworld takes on the character of deception, of objectively false consciousness.' Habermas goes so far as to describe this process as 'structural violence' exercised over intersubjective forms of understanding 'by way of systematic restrictions on communication; distortion is anchored in the formal conditions of communicative action in such a way that the interrelation of the objective, social and subjective worlds gets prejudged for participants in a typical fashion' (p. 187).

By analogy with what Lukács called 'forms of objectivity', predefining the individual's relationship to reality, Habermas speaks of forms of understanding: 'a compromise between the general structures of communicative action and reproductive constraints unavailable as themes within a given lifeworld' (p. 187). Habermas gives the example of the ideological role taken on by 'religious-metaphysical worldviews', the process of sociodicy analysed by Weber in which religious systems justify social inequality and political order, thus meeting a need for legitimation which is absent from tribal societies. The basic pattern is one in which a stratified social order is presented as being in harmony with the fundamental order of the world.[15] But how can these accounts 'be sustained against all appearances of barbaric injustice' (p. 189)? Because, Habermas suggests, these religious systems (or the validity-claims they raise) are too undifferentiated to be accessible to rational critique; the ideological message, in other words, is wrapped up in a mishmash of sacred and profane beliefs.

As in his account, earlier in the book, of the extent to which world-views make possible a decentred understanding of the world, Habermas now sketches out a rough typology of dominant forms of mutual understanding. He stresses that these do not directly correspond to the structures of dominant world-views, since 'established interpretive systems do not pervade all areas of action with the same intensity' (p. 190). Figure 2 illustrates the differentiation of these spheres.

What follows from all this for the relation between social and system integration? Basically, Habermas is restating the thesis of the *Communist Manifesto* that in bourgeois society the old veils of oppression are ripped away. The 'competition' between system and social integration becomes 'more visible'.

> In the end, systemic mechanisms suppress forms of social integration even in those areas where a consensus-dependent coordination of action cannot be replaced, that is, where the symbolic reproduction of the lifeworld is at stake. In these areas the mediatization of the lifeworld assumes the form of a colonization. (p. 196)

How might one theorize this process? Talcott Parsons, Habermas reminds us, moved from action theory, within which he could not derive an adequate concept of society, to stressing the primacy of systems theory, though he retained the more traditional theory of culture which had created problems for his original model of society. Lacking, as Habermas sees it, an adequate account of culture as part of the lifeworld, 'Parsons has no theoretical tools at his disposal with which to explain the resistance that cultural patterns with their own independent logics offer to functional imperatives' (p. 231). Eventually Parsons got off this hook by simply redefining culture as one system among others in a general theory of action systems (pp. 235–6). This in turn creates problems for his theory of modernity:[16] 'Parsons has to reduce sociopathological phenomena to systemic disequilibria; what is specific to social crises gets lost in the process' (p. 192).

In the final chapter of *The Theory of Communicative Action* Habermas therefore returns to Weber, armed with the

Domains of action / Differentiation of validity spheres	Sacred		Profane	
	Cultic practice	World-views that steer practice	Communication	Purposive activity
Confusion of relations of validity and effectiveness: performative-instrumental attitude	1 Rite (institutionaliza-tion of social solidarity)	2 Myth	—	—
Differentiation between relations of validity and effectiveness: orientation to success *v.* to mutual understanding	5 Sacrament/prayer (institutionalization of paths to salvation and knowledge)	6 Religious and metaphysical world-views	3 Communicative action bound to particular contexts and with a holistic orientation to validity	4 Purposive activity as a task-oriented element of roles (utilization of technical innovations)

Differentiation of specific validity-claims at the level of action: objectivating v. norm-conformative v. expressive attitudes	9 Contemplative presentation of auratic art (institutionalization of the enjoyment of art)	10 Religious ethics of conviction, rational law, civil religion	7 Normatively regulated communicative action with an argumentative handling of truth-claims	8 Purposive activity organized through legitimate power (utilization of specialized practical-professional knowledge)
Differentiation of specific validity-claims at the level of discourse: communicative action v. discourse	—	—	11 Normatively unbound communicative action with institutionalized criticism	12 Purposive activity as ethically neutral purposive-rational action (utilization of scientific technologies and strategies)

Figure 2 Forms of mutual understanding

Source: Habermas, *The Theory of Communicative Action, vol. 2*

Durkheimian–Meadian theory of communicative action and the
system/lifeworld distinction sharpened up in his engagement with
Parsons. Weber's theory of rationalization was shown to suffer from
two problems. First, he 'studies the rationalization of action systems
only under the aspect of purposive rationality'. Second, and
relatedly, he 'equated the capitalist pattern of modernization with
societal rationalization generally'. We must therefore shift the focus
from action orientations to subsystems of purposive-rational action
in order 'to take account of the pathological side effects of a class
structure that cannot be grasped by action-theoretical means alone'
(p. 303). Thus in capitalist and state bureaucracies:

> The basic characteristic of the action orientations of members is not
> purposive-rationality, but the fact that all their actions fall under the
> conditions of organizational membership . . . [in which they] act
> communicatively only *with reservation*. They know they *can* have
> recourse to formal regulations, not only in exceptional but in routine
> cases; there is no *necessity* for achieving consensus by communicative
> means. (pp. 310ff)

Although organizations do of course rely on informal, communicative processes, the point is that these, and the lifeworld itself,
become no more than an environment for the system. The meaning
of an action is given by its role in the system; the subjective meaning
is peripheral and secondary (p. 311). It is an 'open question'
whether 'all integrative operations' would be systematized in a
fully bureaucratized world; the 'methodological weakness of an
absolutized systems functionalism', such as Luhmann's, is that it
behaves as if such an administered world was an accomplished fact
(p. 312).

Similarly, the connection postulated by Weber between
bureaucratization and the loss of freedom is based not on the replacement of value rationality by purposive rationality alone, but
on the uncoupling of system and lifeworld, and the process by
which 'the mediatization of the lifeworld turns into its colonization'
(p. 318). This happens, Habermas argues, via the differentiation of
private and public spheres, centred respectively on the nuclear
family, devoted to consumption and the socialization of its members, and a cultural–media system which delivers mass loyalty to
the state (pp. 318–19).

The roles of employee and state client are organization-depen-
dent, involving detachment from lifeworld contexts and adaptation

'to formally organized domains of action'. However painful may have been the historical process of 'the monetarization and bureaucratization of labor power and government performance', and the concomitant destruction of traditional forms of life, Weber was right that these just are more efficient ways of securing the material reproduction of the lifeworld – 'in Parsons' terms, the functions of adaptation and goal attainment' (p. 321). The roles of consumer and citizen, however, are not externally defined in this way; 'they refer to prior self-formative processes in which preferences, value orientations, attitudes, and so forth have taken shape', reflected in the 'bourgeois ideals' of the sovereign consumer and citizen. These orientations have to be translated into the more abstract terms appropriate to the steering media of power and money before they can be handled in system terms. Where this cannot be fully done, in the spheres of cultural reproduction, social integration and socialization (integration and latency or pattern-maintenance in Parsons's terminology) the result is what we encounter as pathological forms of over-commodification or over-bureaucratization (p. 322; cf. pp. 293–4).

The adaptation of individuals to organizational imperatives and the concomitant elimination of moral-political reasoning account for the two theses that, in Habermas's reconstruction, dominate Weber's diagnosis of modern times: 'loss of freedom' and 'loss of meaning'. Loss of meaning involves the instrumentalization of 'the communicative practice of everyday life' in what Weber called purposive rationality (pp. 325–6), but there is also another aspect to it: the 'cultural impoverishment' of the lifeworld itself. The differentiation of value spheres (science, morality, art) facilitates their individual development, but also the estrangement of these 'expert cultures' from broader cultural traditions. The ideals of the Enlightenment, suggesting a critical reformulation of a shared tradition and the (re)uniting of the private person and the citizen, become a kind of utopian accompaniment to the reification of the lifeworld. Rather than turn to utopian protest, or traditionalistic appeals to simpler forms of life and belief, we should be more precise than Marx, Weber or Durkheim about the causes of the deformations of modernity.

> Neither the secularization of worldviews nor the structural differentiation of society has unavoidable pathological side effects per se. It is not the differentiation and independent development of cultural value spheres that lead to the cultural impoverishment of everyday

communicative practice, but an elitist splitting-off of expert cultures from contexts of communicative action in daily life. It is not the uncoupling of media-steered subsystems and of their organizational forms from the lifeworld that leads to the one-sided rationalization or reification of everyday communicative practice, but only the penetration of forms of economic and administrative rationality into areas of action that resist being converted over to the media of money and power because they are specialized in cultural transmission, social integration, and child rearing, and remain dependent on mutual understanding as a mechanism for coordinating action. (p. 330)

What then produces this colonization of the lifeworld? Habermas turns back once again to Marx, and to his analysis of the commodity form. The theory of value links together the action and system levels, moving from 'the lifeworld of concrete labor to the economic valorization of abstract labor', and thus makes it possible to 'reckon up the costs of capitalist modernization' (p. 383). The theory of value has, however, three weaknesses. First, Marx retains the utopian idea of a totality which would combine system and lifeworld, or rather abolish system processes in a lifeworld of communist *Sittlichkeit*. He thus fails to grasp the positive value of differentiated subsystems such as the market economy and the modern state. Secondly, and relatedly, 'Marx has no criteria by which to distinguish the destruction of traditional forms of life from the reification of posttraditional lifeworlds' (p. 340). 'For this, the concept of alienation is not sufficiently selective' (p. 341). Third, Marx 'overgeneraliz[es] . . . a specific case of the subsumption of the lifeworld under the system' (p. 342). Reification, even if it derives from the commodities and wage relations, is not confined to 'the sphere of social labour'.[17] Here again, as with Weber, it is the purposive-rational model of action, in the sense of creative praxis, which leads Marx astray: 'Marx was unable to conceive the transformation of concrete into abstract labor as a special case of the systemically induced reification of social relations in general because he started from the model of the purposive actor who, along with his products, is robbed of the possibility of developing his essential powers' (p. 342).

Marxism cannot, then, offer 'a satisfactory account of late capitalism' (p. 343). A more adequate one would have to develop a more sophisticated model of system–lifeworld relations than that of base and superstructure, and it would have to come to terms, more seriously than orthodox Marxism has done, with government interventionism, mass democracy and the welfare state. His model, Habermas claims, is better suited to the way in which administrative power is used to mitigate economic crises, albeit at the cost of overloading the administrative systems. The mass-democratic legitimation process is also more central to modern societies and their dynamics than the base–superstructure model admits, and the same goes for the 'social–welfare programs [which] also make legitimation offers that can be checked as to fulfilment' (p. 347). Class conflict is thus diversified as to its objects, and pacified in reformist forms of political action. Its scope too is reduced. Class antagonism resulting from private ownership of the means of production remains central to the economic system, but it no longer dominates the lifeworlds of the citizens of modern welfare states, who perceive themselves as citizens and consumers of public and private goods as well as employees; 'the structures of alienated labor and alienated political participation develop no explosive power' (pp. 348–51).

Thus 'the theory of class consciousness loses its empirical reference' (p. 352), as does the theory of ideology; culture becomes too disenchanted (*entzaubert*) to be 'capable of taking on ideological functions' (p. 353). Both the original bourgeois ideologies and the nineteenth-century critiques of one aspect or another of modernization had a totalizing form, and this has nothing to latch on to in the more fragmented structures of modern consciousness (p. 354). Instead, late capitalist modernity is stabilized by the 'fragmentation' of everyday consciousness, in which 'everyday knowledge . . . remains diffuse, or at least never attains that level of articulation at which alone knowledge can be accepted as valid according to the standards of cultural modernity. . . . It is only with this that the conditions for a colonization of the lifeworld are met . . . [in which the] scattered perspectives of the local culture cannot comprehend the intrusion of system imperatives' (p. 355).

This is one of the points at which Habermas's diagnosis coincides with postmodernist accounts of 'the end of grand narratives' (Jean-François Lyotard) and the flattening effect of mass culture (Jean Baudrillard). He concludes, plausibly enough, that

the theory of late-capitalist reification, reformulated in terms of system and lifeworld, has to be supplemented by an analysis of cultural modernity, which replaces the now superseded theory of consciousness. Rather than serving a critique of ideology, this analysis would have to explain the cultural impoverishment and fragmentation of everyday consciousness. Rather than hunting after the scattered

traces of revolutionary consciousness, it would have to examine the
conditions for recoupling a rationalized culture with an everyday
communication dependent on vital traditions. (pp. 355–6)

As an illustration of the sort of processes described by his concept
of internal colonization of the lifeworld, Habermas examines the
juridification (*Verrechtlichung*) of communicatively structured
spheres of action as exemplified by the growth of law, especially
family and educational law in Germany. This is part of a broad
process of extension and deepening of the sphere of law, in which it
comes to cover more and more areas of life in greater and greater
detail.[18] He distinguishes four phases or waves (*Schübe*) of
juridification. The first is that of the institutionalization of the bourgeois economy and state in early modern, largely absolutist Europe.
The law came to regulate dealings between individuals and to express the sovereignty of the state and its distinctness from civil
society. Hobbes's Leviathan is the clearest intellectual expression of
this phase; the lifeworld is 'placed at the disposal of the market and
of absolutist rule' (p. 359).

Subsequent phases of juridification can be seen as a process in
which the lifeworld makes its own claims for legal recognition. In
the bourgeois constitutional state (*Rechtsstaat*) 'citizens are given
actionable civil rights against a sovereign – though they do not yet
democratically participate in forming the sovereign's will' (p. 359).
The state comes to acquire 'a legitimacy in its own right', based on
its protection of the citizens: 'legitimation on the basis of a modern
lifeworld' (p. 360). The democratic *Rechtsstaat* emerging from the
French Revolution takes the further step of juridifying the process
of legitimation, in the extension of the vote and freedom of association; legislation is now supposed to have democratic support.

Just as these last two phases of juridification limited the powers
of the state, the final one, that of the welfare state, limits the operation of the economic system. 'The development toward a democratic welfare state [*zum sozialen und demokratischen Rechtsstaat*] can
in fact be understood as the institutionalizing in legal form of a
social power relation anchored in class structure' (p. 361). But the
interventions of the welfare state have an ambiguous character;[19]
they may guarantee freedoms in a way that 'endangers the freedom
of the beneficiaries' – especially in the case of social-welfare politics.
The whole framework of legal entitlements geared to bureaucratic
intervention, often taking the form of monetary compensation, may
fail to meet the needs of welfare clients; this then gives rise to

therapeutic services which constitute a further threat to what they aim to promote, namely 'the client's independence and self-reliance' (p. 363).

How might one distinguish these two aspects of juridification, the expansion and restriction of freedom? Habermas mentions two possible criteria. The first draws on 'the classical division of fundamental rights into liberties and participatory rights; one might presume that the structure of bourgeois formal law becomes dilemmatic precisely when these means are no longer used to negatively demarcate areas of private discretion, but are supposed to provide positive guarantees of membership and participation in institutions and benefits' (p. 364). This would suggest that signs of the restriction of freedom would appear as early as the third (democratizing) phase of juridification. But although the forms of political participation are in many ways restrictive (machine policies, parliamentary elitism, etc.) the principles of liberal and democratic freedoms are unambiguously liberatory.

The second possible criterion relates to the legitimation of legal norms: 'whether they can be legitimized only through procedure in the positivist sense, or are amenable to substantive justification' (p. 365). In fact, however, legal institutions always require a more than procedural legitimation. Where, however, as in the area of social welfare, the law intervenes in communicatively structured areas of the lifeworld which have not been formally organized, there arise 'reification effects' explained by the use of social-welfare law as a medium (p. 367), 'the superimposition of legal norms' (p. 369). Family law, for example in child custody cases, brings out the limits of the law as a medium and the way in which it 'violates the communicative structures of the sphere that has been juridified' (p. 370). In a switch into a normative mode that prefigures the final section of the book, Habermas draws the policy conclusion:

> If one studies the paradoxical structure of juridification in such areas as the family, the schools, social-welfare policy, and the like, the meaning of the demands that regularly result from these analyses is easy to decipher. The point is to protect areas of life that are functionally dependent on social integration through values, norms, and consensus formation, to preserve them from falling prey to the systemic imperatives of economic and administrative subsystems growing with dynamics of their own, and to defend them from becoming converted over, through the steering medium of the law, to a principle of sociation that is, for them, dysfunctional. (pp. 372–3)

The tasks of critical theory

In the final section of *The Theory of Communicative Action*, 'The tasks of a critical theory of society', Habermas compares his own systems theory with Marx's theory of value and with the development of Marxism in the Frankfurt Institute for Social Research. Like the Marxist theory of value, Habermas's theory focuses on the replacement of communicative action by media-steered interaction. But

> the conversion to another mechanism of action coordination, and thereby to another principle of sociation, results in reification – that is, in a pathological de-formation of the communicative infrastructure of the lifeworld – only when the lifeworld cannot be withdrawn from the functions in question, when these functions cannot be painlessly transferred to media-steered systems of action, as those of material reproduction sometimes can. (pp. 374ff)

Despite these differences, the basic structure of Habermas's theory of capitalist modernization

> does follow the Marxian model. It is critical both of contemporary social sciences and of the social reality they are supposed to grasp. It is critical of the reality of developed societies inasmuch as they do not make full use of the learning potential culturally available to them, but deliver themselves over to an uncontrolled growth of complexity. (p. 375)

There are 'three main lines of inquiry occupied with the phenomenon of modern societies' (p. 375), covering different domains as a 'result of one-sided abstractions that unconsciously cut the ties between system and lifeworld constitutive for modern societies' (p. 376). The history of society (*Gesellschaftsgeschichte*) of such writers as Reinhard Bendix and Barrington Moore gives primacy to structural differentiation but cannot provide an adequate account of the pathologies of modernity.[20] The same is true of the systems theory prominent in economics, organizational studies and Luhmann's sociology. The third approach, interpretative sociology, can describe aspects of contemporary pathologies but not the basic dynamic processes of both systems and lifeworlds. 'As a result, the subcultural mirrorings in which the sociopathologies of modernity are refracted and reflected retain the subjective and accidental character of uncomprehended events' (p. 377). Habermas's reworking of a fourth approach, 'the genetic structuralism of developmental psychology', via Mead and Durkheim into a new reading of Weber's theory of rationalization, aims to capture the 'paradoxical' situations 'in which systemic relief mechanisms made possible by the rationalization of the lifeworld turn around and overburden the communicative structure of the lifeworld'(p. 378).

What of Habermas's predecessors in critical theory and their extension of a Marxist approach into new areas of inquiry? The early work of the Institute for Social Research covered six main themes: 'the forms of integration in postliberal societies; family socialization and ego development; mass media and mass culture; the social psychology behind the cessation of protest; the theory of art and the critique of positivism and science' (pp. 378–9). This work relied on a 'Marxist philosophy of history'[21] involving the radicalization of bourgeois thinking and hence a 'trust in the rationality potential of bourgeois culture', but 'the critiques of ideology carried out by Horkheimer, Marcuse and Adorno confirmed them in the belief that culture was losing its autonomy in post-liberal societies and was being incorporated into the machinery of the economic-administrative system (p. 382).

Thus the philosophy of history which critical theory required as a foundation 'was not able to support an empirical research program' (p. 382). And there was a further weakness at the level of social theory – an inability to analyse the structures of social action in which processes of rationalization and also reification are located. Once again we find the conjunction of Habermas's two bugbears, the philosophy of history and the influence of the philosophy of consciousness. 'The basic concepts of critical theory placed the consciousness of individuals directly *vis-à-vis* the economic and administrative mechanisms of integration, which were only extended inward, intrapsychically' (p. 383).[22]

Habermas's alternative method of reconstructing 'structures of action and structures of mutual understanding that are found in the intuitive knowledge of competent members of modern societies' is an attempt 'to free historical materialism from its philosophy of history ballast' (p. 383). Referring back to *Communication and the Evolution of Society* for the basic evolutionary model, he stresses that

A theory developed in this way can no longer start by examining concrete ideals immanent in inherited[23] forms of life. It must orient itself to the range of learning processes that is opened up at a given time by a historically attained level of learning. It must refrain from

critically evaluating and normatively ordering totalities, forms of life
and cultures, and life-contexts and epochs as a whole. And yet it can
take up some of the intentions for which the interdisciplinary research program of earlier critical theory remains instructive. (p. 383)

Habermas sketches out how such a theory might look in relation
to the six areas which he had distinguished in Frankfurt School
theory. First, the issue of integration. Post-liberal societies have
developed either along the path of state economic intervention and
(fascism apart) welfare-state mass democracy, or via bureaucratic
socialism and 'a political order of dictatorship by state parties'
(p. 384). In capitalism, the economic system takes the lead; in socialism the administrative system.

> According to whether the economic system or the state apparatus
> attains evolutionary primacy, either private households or politically
> relevant memberships are the point of entry for crises that are shifted
> from the subsystems to the lifeworld. In modernized societies dis-
> turbances in the material reproduction of the lifeworld take the form
> of stubborn systemic disequilibria; the latter either take effect directly
> as crises or they call forth pathologies in the lifeworld. (p. 385)

Thus the steering crises of the capitalist business cycle are parallelled by the unintended consequences of state socialist planning.
And just as the capitalist economy 'relies on organizational performances of the state', and thus displaces crises on to the state
apparatus (as he had argued in *Legitimation Crisis*), so 'the socialist
planning bureaucracy has to rely on self-steering processes of the
economy'. Here, the society/social integration axis is the crucial
one, though disturbances may initially be 'pushed to the periphery
– before anomic conditions arise there are appearances of withdrawal of legitimation or motivation' (p. 385). And, as described in
Legitimation Crisis, these crises can in turn give rise to motivational
crises: culture and personality take the strain, as it were. 'Instead of
manifestations of anomie . . . phenomena of alienation and the un-
settling of collective identity emerge. I have traced such phenomena
back to a colonization of the lifeworld and characterized them as a
reification of the communicative practice of everyday life' (p. 386).[24]

Habermas then turns to the second sphere of activity of earlier
critical theory: family socialization and ego development. As we
noted earlier, his view is that the Institute's basic model was one of
a direct and largely pathological effect of the economic system on
the individual psyche.

If, by contrast, we *also* recognize in the structural transformation of
the bourgeois family the inherent rationalization of the lifeworld; if
we see that, in egalitarian patterns of relationship, in individuated
forms of intercourse, and in liberalized child-rearing practices, some
of the potential for rationality ingrained in communicative action is
also released; then the changed conditions of socialization in the
middle-class nuclear family appear in a different light. (p. 387)

As a result, he suggests, neuroses resulting from Oedipus conflicts
and authoritarianism are on the decline, and narcissistic disturbances and adolescent crises are growing. Habermas suggests that
the theory of communicative action, which makes 'socializatory
interaction'

the point of reference for the analysis of ego development, and systematically distorted communication – the reification of interpersonal relations – the point of reference for investigating pathogenesis
. . . provides a framework within which the structural model of ego,
id, and superego can be recast. Instead of an instinct theory that
represents the relation of ego to inner nature in terms of a philosophy
of consciousness – on the model of relations between subject and
object – we have a theory of socialization that connects Freud with
Mead, gives structures of intersubjectivity their due, and replaces
hypotheses about instinctual vicissitudes with assumptions about
identity formation. (pp. 388–9)

In the third area, that of the mass media and mass culture,
Habermas suggests a more nuanced model than that in which the
public sphere is swamped by a media flow passively absorbed by a
massified public. In addition to the empirical qualifications which,
as we saw in chapter 1, have been placed on this model, there is also
a theoretical point emerging from Habermas's theory of media in
the broader sense. Using his distinction between 'steering media,
via which subsystems are differentiated out of the lifeworld', and
'generalized forms of communication, which do not replace reaching agreement in language but merely condense it, and thus remain
tied to lifeworld contexts' (p. 390), he argues that 'The mass media
belong to these generalized forms of communication. They free
communication processes from the provinciality of spatiotem-
porally restricted contexts and permit public spheres to emerge.'
These publics are structured by those who control the media, but
not entirely so – 'and therein lies their ambivalent potential' (p. 390).
Thus although subsequent research has supported much of the

Frankfurt School critique of the culture industry it has also documented a number of countervailing tendencies (p. 391).

On the fourth issue, that of protest potential, Habermas insists
that 'one major difference' between the Frankfurt critique of instrumental reason and his own critique of functionalist reason is
that 'processes of reification do not appear as mere reflexes – as
manifestations of a repressive integration emanating from an
oligopolistic economy and an authoritarian state, (p. 391). Here, as
in the case of the media, we in fact have to deal with conflicting
tendencies. Protest certainly exists, increasingly in the areas of
cultural reproduction, social integration and socialization, in
response to

> a reification of communicatively structured domains of action that
> will not respond to the media of money or power. The issue is not
> primarily one of compensations that the welfare state can provide,
> but of defending and restoring endangered ways of life. In short, the
> new conflicts are not ignited by distribution problems but by ques-
> tions having to do with the grammar of forms of life. (p. 392)

Habermas endorses R. F. Inglehart's thesis of a 'silent revolution',
a shift from the 'old' politics of bread-and-butter issues to a 'new
politics' concerned with broader questions about ways of life.
'These phenomena tally with my thesis regarding internal colonization' (p. 392).[25] Within the mass of protest movements, Habermas
differentiates 'emancipatory potentials from potentials for resistance and withdrawal'. Feminism alone 'stands in the tradition of
bourgois-socialist liberation movements'; the other social movements 'have a more defensive character' (p. 393). Within resistance
movements, one can differentiate further between those defending
tradition and property, such as middle-class tax and environmental
protests, and 'a defence that already operates on the basis of a
rationalized lifeworld and tries out new ways of cooperating and
living together' (p. 394) – as found in youth, green and peace movements. These movements are oriented to three related groups of
problems in particular: specifically environmental problems, risks
arising from excessive complexity, and what he calls the 'overbur-
dening of the communicative infrastructure', in which the 'culturally impoverished and one-sidedly rationalized practice of
everyday life' gives rise to particularistic subcultural communities.
The innovative movements as a whole usually aim to dediffer-
entiate formally institutionalized activities such as 'work' and 'poli-

tics' and to return them to the sphere of communicative action. It is crucial, he insists, to distinguish between 'the communicative rationality of cultural modernity' and the functionalist rationality of self-maintaining economic and administrative action systems. The conflation of these two distinct aspects of modernity, 'the rationalization of the lifeworld' and 'the increasing complexity of the social system', underlies much of the confusion around the theme of postmodernity (p. 396).

In addressing the final two areas of interest for the first-generation critical theorists, art and (philosophy of) science, Habermas argues that critical theory no longer needs to unmask the social content of philosophical theories but can co-operate with philosophy in the study of different aspects of rationality. The differentiation, in modernity, of various aspects of intellectual life needs no justification, and no philosophical foundation. What remain are the questions '(i) whether a reason that has objectively split up into its moments can still preserve its unity, and (ii) how expert cultures can be mediated with everyday practice' (pp. 397–8).[26] Habermas's formal pragmatics, he reminds us, examines the differentiation of validity-claims, but even when one validity-claim is primary the others also play a role. Thus moral and aesthetic issues enter into discussions in the human sciences, issues of needs and desires enter into moral reasoning, and cognitive and moral-practical issues enter into aesthetics. 'It seems as if the radically differentiated moments of reason want in such countermovements to point toward a unity not a unity that could be had at the level of worldviews, but one that might be established this side of expert cultures, in a nonreified communicative everyday practice' (p. 398).

If these considerations give a special role to philosophy, it is a different one from the foundationalism rightly criticized by pragmatism and hermeneutics. What Habermas is arguing for is a philosophy which combines with empirical science, not just in an interdisciplinary sense but in 'approaches, which are simultaneously empirical and reconstructive', such as those of Mead, Weber and Durkheim, or, more recently, Piaget (p. 399). Nor can such a reconstructive theory ignore the fact that humanity has unlearned a great deal in the course of its development (p. 400). It must also recognize that it aims to explicate a background knowledge available to human beings in the lifeworld, and its operations can only be selective. What justifies these selections is ultimately the present state of society, as in Marx's concept of 'real abstraction': 'the development of society must itself give rise to the problem situations that objectively afford contemporaries a privileged access to the general structures of the lifeworld. . . . It may be that [the] challenge that places the symbolic structures of the lifeworld as a whole in question can account for why they have become accessible to us' (p. 403).

7

The Theory of Communicative Action: An Assessment

How might one begin to assess a work of this scope and ambition?[1] The first step is to reflect on what sort of theory Habermas is putting forward. It is, in his terms, a reconstructive theory, reconstructive in the sense both of recovering and bringing out (and perhaps contributing to) the practical development of human capacities for communicative action, and of aiming to reconstruct historical materialism and the Western Marxist critique of capitalist reification.[2] A reconstructive theory will not be expected to display what Giddens has called the 'enormous revelatory power' of natural-scientific theories, and, although a new theory of action is as broad a project as one could imagine, it will still be telling us how we do something we know we do already. But this is in a way what the bulk of social theory has always sought to do, to show how it is that man is born free but is everywhere in chains, how social order is possible in a society of egoists, how reason and the realization of freedom can progress, how free exchange of labour for wages gives rise to exploitation, and so on.[3]

If there is a common theme to the criticisms which have been addressed to Habermas, it is, not surprisingly, that things are not quite so cut and dried as he presents them. In practice this critique takes two forms. Detailed criticisms of particular arguments tend to suggest, as we have seen, that the adoption or rejection of Habermas's theory depends more on holistic judgements at the level of social theory than on the piecemeal acceptance of successive philosophical arguments. The other outcome is the suggestion that some of the social processes he describes are themselves more ambiguous and contradictory than he recognizes.

We have already seen Habermas concede that the distinction between illocutionary and perlocutionary speech acts does not so much underwrite, as itself depend on that between communicative and strategic action. This is one example of the holistic shift or the shift of emphasis from philosophical to sociological analysis. Another would be Herbert Schnädelbach's argument (which in fact Habermas rejects) that there is not such a direct relation as Habermas believes between understanding or describing reasons and evaluating or accepting them. If Schnädelbach is right here, as I think he is, it follows that the normative basis for Habermas's theory may lie, not in his universal or formal pragmatics, but in his substantive account 'of the relation between communicative action and lifeworld' (p. 16).

The most central issue to examine is perhaps the one noted at the beginning of chapter 5. Is there really such a thing as communicative action or action oriented to/by understanding? In chapter 5 we gave Habermas the benefit of the doubt on this issue, but we cannot deny that there is a substantial body of theory which sees all social action as, in Habermasian terms, strategic, treating normatively regulated and communicative action as at best marginal deviations from the strategic principle of the pursuit of rational self-interest. The rational-action theorist may concede that, phenomenologically, social action seems to fall into the boxes which Habermas provides, but the real story is written in the language of strategic reason. For the sociobiologist, the real explanation lies even deeper, at the level of 'the selfish gene'. Neither a typology of forms of social interaction nor a phenomenology of introspected motives will help here.[4]

Habermas's response has tended to be that rational-action theories of this kind are too simplistic. He concedes, for example, a major role to compromises and bargaining in political decision-making, but stresses that we can still ask how far such compromises involve a 'fair balancing out of interests', and *this* question can be answered in terms of moral-practical rationality, where our judgements are not based on self-interest.[5]

Habermas tried, of course, to use speech-act theory to mark off strategic action as deceptive and parasitic on communicative action, but he was forced to concede, as we saw earlier, that 'one can no longer consider *all* perlocutions to be latent "strategic action"' (p. 240). The most serious objections to Habermas's model come from those who start from the premise, which he shares, that 'both models of action (communicative and strategic) impute to the actors a capacity for setting ends and for goal-oriented action as well as an interest in executing their own plans for action'. Such critics go on, however, to merge the two models of action in an 'impermissible' manner (p. 241).

In justifying this prohibition, however, Habermas is again led to speak of different worlds. The lifeworld is 'linguistically constituted':

> the medium of language and the telos of reaching understanding intrinsic to it reciprocally constitute one another. The relation between these is not one of means and ends. As a consequence, 'aims' which an actor pursues in language and can only realize together with Alter cannot be described as if they resembled conditions which we can bring about by intervening causally in the world. For the actor, the aims of action oriented towards success and reaching understanding are situated on different levels: either in the objective world or, beyond all entities, in the linguistically constituted lifeworld. (p. 241)

But, even if the reality of communicative action is conceded, it is still not clear just what constrains actors to adopt a performative attitude and to engage in communicative action. There is a parallel here to the analysis in philosophical ethics of 'taking the moral point of view', for example recognizing that moral judgements must be universalizable. If actors refuse to take this first step, the whole game cannot begin. Habermas rightly resists those readings which assimilate his model of communicative action to that of moral reasoning at the level of *contents*, since these are only one variant of validity-claims, but there still seems to be a structural similarity in their form.

Perhaps at this point Habermas can only move a Hegelian direction, asserting that we have a set of institutionalized practices which correspond to his description of communicative action, and in relation to which normatively regulated and expressive (dramaturgical) action can be seen as limit cases (p. 242). Just as it is possible for someone to refuse to adopt the moral point of view, it is similarly possible for someone to refuse to engage in a specific form of communicative action, or merely to *simulate* what would be required by communicative action in a performative attitude. But this is the homage which vice pays to virtue, or lies to truth. This is roughly the line Habermas now takes. He is not, he insists, saying that people ought to act communicatively, but that they *must....* When parents educate their children, when living generations appropriate the knowledge handed down by their predecessors, when individuals cooperate, i.e. get on with one another without a costly use of force, they must act communicatively. There are elementary social functions which can only be satisfied by means of communicative action.[6]

Communicative action, he insists, is not the same as argumentation; the latter term denotes specific forms of communication: 'islands in the sea of praxis'.

The other possible line of argument gives Habermas's claims a Kantian twist, suggesting that, however elusive genuine communicative action may be, it is what we *should* be doing. Then we really are back with the 'moral point of view' analogy. This is the line taken by Habermas's close collaborator, the philosopher Karl-Otto Apel, and Habermas also seems to feel a pull in this direction, in his analyses of law, morals and *Sittlichkeit* and the theory of argumentation. Even in the case of the law, however, he stresses how far we have come already with an approach to the consensual regulation of basically strategic action:

> Legal norms can only be compelling in the long term if the processes by which they come into existence are accepted as legitimate. This process of acceptance involves a communicative action that appears as such, so to speak, at the other end of the legal system, on the side of democratic will formation and political legislation.[7]

Although Habermas's detailed arguments for the primacy of communicative action are not entirely successful, he has surely identified an important sphere of human action which connects in important ways with our intuitions about consensual decision making and participatory democracy, as well as about our use of language.[8] What this is not, as Hans Joas has pointed out, is a comprehensive theory or typology of action, 'but rather a classification that aims from the start at Habermas's distinction, admittedly a convincing one, of various kinds of possible relations to the world' (p. 101). This critique, which incidentally Habermas brushes aside with the objection that he is 'not concerned with constructing an anthropology of action as a whole' (p. 249), suggests once again that one has to accept or reject the whole package. Joas also suggests, however, like many other critics, that Habermas should distinguish, more carefully than he did in earlier presentations, between types of action and types of action co-ordination.

Habermas now accepts this (p. 291, n. 60). As Joas notes, however, he still tends to assume 'a linear relationship of correspondence among types of action, types of coordination of action, and societal domains' (p. 104). And this slide, even if it is not as automatic as Joas claims, does tend to pervade Habermas's analysis. Habermas recognizes that 'action domains of the lifeworld which are primarily integrated socially are . . . neither free of power nor of strategic action' (p. 258), but he still defines ' the mechanisms of social integration . . . in such a manner that they rest on the structures of action oriented towards reaching understanding'(p. 254).⁹

A further area where Joas feels that Habermas has run together separate issues is in linking the critique of the philosophy of consciousness so closely to the model of communicative action. The history of pragmatism, he notes, shows that they are distinct (p. 101). This is more than just a point of historical scholarship, since Joas argues that, if he had distinguished these two strands more clearly, Habermas would have formulated his action theory differently.¹⁰

The issue which, as Habermas notes (p. 250), has aroused more criticism than his theory of communicative action as such is the lifeworld/system distinction. Doubts have focused around three main questions: the unclarity or incoherence of Habermas's concept of the lifeworld, the way he specifies the relations between system and lifeworld and his recourse to systems theory altogether. And of course discussion of these issues moves rapidly on to the substantive questions raised by his account of capitalist modernity, economy–state relations, and so on.

First, the lifeworld. Disagreement centres on whether Habermas is inconsistent in his usage, or whether, as he himself believes, he is simply operating with two distinct concepts of the lifeworld, a quasi-transcendental or formal-pragmatic concept in which it forms a shared background to communicative action, and the everyday or sociological concept which is relevant to discussions of its colonization and other aspects of system–lifeworld relations. Even if we make the charitable assumption that Habermas was the innocent victim of misreading by many of his commentators, it remains the case that the formal-pragmatic concept does not in the end do much work in his theory, and may in fact, as Schnädelbach suggests, collapse into the everyday concept (p. 18). It remains, however, like the smile on the face of the Cheshire Cat, giving the real lifeworld a spurious veneer of mutuality. Habermas writes in his 'reply' that 'the formal-pragmatic concept of lifeworld', in which it is viewed from the actor's perspective, should be distinguished from the corresponding sociological concept (p. 247).

It is certainly true that hasty readers came away with the misconception that the message of the book was 'system bad, lifeworld good', with all that would imply for evaluations of clitoridectomy, marital violence, and other repellent traditional practices. It is doubtful, however, whether this is entirely a matter of misunderstanding. As we have seen, Habermas, though differentiating clearly between normatively regulated and communicative action, lays great stress on the Parsonian theme of social integration by means of norms. And, for all his critique of the 'culturalistic' narrowness of *verstehende* sociology,[11] there remains a suspicion, not confined to what Habermas rather dismissively calls 'objections which are in part normative and in part inspired by Marxism' (p. 251), that in his two-track reconstruction of historical materialism the rails of normative evolution are carrying an unfairly large share of the traffic.

Several of the essays in *Communicative Action* bear on this theme. Günther Dux questions the way in which Habermas 'allows social world and legitimate order to merge' and the centrality which he attributes to communicative action in the emergence and maintenance of human society.[12] Early societies were egalitarian *and* communicatively structured, but not in the strong Habermasian sense in which individuals dispassionately compare their own interests with those of others (p. 95). Joas, as we have seen, finds Habermas's concepts of social action somewhat impoverished, and contests the need for his recourse to systems theory:

> Habermas confounds the distinction between the theory of action and the theory of social order with, on the one hand, the solution to the problem of social order provided by functionalist systems theory and, on the other hand, with the substantive question of the extent to which societal processes occur independently of the intentions of individual actors. (p. 105)

Habermas, says Joas, skews his interpretations of social theory to support his claim that action theory is not enough. Many writers stress unintended consequences of action without seeing them as entailing functionalism, and some indeed see them as having *anti*-functionalist implications.[13] Although Max Weber's concept of meaning is indeed limited by its roots in a philosophy of consciousness, his concept of action is not monological in the way Habermas implies (p. 103), and he has a theory of social order as well as action (p. 106). Nor is Mead's concept of social integration so limited to the immediacy of the lifeworld (p. 108). Although Mead fits Habermas's argument for a paradigm shift to communicative action, Durkheim remains within the philosophy of consciousness. As we saw earlier, 'Habermas identifies in a misleading fashion a typology of action with the distinction among types of coordination of action' (p. 104). Finally, there was not such a rupture in Parsons's thought as Habermas believes; he always upheld 'not only a voluntaristic theory of action, but also a normativistic theory of social order' (pp. 109–10). While Habermas rejects 'the claim of functionalist analysis to be exhaustive of the social totality' (p. 110), he needlessly accepts that reproduction processes must be based on differentiated societal subsystems, and he expands David Lockwood's analytical distinction between system and social integration into distinct spheres of society whose relations change in the course of history. Habermas has ignored his own earlier critiques of functionalism, and others such as Giddens's, in his desire to avoid what he sees as the reification of collective actors and their actions.[14]

Thomas McCarthy, the heroic (and excellent) translator of *The Theory of Communicative Action*, argues in similar terms against the need for systems theory (p. 138), though he is less hostile than Joas to a modestly functionalist framework of interpretation of the kind Habermas flirted with in *On the Logic of the Social Sciences*. He questions in particular Habermas's rather hasty assimilation of economic and political systems. Johannes Berger, too, argues that Habermas exaggerates the smoothness with which the subsystems operate, and neglects the ways in which the lifeworld can intrude into subsystems as well as vice versa (cf. pp. 106–7 above).

In his reply to this group of criticisms, Habermas makes clear that he now at least sees system and social integration as analytically distinct aspects of social integration, measured respectively by external stabilization and boundary maintenance on the one hand, and 'internal stabilization and the preservation of ego and group identities' (p. 252) on the other.

That which, in borderline cases, becomes respectively subject to crises and threatened in its existence (*Bestand*) is in the one instance limited to the self-understanding of those concerned and, in the other, accessible only to objective observation. It is always *the same* society which is caught in the grips of such crises of identity or steering, but each of these processes can be grouped only in terms of one of the two aspects of societal integration. (p. 253)

These now appear as two different perspectives, more or less appropriate depending on whether the process under investigation is primarily one of material reproduction or more a matter of 'cultural tradition, social integration and socialization'. The more differentiated the society, the more processes of the former type demand a systems approach if they are not to be 'inadmissibly foreshortened' (p. 253). One such case is that of the integration of 'aggregated action consequences', even though these *can* be studied in a lifeworld perspective. (An analogy might be with someone who can just about see to drive with their reading glasses, but who really needs long-distance ones.)[15]

We have already noted Habermas's clarification that the lifeworld is by no means free of domination and (self)-deception, so that mechanisms of integration do not directly map on to types of action. Having loosened things up to this extent, Habermas does, however, want to stress that system differentiation is not just a matter of analytical perspective but a real historical process, reflected in the philosophical discourse (including the social theory) of modernity. Once these subsystems are constituted, by legal means, they ultimately rely on formal economic or administrative processes rather than normative/communicative understandings. 'One can, therefore, define the lifeworld *negatively* as the totality of action domains which cannot be bent to conform to a description of media-steered subsystems' (p. 257). Once such subsystems are established, 'media-guided interactions no longer embody an instrumental, but rather a functional form of reason' (p. 258).[16]

Reasonably enough, Habermas does not respond in detail in *Communicative Action* to the empirical issues raised about modern societies. He admits, in reference to McCarthy, that 'the political system, owing to the nature of the medium of power and the way in which it is institutionally anchored in the lifeworld, remains far more dependent on its environments than does the economic system' (p. 259). More generally, he says, he reacts 'utterly pragmatically' to McCarthy's question of how much one should borrow from systems theory. As for the role of media-guided subsystems themselves, he reiterates his claims 'that the media framework cannot be transposed onto the domains of cultural tradition, social integration, and socialization, and . . . that these three functions can be fulfilled only via the medium of communicative action and not via the steering media of money and power: meaning can neither be bought nor coerced' (p. 259). Johannes Berger is right, he admits, to attack the notion of smoothly 'self-propelling' subsystems, but wrong to ascribe it to him (p. 260). Nor does he see the subsystem formation process as completed (p. 259); there are counter-trends to these processes which are still operating.[17] To recognize these 'structurally anchored developmental trends' (p. 260) is not to abandon socialism or radical democracy. But the most we can reasonably aim at is the 'defensive re-steering' of the neo-capitalist economy and the interventionist state: 'I believe for empirical reasons that there is no longer much prospect of the democratic reshaping from within of a differentiated economic system solely by means of worker self-management, in other words by switching its steering from money and organizational power *completely* over to participation' (p. 261).

In view of Habermas's focus on issues to do with the welfare state towards the end of *Theory of Communicative Action* and, even more, his systematic claim that one of the principal contradictions in modern liberal democracies arises from the impossibility of solving lifeworld problems with the means of money and power, it is worth examining an article of 1985, 'The crisis of the welfare state and the exhaustion of utopian energies', reprinted in *The New Conservatism*. The term *Unübersichtlichkeit* – 'obscurity' rather than 'conservatism' – in the original title of this volume of essays denotes the inability of contemporary intellectuals and politicians to come to terms with the massive problems of environmental crisis, military threats, global poverty, unemployment and so forth.[18]

All this is one reason for the 'exhaustion of utopian energies', but there is also another, more precise cause: the end of a specific utopia based on the potential of the 'employment society' (*Arbeitsgesellschaft*). As work loses its determinant role in modern societies,[19] so does the utopian project focused on the reform of work relations and the welfare state. Even if state intervention is capable of curbing and humanizing the capitalist economy, in the face of such constraints as the internationalization of commodity and labour markets which make it impossible to guarantee full employment, and the further threat of tax backlashes, there is a more fundamental problem: whether political power is in any case the right means to secure more human and emancipated 'forms of life'.[20] Whereas social reformers (from, say, the 1860s to the 1960s) had mostly seen welfare-state intervention in private life as unproblematically beneficial, there is now growing anxiety about what the New Right calls welfare dependence and Foucauldian radicals call surveillance and the panoptical society.[21] These pathologies of the welfare state are paralleled by, and interact with, its liberal-democratic political shell, in which parties compete for 'mass loyalty' as corporations compete for market shares.

Harry Kunneman, in one of the most stimulating and creative commentaries on Habermas's recent work,[22] brings out very well the implications of Habermas's occasional remarks about, for example, the welfare-state therapeutocracy for his work as a whole. Kunneman's book is organized around the title metaphor of a 'truth-funnel' in which modern natural and social science filter and reformulate what can be accepted as 'valid' knowledge. While he sees Habermas's stress on communicative consensus between scientists, and his insistence that normative validity and expressive authenticity are no less important than factual truth, as a welcome corrective to dominant models of science, he feels that Habermas remains too sanguine about the objectifying role of science in general and more specifically the active contribution of the social sciences to the colonization of the lifeworld. Whereas Habermas tends to regard this colonization process as the replacement of one principle of sociation by another, Kunneman stresses the aspect of 'pseudo-communication which marks the application of social-scientific knowledge within the exchange relations between system and lifeworld'.[23]

In other words, whereas Habermas tends to praise Foucault's detailed analysis of communicative pathologies while rejecting his allegedly nihilistic resignation in the face of the ubiquity of strategic action, Kunneman stresses the normality of what Habermas sees as the deviant and pathological category of 'latently strategic action'. This becomes increasingly important when, as in Western societies in the last twenty years, authority relations in organizations, or at least their expression in concrete interaction, have become more informal and apparently consensual or, in a loose sense, democratic. This is, however, something of an illusion.

> The role of communicative processes in formal organizations can . . . be analysed more closely if one represents the formal, juridically structured framework of enterprises and state bureaucracies as a 'container' into which communicative processes are squeezed in and dammed up. As soon as these threaten to become dysfunctional for the goals of the organization, sanctions which are not communicatively criticizable can be brought into play.[24]

A similar process occurs in the 'caring' professions, where practitioners are structurally constrained both to identify with their clients and the clients' own definitions of their situation and to override these identifications when they use their monopoly of specialized knowledge, usually in response to external constraints.[25]

Kunneman sketches out the ways in which the roles of client, consumer and citizen are affected by processes of pseudo-communication. Without going into details here, it should be clear that Habermas needs Foucault more than he has recognized, even in his most recent work. As Kunneman puts it, it is because Habermas's conceptual scheme denies 'a structural role for latent strategic action in the symbolic reproduction of the lifeworld [that] he cannot recognize, at the empirical level, the important contribution of pseudo-communication to the colonization of the lifeworld'.[26] The converse is, however, also true: Foucault's undifferentiated concept of disciplinary power must be refined in terms of distinctions implicit in Habermas's work, though not yet fully articulated.

Some of the issues raised in the critical discussion of *The Theory of Communicative Action* concerning modernity and postmodernity, and the critique of metaphysics, are better left to the next chapter, but it is possible here to draw together some threads. First, Habermas has brought out the unity of his preoccupations over the past thirty years and developed a theory of magnificent scope and power. It is clear, I think, that the two volumes do not have the sort of sequential flow that Habermas implies, but his engagement with Weber is of enormous importance and the incorporation of Mead, Durkheim and Parsons, though problematic, is not without interest. And more interesting than the linear construction is whether the model in its developed form does help us to understand the pathologies of modernity.

We have already seen the strengths of Habermas's 'discourse ethics', though also some of its weaknesses. In some ways, though he rejects this vocation, it is as a normative ethical-political theory that his work seems most convincing.[27] Taking it as a social theory of modernity, we must ask whether the pathologies of reification on which he focuses are really more urgent than those of poverty and exploitation (both intra- and international), or of disorganization and 'risk'.[28] It is easy to get the impression from *The Theory of Communicative Action* that Habermas believes that the main problems of our age are the contradictions of the capitalist welfare state, whose solutions are to be found in the global diffusion of a more radically social and democratic social democracy. In the short run, this is of course a terribly limited perspective, with little or nothing to say about the problems of what one might loosely call the South and the Earth, the 'Third World' and the environment. Habermas is far from unaware of these issues, and various thinkers influenced by his work have developed recognizably Habermasian themes in more concrete directions: Ulrich Beck into the areas of environmental and other risks and personal decision-making, Claus Offe from crisis tendencies in welfare capitalism to a more global analysis of capitalist production, David Held in democratic theory.

The relevance of Habermas's analysis must, I think, be seen in a longer-term perspective. We do not at present have any well-developed alternatives to the social-democratic amelioration of capitalism, and while religious fundamentalism, ultra-Leninism and nationalistic populism may attract support it is difficult not to see them as regressive forms of political organization. Globalization means *par excellence* the globalization of a particular model of social and economic organization, and an important role for intellectuals in metropolitan countries, including increasingly Japan, may be to preserve and develop a political culture which recognizes the responsibilities of this situation. Generalizing the medical motto, 'to do the sick no harm', we might say that an important political task in the richer countries of the world is to make sure that we do the rest of the world, and the world itself, as little further damage as possible. It is in this somewhat indirect way that a Habermasian programme may have a wider application.

Habermas's thinking goes along with those who increasingly see modern politics in terms of communication and culture – not the communication of trivial packaged 'messages' from politicians but broader shifts of opinion such as those brought about by feminist and ecological movements.[29] The present eclipse of Marxism does not guarantee capitalism eternal vigorous life, nor is it clear that capitalism can preserve liveable conditions on the planet. What Habermas offers, perhaps, is a social theory which provides an intellectual basis for, and is made in the image of, the active (though not only participatory) democratic politics, without the attendant revolutionary rhetoric, which we still associate with the late 1960s. If this sort of politics is the place to look for a solution to our problems, then perhaps Habermas's theory of communicative action is the right way, or a right way, of posing the question. Like many of the most creative theorists of our age, Habermas does not offer ready-made solutions so much as possible ways of developing what he sometimes calls the grammar of our ways of life.

8

Modernity and Philosophy

The philosophical discourse of modernity

In September 1980, when he received the Adorno Prize in Frankfurt, Habermas delivered a speech with the title 'Modernity – an incomplete project'.[1] Here, he fired a warning shot against the French thinkers associated (outside France) with the label 'post-structuralism', and the concept of 'postmodernity' which Jean-François Lyotard and others had established as a major reference point of contemporary thinking.[2] The relationship between these two terms has been characterized in very different ways. Post-structuralism can best be understood as a movement in French thought in the late 1970s which radicalized certain themes found in (though also prior to) the heyday of structuralism in the previous decade. It retained structuralism's reductive analysis of meaning and subjectivity, while abandoning the structuralist search for an underlying logic of basic oppositions (and indeed the very idea of clear-cut binary oppositions). This suspicion of system and theory had affinities with, on the one hand, artistic postmodernism, notably in architecture, and on the other with the critique of modernity as a form of society and thought. Lyotard's book served as a useful reference point for many of these wide-ranging ideas; he combined a scepticism about science with a more fundamental rejection of the ideologies and philosophies of history, the 'grand narratives' of progress, emancipation, and so on, with which Western modernity had sustained and consoled itself.

Some of these themes were close to Habermas's own preoccupations. His growing suspicion of what he had earlier upheld as 'philosophy of history with a practical purpose' parallels that of Lyotard; he had never had much time for the scientistic pretensions of structuralism, and his developing critique of metaphysical philosophy had some affinities with that of Martin Heidegger and Jacques Derrida. On the other hand, Habermas reacted very badly to what he saw as a frivolous and politically irresponsible attack on the rationalist and humanist ideals of the Enlightenment; the engaging and provocative hyperbole of Paris recalled more sinister intellectual and political currents of counter-Enlightenment thought in Germany. Habermas's tendency for a time to lump the post-structuralists together with the ultra-conservative 'new philosophers' made them seem even more suspect.

A second article, 'The entwinement of myth and enlightenment', published in both German and English in 1982, was followed by further lectures delivered at the Collège de France, Cornell University and Frankfurt in 1983–4 and published in 1985 as *The Philosophical Discourse of Modernity*. Habermas describes this as a 'reconstruction' of the way in which 'modernity, since the late eighteenth century, has been elevated to a philosophical theme'.[3]

Habermas begins *The Philosophical Discourse of Modernity* by sketching out the way in which the modernization theory of the 1950s 'separate[s] the concept of "modernity" from its modern-European origins and turns it into a spatially and temporally neutralized model for all processes of social development' (p. 2). The more modernization is treated as an automatic evolutionary process, the more separate becomes modern culture – washed up, its possibilities exhausted, in Arnold Gehlen's term 'crystallized'. Whereas Gehlen's neo-conservative version of postmodernity or 'posthistory' implies that we should simply make do with what we have, a more anarchistic or subversive account of postmodernity aims to transcend modernity's instrumental or technical rationality, its will to power. Habermas's suspicion – and this is what drives his sometimes excessive anxiety about contemporary intellectual trends – is that these sceptical backward glances are merely restating anti-modern themes of the 'counter-Enlightenment'.

The modern conception of time, which expresses itself in a constant rehistoricization of intellectual life, is based on the awareness that, as Hegel put it in the Introduction to *The Phenomenology of Mind*, 'something new is on the way' and that we are on our own, free to make our own history. What Hegel calls the principle of the freedom of subjectivity is expressed in crucial events such as the Reformation, the Enlightenment and the French Revolution, and in cultural forms such as modern science (where freedom comes from knowing the laws of nature), morality and romantic art. But the differentiation of these various spheres, as in Kant's system of pure reason, practical reason and judgement, brings out the one-sidedness of subjectivity as a unifying principle. For Hegel, Habermas argues:

> It does possess, to be sure, an unexampled power to bring about the formation [*Bildung*] of subjective freedom and reflection and to undermine religion. . . . But the principle of subjectivity is not powerful enough to regenerate the unifying power of religion in the medium of reason. (p. 21)

But, having recognized this problem at the beginning of his philosophical career, Hegel gradually slides into the illusory solution provided by his concept of absolute knowledge, thus conceiving, Habermas maintains, 'the overcoming of subjectivity within the limits of the philosophy of the subject' (p. 22). Given Hegel's massive influence on most subsequent philosophy, this is a serious matter. The 'first philosopher to develop a clear concept of modernity' (p. 13) has ended up with a philosophical system which abandons it. 'However the temporal, empirical present may find its way out of its division [*Zwiespalt*], how it may form itself is to be left to it and is not an immediately practical affair and concern of philosophy.'[4] Habermas concludes:

> The philosophical discourse of modernity begins, then, with Hegel's legacy. The discourse of modernity, which we are still conducting down to our own day, is also marked by the consciousness that philosophy is at an end, whether this is seen as a productive challenge or only as a provocation. (pp. 51–2)

Even the personnel become more diversified: as other disciplines become more professionalized, philosophy becomes less so. Independent scholars such as Marx, Kierkegaard and Nietzsche play a larger part than academic philosophers, and so do people like Darwin and Freud developing independent branches of science. This makes the common features of this discourse all the more striking: Enlightenment reason is seen as an illusory phenomenon with a narrow, and ultimately authoritarian, subjective conception of rationality (pp. 55–6). In this sense, Habermas argues, 'we remain contemporaries of the Young Hegelians' (p. 53). Subsequent thinkers, down to Theodor Adorno, Arnold Gehlen and Michel Foucault, lie in three broad lines of development.

> Left Hegelian critique, turned toward the practical and aroused for revolution, aimed at mobilizing the historically accumulated potential of reason (awaiting release) against its mutilation, against the one-sided rationalization of the bourgeois world. The Right Hegelians followed Hegel in the conviction that the substance of state and religion would compensate for the restlessness of bourgeois society, as soon as the subjectivity of the revolutionary consciousness that incited restlessness yielded to objective insight into the rationality of the status quo. . . . Finally, Nietzsche wanted to unmask the dramaturgy of the entire stage-piece in which both – revolutionary hope and the reaction to it – enter on the scene. . . . Reason is nothing else than power, than the will to power, which it so radiantly conceals. (p. 56)

If this reads like a (rather brisk) exercise in distanced intellectual history, it is not intended to be: Habermas stresses that we cannot step outside the discourse of modernity (p. 59). He offers his account as a 'participant's perspective' on the problems inherent in these three movements (p. 59). 'Left Hegelianism' develops into neo-Marxist 'praxis philosophy'.[5] As the rather compressed meat in this sandwich, Marx himself is presented as being, like Hegel, 'weighted down by the basic conceptual necessities of the philosophy of the subject', albeit 'grounded in the practice of a producing subject rather than in the reflection of a knowing subject' (p. 63).[6]

In the other corner, the Right Hegelian tradition runs through to the conservative sociologist Hans Freyer and, more recently, the historian of philosophy Joachim Ritter. This neo-traditional and anti-intellectual reaction is, however, less of a challenge to the discourse of modernity than that following from Nietzsche, whose critique of reason appears, prima facie, to be a real attempt to break out of the philosophy of the subject (p. 74). Whereas both Left and Right Hegelians basically accepted the superiority of modernity to traditional ways of life, Nietzsche both generalizes (to earlier historical periods) and undermines the rationality which had been imputed to modernity. 'Nietzsche owes his concept of modernity, developed in terms of his theory of power, to an unmasking critique of reason that sets itself outside the horizon of reason' (p. 96). Habermas sees an ambivalence in Nietzsche, again no doubt arising from the Hegelian end-of-philosophy problematic, which develops into a second major branching point in modern philosophy.

> Nietzsche's critique of modernity has been continued along [two] paths. The sceptical scholar who wants to unmask the perversion of the will to power, the revolt of reactionary forces, and the emergence of a subject-centred reason by using anthropological, psychological, and historical methods has successors in Bataille, Lacan, and Foucault; the initiate-critic of metaphysics who pretends to a unique kind of knowledge and pursues the rise of the philosophy of the subject back to its pre-Socratic beginnings has successors in Heidegger and Derrida. (p. 97)

Before following these two directions, Habermas interposes his earlier essay on 'The entwinement of myth and enlightenment', in which he examines 'Horkheimer and Adorno's ambiguous attempt at a dialectic of enlightenment that would satisfy Nietzsche's radical critique of reason' (p. 105). Habermas stresses the 'thoroughly philosophical' intention of *Dialectic of Enlightenment*:

> Reason itself destroys the humanity it first made possible . . . from the very start the process of enlightenment is the result of a drive to self-preservation that mutilates reason, because it lays claim to it only in the form of a purposive-rational mastery of nature and instinct – precisely as instrumental reason. (pp. 110–11)

In the rest of the book Horkheimer and Adorno aim to justify the claim that 'reason remains subordinated to the dictates of purposive rationality right into its most recent products – modern science, universalistic ideas of justice and morality, autonomous art' (p. 111). This 'astoundingly' (p. 112) oversimplified account of modernity, Habermas argues once again, 'does not do justice to the rational content of cultural modernity that was captured in bourgeois ideals (and thus also instrumentalized along with them)' (p. 113). The critique of ideology 'outstrips itself' (p. 127) in a Nietzschean manner that makes one 'insensitive to the traces and the existing forms of communicative rationality' (p. 129).

Whereas Habermas's discussion of Horkheimer and Adorno covers familiar ground, his account of Heidegger's 'Undermining of Western rationalism through the critique of metaphysics' takes us into a very different intellectual universe, of which I shall give only an outline. Habermas of course approves of Heidegger's critique of the subjectivism of Western metaphysics. He refers favourably to the chapter in Heidegger's 1939 lectures on Nietzsche entitled 'Mutual understanding and calculation', which contrast the strategic model of the subject, for which mutual understanding just means being able to count on others, with a fuller conception of agreement and disagreement: 'the approach of human beings toward one another in their selfsameness and selfhood has first to be grounded in mutual understanding' (p. 130). But Heidegger's intuitions about communicative rationality, like his critique of modernity (which had been a strong impulse in Habermas's own early thought), are set against the background of an overblown conception of philosophy and a messianic mysticism reduced to absurdity in Heidegger's nasty and brutish, if short, identification with Nazism and his subsequent 'turn' to a 'philosophy of origins'. Against this, Habermas insists on the possibility of less dramatic but more secure ways out 'of the philosophy of the subject' (p. 137).

Habermas's evaluation of the contemporary French philosopher Jacques Derrida runs along similar lines. Derrida too develops a critique of Western metaphysics in the form of a critique of the primacy accorded to speech and presence. Derrida's critique of Husserl's theory of meaning in 'La voix et le phénomène' brings out the problems of Husserl's concept of essence and their metaphysical roots, but he fails to take a more obvious and promising alternative starting point: to analyse the production of meaning in intersubjective terms rather than as 'the world-constituting performances of subjectivity' (p. 172). Thus Derrida's thought is characterized by an 'inverted foundationalism' (p. 167); he 'inherits the weakness of a critique of metaphysics that does not shake loose of the intentions of first philosophy (*Ursprungsphilosophie*)' (p. 181).

Habermas's critique is a little brisk, though it should not be too shocking in an Anglo-Saxon intellectual climate in which it never took much courage to say boo to a logos.[7] But whatever one makes of Derrida's basic philosophical orientation it is his deconstructive research programme which has been more influential on the world stage. Habermas notes the affinities between Derrida's deconstruction and Adorno's negative dialectics. Both engage in a self-critique of reason which is fully aware of its paradoxical character; 'the tools of thought, which miss the "dimension of nonidentity" and are imbued with the "metaphysics of presence", are nevertheless the only available means for uncovering their own insufficiency' (p. 185). Though Adorno's diagnosis is tragic, and his aesthetic utopianism desperate, by comparison with Derrida's Heideggerian acceptance of reality *(Gelassenheit)*, they both reject

Heidegger's pseudo-profundities as a possible solution and 'are sensitized in the same way against definitive, totalizing, all-incorporating models' (p. 187). But Derrida's nihilism about interpretation, like his inflation of the category of rhetoric in his attempt to efface or 'level down' the generic distinction (*Gattungsunterschied*) between philosophy and literature, fails to capture the nature of these enterprises (pp. 188–9). Similarly, and more generally, Derrida's pan-rhetoricism misses the different status of philosophy and literary criticism 'as mediators between expert cultures and the everyday world' (p. 207). To move from identifying the rhetorical elements which are undoubtedly present in all discourse to saying that everything is rhetorical in the same way is to remove the point of the claim (p. 210).[8]

After following Derrida into recent debates in literary theory, Habermas turns back to the French surrealist writer Georges Bataille. This somewhat surprising object-choice, which in some ways recalls Adorno and Horkheimer's use of the Marquis de Sade in *Dialectic of Enlightenment*, is partly explained by Bataille's role in transmitting Nietzschean influences to a later generation of thinkers, notably Foucault (pp. 238–9). But Bataille is also important in his own right in the philosophical discourse of modernity. Sharing with Adorno and Horkheimer a suspicion of the self-domination of Western rationality, especially in its ethical dimension (pp. 213ff), Bataille looks for a way out which parallels Heidegger's, but where transcendence takes the form of transgression, excess, waste and, at the limit, ritual sacrifice. Just as Heidegger had one foot in poetry, Bataille had one in philosophy, but in the end he rejects the systematic pursuit of knowledge as something also trapped in utilitarian calculation; 'the supreme moment necessarily transcends the philosophical problematic' (quoted by Habermas, p. 237).

Habermas's engagement with Michel Foucault is more substantial. In Foucault's thought, 'the radical critique of reason' takes 'the form of a historiography of the human sciences' (p. 247), 'a kind of antiscience' (p. 242) which anatomizes their will to power both at the empirical level, in medicine, psychopathology, criminology, penology, etc., and at the metatheoretical level of the constitution of their basic conceptual orientations.[9] Habermas notes that, as he showed in *Knowledge and Human Interests*, this is only part of the story: 'in the 1970s objectifying approaches no longer dominated the field in the human sciences; they were competing instead with hermeneutical and critical approaches that were tailored in their forms of knowledge to possibilities of application other than manipulation of self and of others' (pp. 272ff). But there is a more fundamental problem in Foucault's thought – the same paradox of self-reference which we have encountered throughout. The attempt to step out of modernity in a genealogical historiography grounded on the theory of power ends up as precisely the presentistic, relativistic, crypto-normative illusory science that it does not want to be (pp. 275–6).

Once again, as we saw in relation to literature, the problem is that 'the internal aspects of meaning, of truth-validity, and of evaluating do not go without remainder into the externally grasped aspects of practices of power' (p. 276). First, Foucault cannot undercut the hermeneutic predicament in his search for a real history of underlying practices which goes below or behind the self-understandings of actors. These practices have no meaning except in relation to earlier and later ones and, from our point of view, to the present. To ignore this problematic is to fall victim to it: 'The unmasking of the objectivistic illusions of any will to knowledge leads to agreement with a historiography that is narcissistically oriented toward the standpoint of the historian and instrumentalizes the contemplation of the past for the needs of the present' (p. 278). Nietzsche rides again.

Secondly, genealogical historiography succumbs to a 'relativistic self-denial' (p. 281): 'if the truth claim that Foucault himself raises for his genealogy of knowledge were in fact illusory and amounted to no more than the effects that this theory is capable of releasing within the circle of its adherents, then the entire undertaking of a critical unmasking of the human sciences would lose its point' (p. 279). Foucault flirts with a Lukácsian argument to the effect that genealogy recovers subjugated or disqualified knowledge-forms, but he cannot give these the kind of 'cognitive privilege' that was afforded to the proletariat in Lukács's philosophy of history (p. 281). Third, Foucault's apparently value-free or supra-normative position which 'resists the demand to take sides' masks a very clear critical standpoint, that of 'a dissident who offers resistance to modern thought and humanistically disguised disciplinary power' (p. 282). But Foucault cannot ground resistance and critique without moving on to the terrain of normative argument.[10] Of this we have only fragments (p. 284).

This attempt to eliminate 'the categories of meaning, validity and value . . . not only on the metatheoretical, but on the empirical level as well' leaves Foucault 'with an object domain from which the theory of power has erased all traces of communicative actions entangled in lifeworld contexts' (p. 286). Habermas illustrates this claim with reference to the classic sociological problems of social order and the relation between the individual and society. Following Axel Honneth's argument in *Critique of Power*, Habermas asks how Foucault can explain the way in which permanent power struggles lead to stabilized networks of power or how socialization can mean individuation as well as subordination, or that the bourgeois constitutional state is more than just 'a dysfunctional relic from the period of absolutism' (p. 290). Foucault's neglect even of penal law means that he overlooks not only the possibilities of law-based counter-movements, in which he was himself active, but also, more fundamentally, the fact that 'it is the legal means for securing freedom that themselves endanger the freedom of their presumptive beneficiaries' (p. 291).[11]

Despite the severity of his critique of Foucault, it is clear that Habermas has learned a lot from him, not just, as we saw in the last chapter, at the empirical level of the critical examination of welfare techniques, but also from his 'illuminating critique of the entanglement of the human sciences in the philosophy of the subject' (p. 294). Foucault's own critique, however, does not escape the same problem. He attempts 'to preserve the transcendental moment proper to generative performances in the basic concept of power while driving from it any trace of subjectivity' (p. 295). This, Habermas believes, leads Foucault into the subjectivist paradoxes noted above.

Habermas's critique of Foucault raises a broader issue which I shall return to later in this chapter: his way of reading the (largely French) critics of modernity. It is not easy to separate out the rhetoric underlying much of this discourse from the substantive underlying claims, but I share Richard Bernstein's preference for a more sympathetic reading of Foucault's thought: 'instead of claiming that Foucault is flatly contradicting himself on the question of the subject, truth, and freedom, we can read him in a different way – as deliberately using hyperbolic rhetorical constructions in order to compel us to disrupt and question our traditional understandings of these key concepts. And he effectively does this by showing us the dark ambiguities in the construction of these concepts and the role they have played in social practices.'[12] A reading like this brings Foucault closer to Adorno and the tradition of critical theory, and reveals him as a thinker whose focus on social conflict offers a crucial counterpoint to Habermas's communication theory.[13]

Habermas suggests that Foucault's 'acute diagnosis' of the 'basic conceptual aporias of the philosophy of consciousness', together with those of his own philosophy of power, point the way for his own project of replaying the philosophical discourse of modernity so as to find 'other ways out of the philosophy of the subject'.

> With Hegel and Marx it would have been a matter of not swallowing the intuition concerning the ethical totality back into the horizon of the self-refence of the knowing and acting subject, but of explicating it in accord with the model of unconstrained consensus formation in a communication community standing under cooperative constraints. With Heidegger and Derrida it would have been a matter of ascribing the meaning-creating horizons of world interpretation not to a Dasein heroically projecting itself or to a background occurrence that shapes structures, but rather to communicatively structured lifeworlds that reproduce themselves via the palpable medium of action oriented to mutual agreement. (p. 295)

In other words, rather than oscillating between the inflation of the human knowing subject and a radical scepticism about its reality, we should hold on to a model in which 'participants in interaction . . . coordinate their plans for action by coming to an understanding about something in the world' (p. 296). In the reconstruction of these practices, 'the ontological separation between the transcendental and the empirical is no longer applicable' (pp. 297–8). Similarly, the relation between the unconscious and the conscious, and the making conscious of what is unconscious, cease to be seen as 'heroic exertion' of the subject, but rather as part of the process of coming to understanding (p. 298).

The idea of self-reflection, inherited from the philosophy of consciousness, gives rise to two distinct operations, the rational reconstruction of formal rule systems and a more totalizing process of methodical self-criticism which bears on entire forms of life (p. 300). This does not mean, Habermas insists, that 'the purism of pure reason is . . . resurrected again in communicative reason' (p. 301). But, in opposition to totalizing critiques of rationality and logocentrism, Habermas is offering a 'less dramatic' critique which

> starts from an attack on the abstractions surrounding logos itself, as free of language, as individualist and as disembodied. It conceives of intersubjective understanding as the telos inscribed into communication in ordinary language, and of the logocentrism of Western

thought, heightened by the philosophy of consciousness, as a systematic foreshortening and distortion of a potential always already operative in the communicative practice of everyday life, but only selectively exploited. (p. 311)

This points the way to Habermas's own approach: an analysis focused not on judgements or sentences but on speech acts, in which, contra conceptions of language as just a factual representation of states of affairs, or their negative counterpart in which it is seen as mere rhetoric, the three validity-claims of truth, normative rightness and expressive truthfulness or sincerity are given equal importance. The phenomenological concept of the lifeworld must be expanded to cover not just background knowledge 'but also normatively reliable patterns of social relations . . . and the (communicative) competences acquired in socialization processes' (p. 314). Rationality, too, must be understood not just in terms of the knowing (and purposively acting) subject, but in procedural terms as a capacity to respond to the full range of validity-claims. 'Communicative reason finds its criteria in the argumentative procedures for . . . redeeming claims to propositional truth, normative rightness, subjective truthfulness, and aesthetic harmony' (p. 314). It thus 'recalls older ideas of logos' in its orientation to consensus and 'a decentered understanding of the world' (p. 315).

This in turn sheds a new light on the critique of instrumental reason, addressed in the final lecture, entitled 'The normative content of modernity'. Adorno, Foucault and Derrida cannot adequately locate their own positions, either in terms of the conventional classifications of the sciences – which they resist but by which they are none the less governed in their academic reception – or in the content of their thought. 'That the self-referential critique of reason is located everywhere and nowhere, so to speak, in discourses without a place, renders it almost immune to competing interpretations' (p. 337). These 'variations of a critique of reason with a reckless disregard for its own foundations' are also all driven by a critique of modernity, 'a special sensitivity for complex injuries and subtle violations', but, having sacrificed such concepts as 'self-consciousness, self-determination and self-realization' (p. 338), they cannot sustain their normative critique with what remains. Thirdly, their critique of modernity is itself overblown and undifferentiated, paying too little attention to its enormous advantages for 'the mass of the population':

To be sure, Adorno's theory of the administered world and
Foucault's theory of power are more fertile, and simply more in-
formative, than Heidegger's or Derrida's lucubrations on technology
as an instrumental frame [*Gestell*] or on the totalitarian nature of the
political order. But they are all insensitive to the highly ambivalent
content of cultural and social modernity. (p. 338)

These discourses, Habermas suggests, neglect the 'everyday
practice' of problem-solving and mundane learning processes 'as
something derivative or inauthentic' (p. 339).[14] The specialization of
artistic, legal, scientific and other forms of expertise is of course a
fact, and one which has given rise to 'an increase in knowledge that
is hard to dispute' (p. 340). This specialization and abstraction
should not be seen 'per se as phenomena of decline symptomatic of
subject-centred reason' (p. 339): it is only the modalities of interchange between these knowledge systems and everyday practice
that determine whether the gains from such abstraction affect the
lifeworld destructively' (p. 340).

> Horkheimer and Adorno have, like Foucault, described this process
> of a self-overburdening and self-reifying subjectivity as a world-
> historical process. But both sides missed its deeper irony, which
> consists in the fact that the communicative potentiality of reason first
> had to be released in the patterns of modern lifeworlds before the
> unfettered imperatives of the economic and administrative subsys-
> tems could react back on the vulnerable practice of everyday life
> and could thereby promote the cognitive-instrumental dimension
> to domination over the suppressed moments of practical reason.
> (p. 315)

How does this model relate to the philosophy of praxis developed out of the Marxist tradition, which Habermas examines in
The Theory of Communicative Action? They share a focus on the embodiment of rational practice 'in history, society, body, and language'. But praxis philosophy, in Habermas's view, remains
dominated by the philosophy of the subject in the form of philosophical anthropology; history, society and the body are dualisti-
cally conceived either as conditions given to the subject or as its
production. 'Thought that is tied to the philosophy of the subject
cannot bridge over these dichotomies but, as Foucault acutely diag-
nosed, oscillates helplessly between one and the other pole' (p. 317).
Language, too, is conceived either as a vehicle for the creation of
meaning or as something which happens behind our backs. Either

way, 'the connection between the disclosure of the world and mundane learning processes is excluded' (p. 319; cf. p. 321).

Habermas stresses the differences between his theory, based on communicative action, and praxis philosophy, based on the concept of social labour. Whereas social reproduction for Marx involves a unity of work and nature, communicative action remains distinct from the lifeworld. Their difference 'is even deepened to the extent that the reproduction of the lifeworld is no longer merely routed through the medium of action oriented to understanding, but is saddled on the interpretative performances of its agents' (p. 342). More concretely, in terms of the Parsonian triad of culture, society and personality, culture tends towards 'the constant revision of traditions that have been thawed, that is, have become reflective', society towards 'the dependence of legitimate orders upon formal and ultimately discursive procedures for establishing and grounding norms', and personality towards 'the risk-filled self-direction of a highly abstract ego-identity' (p. 345). These trends all point towards a situation in which the reproduction of forms of life is secured not by tradition but 'by a risky search for consensus, that is, by the cooperative achievements of those engaged in communicative action themselves' (p. 344). This yields a different model from the 'dialectic of enlightenment' in which subjectivity, 'the principle of modernity', produces divisions and abstractions in itself and in the world which can only be reconciled by a process of self-reflection emanating from, yet going beyond subjectivity' (p. 347).

> As soon as we give up praxis philosophy's understanding of society as a self-referential subject-writ-large, encompassing all individual subjects, the corresponding models for the diagnosis and mastery of crisis – division [*Spaltung*] and revolution – are no longer applicable. Because the successive releasing of the rational potential inherent in communicative action is no longer thought of as self-reflection writ large, this specification of the normative content of modernity can prejudge neither the conceptual tools for diagnosing crises nor the way of overcoming them. (p. 348)[15]

Habermas remains worried that his theory may still be accused of idealism, of failing to explain material reproduction. He stresses that communicative and instrumental action are interlaced with one another. The theory of communicative action recognizes the embodiment of reason(ing) in concrete structures and transcends the traditional philosophical opposition between materiality and 'the transcendent power of abstractive reason' (p. 324). As in *The Theory of Communicative Action*, he attempts to rebut the charge by showing that Marx's dialectic of dead and living labour is just one instance of the relation between systems and lifeworld (pp. 349ff). 'Marx did not distinguish between the new level of system differentiation brought about by a media-steered economic system and the class-specific forms of its institutionalization.' His emancipatory strategy also conflates 'abolishing class structures and melting down the independent systemic logic of functionally differentiated and reified domains of interaction' (p. 354).[16]

In abandoning 'the concepts of praxis philosophy, if not . . . its intentions' (p. 357), we should, Habermas argues, recognize that society cannot be analysed as a subject with knowledge of and influence over itself. Luhmann's system model is right to this extent (p. 357). However, the crises of the modern welfare states and their political systems, their inability to remedy lifeworld problems with system means, have made us 'conscious of the difference between steering problems and problems of mutual understanding. . . . Money and power can neither buy nor compel solidarity and meaning' (p. 363). Once again, as in *The Theory of Communicative Action*, Habermas argues for the need for 'impulses from the lifeworld' to enter and influence, even control, the functional subsystems (p. 364). This in turn requires the development of 'autonomous public spheres', that is, ones 'which are not produced and preserved by the political system for purposes of creating legitimation' (p. 364).

Beyond metaphysics

The Philosophical Discourse of Modernity should be read in conjunction with *Postmetaphysical Thinking* and *The New Conservatism (Die neue Unübersichtlichkeit)*. The latter essays, dating from the first half of the 1980s, have a more contemporary and political relevance, bringing out some of the anxieties which, whether justified or not, motivated *The Philosophical Discourse of Modernity*, while the former elaborate Habermas's conception of postmetaphysical thought in ways which bring out some of the underlying affinities with recent French philosophy. Habermas now views the 'contrast' between German rationalism and French post-structuralism as having been 'quite unnecessarily exaggerated' and as more a matter of 'a difference of rhetorical styles'.[17]

In response to a survey by the newspaper *Le Monde* in 1984, in which he characterizes the new theoretical pluralism and openness as involving also a 'new obscurity',[18] Habermas identifies three interrelated trends. First, contextualism in science: a tolerance of diversity, historical variation and 'soft' sciences and methods. Second, the overcoming of the philosophy of consciousness based on the subject and its self-consciousness – an 'achievement of our age' which Habermas likens to Kant's original introduction of this model. Third, the 'total critique of reason' which 'itself takes on totalitarian characteristics'; even this trend contains a moment of truth, a 'sensitivity to the dialectic of [the] enlightenment.[19] Western 'logocentrism' results from a narrowing-down of the concept of reason rather than its over-extension, its cognitivistic restriction to the isolated domains of ontology, epistemology and semantics at the expense of a broader perspective of the kind found in pragmatism and related movements. This restriction reflects the one-sided capitalist modernization of the lifeworld and therefore cannot be overcome on the terrain of philosophy or social science – though these can help in the recovery of lost dimensions of reason.[20]

Attempts to rehabilitate metaphysics, whether in the traditional mode of transcendental philosophy, as in the work of Dieter Henrich, or in more innovative and fashionable variants building on Heidegger's later philosophy, attribute to philosophy a privileged method and domain which it can no longer aspire to without anachronism.[21] In opposition to this love–hate relationship to metaphysics found in some contemporary philosophy, we find a more genuinely anti-metaphysical radical contextualism represented in Richard Rorty's neo-pragmatism. Rorty's critique of philosophical foundationalism in *Philosophy and the Mirror of Nature* has developed into an ultra-tolerant liberal pragmatism open to all contributions to the 'conversation', and in which 'truth' is nothing more than a nod of approval. Here Habermas takes up and develops an argument made by Hilary Putnam. When Rorty claims that we cannot mean by truth anything more than truth 'for us', though we can aim to extend the scope of 'us' by pursuing intersubjective agreement, Habermas argues that we could not understand the way we criticize and modify our established standards of rationality and justification if we did not take seriously the idea of a possible consensus which would transcend the opposition of 'us' and 'them'. In other words, although our validity-claims are always made in specific contexts, the validity which they claim transcends time and space.[22]

In social theory, Habermas argues, the current valorization of contradiction and difference derives partly from a still unclarified relation to metaphysics, but even more to a recognition of the complexity, differentiation and decentredness of modern societies, in which the state no longer acts as a centre for social functions and '*everything* appears to have become part of the periphery'.[23] Yet we cannot sustain our own self-understanding without a corresponding image of our societies and their possible futures; even a decentred society needs as a reference point 'the projected unity of an intersubjectively formed common will'.[24] Thus Habermas aims 'to make plausible a weak but not defeatist concept of linguistically embodied reason'[25] which preserves from the metaphysical tradition the ideas of the rational understanding of reality and the unconstrained harmony of individual and society in a way which is sceptical and fallibilist enough to fit the reality of the contemporary situation.

In the past few years some of the steam has gone out of the radical critique of reason in its 'French' form, though Rortyan pragmatism remains attractive to many contemporary thinkers.[26] Once the noise on the translation channel has been filtered out, many of these positions seem much closer than their protagonists believed. Manfred Frank, for instance, has plausibly suggested that the prima facie opposition between Habermas's model of the harmonious pursuit of communicative consensus, free from violence, and Lyotard's postulate of irreconcilable conflicts (*différends*) is not necessarily as stark as it appears. Lyotard can be seen as accentuating the conflictual character of dialogue in a way which offers a useful corrective to Habermas's model, rather than a root-and-branch alternative.[27] Habermas's own critique inevitably begins to look, even more than it did before, like the American and Soviet anti-guerrilla campaigns which unsuccessfully deployed what should have been devastating firepower against an army which refused to stand still and be shot at. It should be clear, I think, that Habermas is right to deny that he is 'advocating a linear continuation of the tradition of the Enlightenment',[28] and the mutual accusations of totalitarianism on the part of impeccably humane and liberal thinkers seem a little hollow against the background of the real collapse of the last would-be totalitarian regimes and the increasingly bloody conflicts between their heirs. But Habermas's positive ideal of a philosophy which is post-metaphysical yet not post-rational remains both attractive and plausible.

9

Law and the State

A major task for Habermas was to assess the implications of his developed theories of communicative action and discourse ethics for his continuing concern with the public sphere in advanced capitalist democracies. The big question for him has always been the conditions which (would) make possible rational discussion of public affairs and democratic decision-making. Some of his readers have put it more sharply: how could the apparently utopian notions of emancipatory knowledge and practice, of ideal communicative situations and of communicative action and discourse ethics cope with the grubby reality of self-interested conduct, self-serving institutions and political horse-trading? In some of his political writings in the 1980s, in an introduction to a new edition of his early book on the public sphere, and in interviews such as those in *Autonomy and Solidarity*, Habermas repeatedly gestured towards the implications of what he *does* see as an eminently practical conception.

In particular, his work in this period has focused on legal theory. His *Tanner Lectures on Human Values*, delivered in 1986 and reprinted in 1992 in *Faktizität und Geltung* (*Facticity and Validity*), were titled *Law and Morality*, and attempted to reconstruct the traditional concept of the *Rechtsstaat*, a state embodying the rule of law, in terms of the underlying question: how legal forms of state authority can be legitimate. Max Weber had a short answer to this question: 'it is the rationality inherent in the juridical form itself which provided legitimacy for domination exercised in legal forms.'[1] But Weber's value-free concepts of rationality and of legitimacy are too impoverished, as is shown by the difficulty he has in giving an adequate account of the intrusion of substantive considerations, such as those of welfare, into what is in principle a formal system of law. Weber saw this process as an adulteration of the formal rationality of the legal system. As with economic systems, the choice at the margin between the pursuit of formal and substantive rationality is ultimately a matter of arbitrary decision. For Habermas, by contrast, such 'collisions' between the conflicting principles of substantive considerations of social justice on the one hand, and the formal precision, and therefore calculability, of the law on the other, 'must then be decided from the moral point of view of the universalizability of interests'.[2]

We cannot, then, have a self-legitimating de-moralized rational law; the processes by which legal norms are produced must themselves conform to independent norms of moral-practical procedural rationality (p. 552). This partly means 'moral discourses' (p. 565) in a strict sense, but also democratic processes of legislation (p. 569). This is not just a matter of formal parliamentary procedures. Returning, thirty years on, to the concerns of *Structural Transformation of the Public Sphere*, Habermas stresses the qualitative aspect of the public sphere.

> The rational quality of political legislation does not only depend on how elected majorities and protected minorities work within parliaments. It also depends on the level of participation and school education, the degree of information and the precision with which controversial issues are articulated – in short, on the discursive character of non-institutionalized opinion formation in the political public sphere. (p. 570)

Habermas sweeps aside the claims of system theorists like Luhmann that the complexity of modern societies and their legal systems renders irrelevant the very idea of a justifying law by reference to moral principles. The external approach of system theory cannot account for the demand for validity in law as expressed in the process of legal argumentation, and this process defies all attempts to confine it in purely formal terms. The rationality of law which, as Max Weber rightly insisted, is essential to its independence, cannot be understood as a merely formal or procedural rationality, since law is internally related to morality and politics (p. 580). The *Rechtsstaat* comes to take the place of Kant's rational natural law, but retains the idea that, just as moral principles must be universalizable, the universality or impartiality of judicial decisions demands a complete assessment of claims based on conflicting interests in the light of similarly conflicting principles.

> A legal system is autonomous only to the extent that the procedures institutionalized for legislation and legal decision guarantee a non-partisan formation of opinion and will and thereby give moral procedural rationality access, as it were, to law and politics. No autonomous law without realized democracy. (p. 599)

Habermas repeats this ringing slogan in the introduction to *Faktizität und Geltung* (p. 13).[3] This awareness, that in a sphere of 'fully secularized politics the *Rechtsstaat* cannot be achieved and preserved without radical democracy', is, he suggests, an underlying reason for the lack of direction and self-awareness in contemporary politics. The book aims, then, to demonstrate this principle, while also 'performatively refuting the objection that the theory of communicative action is blind to the reality of institutions' (p. 10). Against a growing scepticism among critical legal theorists about 'the social effectiveness of the normative presuppositions of existing legal practices', against scientistic reductions (Luhmann) and aesthetic assimilations (Derrida), he aims to bring out the centrality of legal thought:

> In the continual controversies since the seventeenth century over the legal institution of the political community, we also articulate a moral-practical self-image of modernity as a whole, expressed both in the testimonies of a universalistic moral consciousness and in the free institutions of the democratic state. (p. 11)[4]

Habermas begins by differentiating his concept of communicative reason from that of practical reason which, in its eighteenth-century context of the philosophy of the subject, treats individuals and states or societies as subjects. Theories of communicative rationality recognize that it is no longer possible to retain a unified Hegelian conception of moral theory, social theory and philosophy of history with direct implications for practice. And to accept the need for a plurality of methods and approaches, those of jurisprudence, the sociology and history of law and of moral and social theory (p. 9), is to accept that we can no longer rely on the old guarantees of philosophy of history, philosophical anthropology or a complacent accommodation to the status quo (p. 16). Moreover, 'modern societies have become so complex' that they can no longer be analysed in terms of the traditional constructs of 'a society centred in the state and a society composed of individuals' (p. 15). Rather than ascribing practical reason to individual actors and/or to states or societies seen as macro-subjects, we should see communicative reason as the result of interactions and ways of life embedded and structured in language.

Whereas traditional practical reason directly yielded norms for action, communicative reason does so only indirectly, via the participants' acceptance of the implications of their actual attempts to come to an understanding.[5] These 'unavoidable idealizations form the counterfactual basis of an actual process of mutual understanding which can *transcend* itself, turning itself critically on its own results. Thus the tension between idea and reality breaks into the facticity of linguistically structured forms of life' (pp. 18–19).

The same tension between facticity and validity pervades the study of politics and law, 'between normativistic approaches which are always in danger of losing contact with social reality, and objectivistic approaches which filter out all normative aspects' (p. 21). And the law itself 'derives its binding force from the alliance between the positivity of law and its claim to legitimacy' (p. 58). Law, in other words, must be both compulsory and compelling, combining the threat of sanctions with an appeal to shared convictions (p. 41). The idea of the *Rechtsstaat* is designed to meet the need to 'legalize' the force underlying the law, in an institutionally differentiated form in which citizens prescribe laws for themselves (p. 58).

Recalling his central claim in *The Theory of Communicative Action* about the coexistence in modern societies of social integration and the system integration via markets and administrative power, Habermas notes that law is implicated in all three means of societal integration, as well as being exposed to demands from a variety of sources. 'The tension between the idealism of contributional law and the materialism of a legal order, especially that of economic law, which merely reflects the unequal distribution of social power, finds its echo in the way the philosophical and the empirical approaches to law drift apart' (p. 60).

Habermas goes on in chapter 2 of *Faktizität und Geltung* to document the failure of philosophical theorists of justice such as Rawls and Dworkin to deal with institutional issues, and the complementary neglect by functionalist sociologists of law of its intrinsic aspect. Law is *both* a system of normative propositions and interpretations *and* an institution, an action system (p. 106). But legal concepts of the body of citizens are 'too concrete for social theory' (p. 107), which must instead see the law as a 'transformer' on the edge between system and lifeworld (p. 108).

Chapters 3 to 6 of the book are devoted to a reconstruction of the intrinsic dimension of legal theory. Habermas begins with the sphere of subjective rights, those 'which citizens must attribute to one another if they wish to legitimately regulate their collective life with the means of positive law' (p. 109). The long-standing dispute over whether these rights should take priority over the legislative system or should be subordinated to a body of positive public law overlooks the more crucial issue of the legitimacy of public law itself (p. 117). Although human rights grounded in the moral autonomy of the individual are complementary to, and rely for their implementation on, the political autonomy of the citizens, we find in both Kant and Rousseau 'an unacknowledged *relation of competition* between the morally grounded *human rights* and the *principle of popular sovereignty'* (p. 123). Here, in other words, is another instance of the collision between competing principles: a conflict which can only be adequately resolved in discourse. This means that the exercise of political autonomy must be grounded in communication, the discursive formation of opinion and policy, rather than an analysis of the form of universal laws (p. 133). We must also distinguish between two types of action-norms: moral and legal. Both are valid, according to Habermas's 'discourse principle D', if 'all those who might be affected could agree to them as participants in a rational discourse' (p. 138).[6] But whereas post-traditional moral norms merely represent 'a form of cultural knowledge' (p. 137), albeit one which may make universalistic claims (p. 139), law is also binding on an institutional level (p. 137).

Habermas notes (p. 140) that the discourse principle, which merely specifies what is implied by the impartial grounding of any norm, must be more sharply distinguished from the moral principle than was the case in his earlier writings. The moral principle must be distinguished from the principle of democracy, which specifies 'a process of legitimate lawmaking. It states . . . that only those laws can claim legitimate validity which can achieve the agreement of all citizens in a discursive process of legislation which is itself legally constituted' (p. 141). Law itself provides a necessary complement to morality, especially a post-conventional and therefore critical one (p. 149).

Habermas goes on to generate a list of basic rights, arising from development of the law, to guarantee: (1) the greatest possible measure of equal subjective freedoms; (2) membership in a free association of citizens; (3) actionable rights and individual legal protection and (4) 'basic rights to equal access to processes of opinion and will-formation, in which citizens exercise their *political autonomy* and through which they enact legitimate law'. Finally, those rights imply (5) basic rights to conditions of life which are socially, technically and ecologically secure to the degree necessary for equal ability to make use of rights 1 to 4 (pp. 155-7).

Framing a system of rights in this way, Habermas suggests, brings out the links between popular sovereignty and human rights, between political and private autonomy (p. 161). This clarifies the apparent paradox 'that the political basic rights must institutionalize the public use of communicative freedoms in the form of subjective rights' (p. 164). We need, in other words, to go beyond a semantic analysis of rights to a pragmatic analysis which takes account of the practical conditions for their exercise; 'legal institutions of freedom collapse without the initiatives of a population which is *used* to freedom' (p. 165). 'Spontaneity cannot be compelled by law; it regenerates itself out of traditions of freedom and preserves itself in associative relations of a liberal political culture' (p. 165).

The dualism running through the law between facticity and validity also applies to the state and its legitimacy. 'Political rule relies on a capacity to threaten which is backed by means of military force; at the same time, however, it has itself *authorized* by legitimate law' (p. 171). To speak of the state is to speak about power, but Habermas distinguishes, once again, between the state's administrative power and what Hannah Arendt called communicative power, the power which 'arises between people when they act together' (p. 182).[7] State power, legally exercised, must also be based on the intuitions of justice embodied in communicative power (p. 183), and Habermas suggests that we should conceive

law as the medium by which communicative power is transformed into administrative power. . . . The idea of the *Rechtsstaat* can then be generally interpreted as the demand that the administrative system, steered by the code of power, should be bound to the law-creating communicative power and preserved from the effects of social power, i.e. the factual impact of privileged interests. (p. 187)

This predominance of communicative power over administrative power should not, however, be understood too concretely:

> In the *Rechtsstaat* as conceived by discourse theory, popular sovereignty is no longer embodied in an identifiable assembly of autonomous citizens. It draws back into the so to speak subject-less communication circuits of forums and associations. Only in this anonymous form can its communicatively fluid power bind the administrative power of the state apparatus to the will of the citizens. (p. 170)

How does communicative power develop? The institutionalization of rights to political participation implies both a cognitive process in which decisions are based on rational arguments and the practical process of the establishment of relations of understanding which develop 'the productive force of communicative freedom' (p. 188). This is even more crucial in the political than in the moral sphere because, whereas it may be possible to separate universalistic moral principles from the collective projects of a given community, political choices inevitably include more detailed and concrete practical local issues. Hence the kind of agreement which is arrived at is more conditional and specific – concerning, in John Rawls's terms, 'obligation' rather than 'natural duties' (p. 194).

It is therefore impossible to apply discourse ethics or a simple concept of discourse directly to democratic politics. Following an earlier essay 'On the pragmatic, ethical and moral use of practical reason',[8] Habermas distinguishes between pragmatic discourses, relating individual or collective choices to given preferences, ethical-political discourses, concerned with the implementation of broader collective ideals, and moral discourses cast in universal terms. 'Ethically relevant' issues include environmental and animal protection, urban planning, immigration policy, the protection of minorities and 'generally issues of political culture'; morally relevant issues would be, for example, abortion law, statutes of limitations of criminal responsibility, or matters of social policy affecting 'the distribution of social wealth and of life and survival chances in general' (p. 204).[9]

In many cases, however, there will be a pragmatic choice to be made between alternatives, opening the way to negotiation and compromise, leading hopefully to an accommodation

(*Vereinbarung*) which balances out conflicting interests.[10] The fairness of such negotiations and compromises is, however, a moral question. The complex relations between these various levels of discourse include 'at least' a 'process model of rational political will-formation' in which pragmatic discourses lead via regulated negotiations and/or ethical-political discourses to moral discourses and finally legal discourses; the latter are concerned essentially with the compatibility of new proposals with established laws and rights (p. 207). This reconstruction allows for familiar institutions such as parliamentary assemblies and majority voting (p. 220). Parliaments are, however, seen not as simply expressing or discovering a hypothetical general interest but as structurally linked (in ways which remain to be decribed in detail[11]) with 'the informal formation of opinion in culturally mobilized publics' (p. 228).

Habermas argues, on the basis of a discussion of the application of law, for a proceduralist conception that incorporates the two approaches which, as we saw earlier, are conventionally opposed to one another: bourgeois formal law and the substantivized law of the welfare state (pp. 239, 271). Such 'legal ideologies' reduce the complexity of judgements; where, however, two or more paradigms conflict, one is forced, as in the case of conflicting moral principles, into a second-order examination of their interrelations. In the case of law, this involves a 'proceduralist conception' of 'reflexive law' which relates these models to 'political conflicts' between alternative models of society (p. 477).

The term 'proceduralist' might seem to suggest the automatic operation of institutionalized procedures. Habermas means just the opposite: a process of interaction, as in the case of political structures, between formal institutions and 'the communications of a . . . public sphere rooted in the private centres of the lifeworld'. Once again, the emphasis is not so much on the competences of actors and institutions[12] as on 'the *forms of communication* on which the interplay of informal and non-institutionalized processes of opinion and will-formation take place' (p. 492). These informal

> structures of mutual recognition . . . and legitimate law . . . spread around the society like a skin. A legal order *is* legitimate to the extent that it secures the equally fundamental private and civic autonomy of its citizens; but at the same time it *owes* its legitimacy to the forms of communication which are essential for this autonomy to express and preserve itself. That is the key to a proceduralist conception of law. (p. 493)

This conception is not only superior to more traditional alternatives; it also responds to the contradiction which arises from the replacement of bourgeois conceptions of law with those which develop along with the interventionist welfare state. 'After the formal-legal guarantee of private autonomy has shown itself to be insufficient, and social steering by legal means endangers the private autonomy which it aims to restore,'[13] 'the only way out is to thematize the connection between forms of communication which simultaneously guarantee private and public autonomy *in their emergence*' (p. 493).

Constitutional law is obviously the sphere where legal and democratic principles are most likely to come into conflict. Habermas focuses on the more fundamental area of the competence of constitutional courts in relation to basic norms. This is particularly important in the case of Germany, where the Federal Constitutional Court reads the constitution as a set of ethical principles rather than as a formal system of rules (p. 309). Controversies in the USA and Germany reveal conflicting conceptions of the democratic process, notably in the contrast between liberal (passive) and 're-publican' (active) models of the citizen. Once again, a proceduralist conception of constitutional law is primarily concerned with the quality of democratic discussion; this of course raises serious empirical questions (pp. 347–8).

In chapters 7 and 8 of *Faktizität und Geltung* Habermas asks how this idealized conception of democratic law-making fits the empirical reality of politics, which seems to be more a matter of power, strategic conflicts and administration. Rather than abstractly confronting the ideal with reality, he aims, in what he describes as a 'reconstructive sociology of democracy', to identify the normative elements built into the factual operation of liberal-democratic political systems (p. 349).

Models of democracy which reduce it entirely to domination and rhetoric[14] cannot explain why people should accept the normative claims, and follow the rules of democracy (p. 358). Discourse theory's 'deliberative' model of democracy incorporates elements both of the liberal conception of politics as the mediation of private interests and of the republican conception of a self-organizing ethical community. It outlines 'an ideal procedure for discussion and decision-making [which] establishes an internal connection between pragmatic considerations, compromises, and discourses of self-clarification and justice' (p. 359). Like republicanism, it centres on the formation of political will and opinion, though treating the

Rechtsstaat not 'as something secondary' but as the necessary institutional framework for these forms of communication, given that
the traditional republican conception of a unified populace at the
centre of the state is no longer tenable (pp. 361–2). This 'higher-
order' subjectless intersubjectivity is centred in a civil society, which
is 'the social foundation of autonomous public spheres' and distinct
from 'the economic system of action and from the public administration' (p. 363). This yields a normative model in which

> The socially integrative force of solidarity, which can no longer be
> drawn solely from sources in communicative action, develops in
> widely differentiated autonomous public spheres and legally
> (*rechtsstaatlich*) institutionalized procedures of democratic opinion
> and will-formation so that it can also hold its own, in the medium of
> law, against the two other mechanisms of social integration: money
> and administrative power. (p. 363)

In this conception, democratic elections do not simply license or
legitimate the actions of power-holders (liberalism), nor do they
merely constitute and reaffirm the political community (republicanism); they also function 'as the most important sluices for the
discursive rationalization of the decisions of a government and
administration bound by law and statute' (p. 364). In this intersubjective reinterpretation of popular sovereignty (p. 365), politics
is internally related to the resources of the lifeworld – 'above all the
initiatives of opinion-forming associations' (p. 366).

Habermas therefore focuses in chapter 8 on civil society and the
public sphere, criticizing the conceptual principles which, along
with the empirical evidence, have led many political sociologists to
give up on normative theories of democracy in favour of more
'realistic' pluralist, economic or systems theories. These models
have in turn failed to satisfy many theorists, and alternatives have
emerged out of these traditions themselves. The Norwegian social
philosopher Jon Elster, for example, has enriched rational action
theory with a non-reductionist model of normative regulated action
and a distinction between 'bargaining' and 'arguing' which, as he
notes himself, converges with Habermas's own thinking (p. 413,
n. 27). Systems theory, too, cannot get its systems to work without
a relation to intersubjective lifeworlds (p. 427), which mediate their
interrelations and their functional overlaps (p. 429).

One can, however, learn from these more sceptical models not to
understand modern states and societies in too concrete a manner.

The public sphere (*Öffentlichkeit*) is not a fixed institution or organization; it is best understood as 'a network for the communication of contents and the expression of attitudes, *i.e. of opinions*, in which the flows of communication are filtered and synthesized in such a way that they condense into *public* opinions clustered according to themes' (p. 436). Public opinion in this sense is the result of a process of communication; it is therefore not to be identified with the collection of individual opinions in surveys – unless of course these follow a process of opinion formation 'in a mobilized public' (p. 438). Similarly 'civil society' in the full modern sense of the term (as opposed to that of Hegel and Marx) is centred on 'a structure of associations which institutionalizes problem-solving discourses on questions of general interest in a framework of organized publics (*veranstalteter Öffentlichkeiten*)' (pp. 443–4).

Civil society and the movements arising from it are a complement rather than an alternative to formally constituted politics; in Jean Cohen and Andrew Arato's phrase, taken from the Polish anti-communist opposition movement Solidarność (Solidarity), they are 'self-limiting' (pp. 448ff). Conversely, the formal political system is not just one of several social subsystems, since it is enmeshed both with other legally regulated (e.g. administrative) systems and with the public sphere. In this context Habermas offers a brief and long-promised reformulation of his well-known model of legitimation crisis. In the original version of the model, as we saw in chapter 4, economic crisis tendencies give rise to rationality crises in state outputs and legitimation crises threatening the withdrawal of popular support. In the new version, Habermas characterizes rationality and legitimation crises in rather more precise terms. The political system's regulatory efficiency is threatened when its instructions are not obeyed, or when they lead to disorganization, or when they overstretch the capacity of the legal system and undermine the normative foundations of the political system itself. The combination of these three problems can lead to what Habermas calls a 'regulatory trilemma' (p. 446). In its other aspect, the political system can fail to preserve social integration if its decisions, however effective, emerge from the independent operation of administrative systems and commercial corporations rather than from a functioning public sphere. 'The independent establishment of illegitimate power and the weakness of civil society and the political public sphere can come to a head in a "legitimatory dilemma" which can in certain circumstances combine with a steering trilemma into a vicious circle. Then the political system is sucked into mutually reinforcing legitimacy and steering deficits' (pp. 466–7).

Thus problems of legitimacy cannot, *pace* system theory, be reduced to the inefficient regulatory outputs of the state, but also arise from 'a disturbance in the democratic origins of law' (p. 518). To treat them just as system problems is to assign to law in the welfare state the role of a mere mediator between conflicting value orientations. But this is to ignore the root causes which have left these orientations and standards to drift apart – the fact that regulative law has been 'uprooted from the soil of legitimate legislation'. These standards arise from the expressed needs of human beings, and, where there is no forum for their expression, political and legal institutions lack the necessary parameters for their activity. Unable to generate these themselves, they fall back into a purely adminstrative disposition over collective goods (pp. 518–19).

These problems are not inevitable results of an overstretched welfare state or of the substantialization of formal law, which in turn results from the increasing complexity of tasks which the state is called upon to perform (in a 'risk society' where it has to consider future generations as well as its immediate clients). The underlying problem is 'the inadequate institutionalization of the principles of the *Rechtsstaat* rather than an overload imposed by these principles on a state activity which has become more complex' (p. 527). To focus solely on complexity, and to use this as an argument against reform, is to 'confuse legitimacy with efficiency and to forget that the institutions of the *Rechtsstaat* were always designed not just to reduce complexity but to preserve it by compensatory adjustment (*Gegensteuerung*), so as to stabilize the tension between facticity and validity inherent in the law' (p. 535).

What is lacking, in other words, is the capacity of legal paradigms to 'illuminate the horizon of a given society' in terms of a system of rights (p. 527). And 'the social basis for the realization for the system of rights is made up of neither the forces of a spontaneously operating market society, nor the measures of an intentionally operating welfare state, but rather the communication flows and mediatized influences which emerge from civil society and the political public sphere and are transformed, via democratic processes, into communicative power' (pp. 532–3).

Once again, in an implicit critique of orthodox systems theory's blindly interacting structures, Habermas stresses that legal and political systems are enmeshed in varying configurations of complex circulatory processes which actors must be able to interpret to themselves in legal and other categories. Behind the varying forms of constitutions lies a single form of practice: the self-determination of free and equal citizens. Starting from their own current activities, participants can achieve an understanding of this general form of democratic practice (p. 467).

In conclusion, Habermas suggests that the model advanced here may give 'a certain coherence' to current concerns for reform. In a post-metaphysical world, the 'state has lost its sacred substance'; this secularization of state power must be compensated by further democratization 'if the *Rechtsstaat* is not to be endangered' (p. 534). This process must go beyond the limits of the nation-state and its sovereignty in the context of the development of a 'world public sphere' (p. 535). Rethinking the *Rechtsstaat* in the way outlined above is not a utopian project, given the importance which civil society, the public sphere and the democratic process now have for the realization of rights.

> In complex societies the scarcest resources are neither the pro-
> ductivity of a market economy nor the steering capacity of public
> administration. What need to be treated with care are above all the
> exhausted resources of nature and a social solidarity which is in a
> process of collapse. And the forces of social solidarity can today be
> regenerated in the forms of communicative practices of self-determi-
> nation. (p. 536)

A reform project based on a procedural concept of law does not specify a particular social ideal or vision of the good life, but merely a means by which those concerned might decide to pursue such goals. It is dogmatic only in its concept of autonomy, according to which human beings are free subjects to the extent that the laws they obey are ones which they give themselves in the light of their intersubjectively achieved insights. And this idea is 'unavoidable' (*unhintergehbar*) for those who have formed their identities in this sort of society.

It will be clear from this brief account that *Faktizät und Geltung* represents a major development in Habermas's work. People can no longer complain that his model of moral reasoning has no implications, or merely anarchistic ones, for legal and political institutions (p. 10). The book is of course only just beginning to be extensively discussed in print, and this discussion will involve a complex division of labour between philosophers and social and legal theorists. A few preliminary comments are in order here.

First, Habermas has offered an enormously rich and carefully elaborated model of the interrelations between politics, morality and law. As with his earlier works, there are questions to be asked about the connections between his various claims. Where Habermas sees a seamless web of argumentation, others tend to see separate claims which must be assessed on their own merits. As Charles Larmore notes, in a contribution to a useful review symposium, Habermas is a little brisk in laying down the law about what one can or cannot meaningfully say in a 'post-metaphysical' context, and this might be better understood as indicating an ineradicable pluralism of competing perspectives rather than a universal paradigm shift common to all except diehard fundamentalists.[15]

Secondly, the precise connections Habermas aims to establish between (subjective) rights and popular sovereignty are likely to give rise to considerable discussion, since his model aims precisely to combine and transcend the liberal and communitarian perspectives and their respective emphases on these two principles. More generally, moral and political philosophers in these two camps have themselves a good deal of room to clarify the implications of their increasingly professionalized and hermetic discussions for concrete issues of social, legal and political theory. In this context Larmore makes the interesting point that the principle of popular sovereignty seems itself to rely upon the recognition of a basic subjective right, the principle of respect for persons, thus shifting the balance back from democratic to subjective rights, where Habermas had attempted to derive subsidiary rights *from* the principle of political autonomy.[16] This may seem like a question of detail, but it has substantial implications both for the structure of Habermas's theory and for his current engagement with the law. The term 'recognition' can serve as a peg for both sets of considerations.

First, Larmore suggests that Habermas cannot put as much weight as he wishes to on the concept of discourse, whether ideal or real, since this relies on the deeper principle of respect for persons. Again, this seems an issue which one should not lose much sleep over, since Habermas can easily agree, and has himself often emphasized, that the willingness to enter into discourse is something which is found only under certain cultural and intersubjective conditions. What we have, in other words, is just another instance of the tension between facticity and validity, between what is logically implied by certain forms of practice and belief and what we actually do.

The more fundamental issue, raised by Peter Dews in the same symposium, concerns the place of law itself in relation to questions of mutual respect, recognition and solidarity. Habermas sees the law in a welfare state as steering a difficult path between a negatively discriminatory approach, which ignores the way factual inequalities limit the freedom of individuals, and a paternalism which overlooks the limits to freedom resulting from state action undertaken to compensate for these same inequalities.[17] What is lacking here as elsewhere, Dews notes, is a more critical assessment of law itself, and in particular of the ways in which it isolates individuals and destroys rather than underpins social integration in the lifeworld.[18]

Sociologists have tended to take a hostile view of law, and have rarely drawn on it as a resource in their theorizing as they have drawn on other bodies of theoretical literature.[19] There was something of a shift in the 1980s, as revolutionary projects of social reconstruction came to seem less viable, and what Marx called 'the narrow horizon of bourgeois right' came to seem rather more attractive than the continuing arbitrariness of post-Stalinist rule. Habermas, it should be stressed, never joined in the rejection of law, either theoretically or practically, but he may partly be trying to counter its residues among those likely to appreciate the underlying radical-democratic thrust of the book. Be that as it may, Dews is surely right that, if Habermas is concerned, as he rightly is , with the loss of social solidarity in modern societies, he needs to look further at the ways in which this can be reinvigorated. Legal and political autonomy are at best necessary and not sufficient conditions for this.[20]

What we need to ask, perhaps, is what forms of social solidarity can be developed, in an increasingly globalized yet fragmented world in which people are both brought together and held apart by the operations of the mass media. What Habermas has done is to show how a set of elaborate but fragmented elements of legal and political theory can be brought into a common framework. But to do this is also to show that, however important these may be as institutional forms, they rely crucially on more informal processes in civil society.

Conclusion: Habermas and the Future of Critical Theory

What, in conclusion, has Habermas achieved, and where is his work going? He has clearly become a classic, often anachronistically set among the previous generation of the founders of Frankfurt School critical theory.[1] In pursuing the project of an interdisciplinary (and still recognizably neo-Marxist) critical theory of society, Habermas has found himself, like the earlier critical theorists, at the centre of contemporary concerns with what we have learned (perhaps too well) to call 'modernity'.[2] The value of a theoretical project of this kind can be questioned from three main directions. First, in terms of narrower conceptions of social science and philosophy such as those of traditional positivism or of systems theorists like Luhmann, whose concept of enlightenment explicitly excludes the idea of 'critique',[3] Habermas goes some way to meet such critics, arguing his position with enormous persistence in relation both to 'big' issues such as value-freedom and to the technicalities of semantics or learning theory. Like Marx, he distinguishes sharply between theories which must be seriously engaged with and 'vulgar' defences of the status quo. In the end, though, he upholds, rightly in my view, the idea of a broadly conceived critical theory of society.

A second direction of criticism is from a more conventional Marxism (the term 'orthodox' has clearly lost all application). Whatever one thinks about the validity of Marxism as a general social theory or as a critique of capitalism, it is clear that Habermas's engagement with specific elements of Marxism has never been as thorough as his alternative 'reconstructions'. More importantly, he has so far had rather little to say about production and class relations even in advanced capitalist societies, let alone the rest of the world, or about human interaction with nature – a topic which Marxism, however inadequately, did address.[4] This is of course a problem only for a theory which aspires to the sort of generality which Habermas's does.

The third line of critique takes issue precisely with Habermas's systematic aspirations, but this time accusing him not of overstepping the limits of scientific rigour but of falling into a scientistic formalism. We need not linger on the more vulgar critiques of this kind, inspired at best by postmodernism and at worst by philistinism. A more serious critique comes from thinkers such as Gillian Rose and Jay Bernstein, who argue instead for a sophisticated neo-Hegelianism which, at least in Bernstein's case, gives an important place to the aesthetic theory developed in Adorno's later work.[5] I shall not discuss this critique in detail here. In a nutshell, my objection is that it ties itself too firmly to a speculative conception of phlosophy, thus falling behind Habermas's powerful attempt to rethink the future of philosophical reflection in relation to the ongoing projects of the human sciences.

A rather more diffuse line of criticism concerns Habermas's partisanship for European modernity, which he seems, in terms of Charles Taylor's useful distinction,[6] to see as an epochal transition in world history rather than as one cultural form among others. Although Habermas firmly refuses to rank forms of life, his theory is clearly partisan in favour of modernity, as characterized by differentiation of value-spheres, post-conventional moral reasoning, and so on. These issues come out most sharply in his ethical theorizing. While recognizing the basis of a 'concern that a formalistic ethics neglects the specific value of cultural forms of life and individual ways of life in favour of moral abstractions',[7] he suggests that this danger only arises if one tries to subject individual or collective ways of life as a whole to moral judgements and overlooks the way in which they 'crystallize around particular identities'. This explains, he says, 'why a rationalization of the life-world does not necessarily – and not even normally – make those affected *happier*'.[8] Qualifications of this kind, though important, hardly meet the broader anxiety about a theoretical model which comes perilously close to treating entire cultures like school-classes. It is easy enough to show that a hyper-tolerant position of the kind advanced by Rorty is in fact no less ethnocentric than a more explicit partisanship for certain traditional European conceptions of rationality and political legitimacy. What is more difficult is to justify such partisanship, or even to decide what sort of justification one might look for. One direction of argument, closest to Habermas's own, is suggested by McCarthy, that we should 'recognize the idealizing elements intrinsic to social practice and build on them'.[9] These forms of socialization may 'foster a capacity for reflection' and, Claus Offe suggests, constitute 'relations of association' which may in turn reinforce relations of mutual respect and mutual aid – but we are a long way from this at present. Another line of argument, though this is also somewhat problematic, is to stress how far a common culture has already been internationalized – how far we already have something like a global public opinion with widely shared conceptions of democracy and human rights. As Habermas recognizes, and as recent events in Eastern Europe and the Middle East show only too clearly, this is an extremely fragile equilibrium, but it may be the only utopia which we can meaningfully envisage.[10]

A final area of anxiety around Habermas's work is almost too familiar to mention: his reticence about practical issues of political organization. The politics of the new social movements which developed from the 1960s alongside and, in the case of the student movement, in close contact with Habermas's work, provided a kind of practical answer to such questions, but a very partial and fragmentary one. It seems at present that Habermas's work has come full circle, with the concerns expressed in his contribution to *Student und Politik* and in *Structural Transformation of the Public Sphere* now returning on the basis of a more developed social and political theory of enormous scope and power. The weight he puts in *Faktizität und Geltung* on the quality of political debate suggests that questions of the cultural mediation of political issues will continue to play a major part in his work.

Having been an unashamed enthusiast for Habermas's work for twenty years, I am delighted that it is now attracting increasing attention across a wide range of disciplines. It is unfortunate that the dimensions and style of his *œuvre*, and especially of his most important books, are such as to deter much of his potential audience. The hope of attracting new readers to Habermas provides some justification for adding to the foothills which surround his towering work.

Notes

Translations not quoted from published English-language editions are my own unless otherwise stated.

Introduction

1 Habermas, *Autonomy and Solidarity*, ed. Peter Dews (1992), p 78
2 Ibid., p. 79.
3 Habermas, *Protestbewegung und Hochschulreform* (Frankfurt, Suhrkamp, 1969), p. 9.
4 Habermas, *Autonomy and Solidarity*, p. 127.
5 Cf. Karl Jaspers, *Wohin treibt die Bundesrepublik?* (Munich, Piper, 1966).

Chapter 1   The Roots of Habermas's Thought

1 For a hostile view, see Therborn, 'Jürgen Habermas: a new eclectic', pp. 69–83.
2 Cf. Anderson, *Considerations on Western Marxism*.
3 Cf. Honneth, 'Communication and reconciliation in Habermas' critique of Adorno', Hohendahl, 'Habermas' critique of the Frankfurt School', and Wiggershaus, *The Frankfurt School*.
4 Habermas, *Autonomy and Solidarity*, p. 97.
5 Ibid., p. 187. Habermas claims that the 'key ideas' of a journal article of 1954 'on rationalization of industry and rationalization of human

relationships . . . contain the kernel of much of what I later came to write in *The Theory of Communicative Action'*.

6 The Federal German polity is of course a particularly clear example of this process, with strong and wealthy parties, with coalition governments sometimes involving both major parties ('grand coalitions') and with a developed system of party balance (and influence) in public appointments. See Klaus von Beyme, *Politik im Parteienstaat* (Frankfurt, Suhrkamp, 1993).

7 Habermas, *Student und Politik*, p. 34.

8 Habermas, *The Structural Transformation of the Public Sphere*, p. 236. Page references to this publication are hereafter given in the text in parentheses.

9 Robert C. Holub's *Jürgen Habermas: Critic in the Public Sphere* uses this theme to organize an interesting discussion of Habermas's *œuvre* as a whole, focusing on his public exchanges in the 'positivism dispute' and the more recent 'historians' dispute' and with the student left, Gadamer, Luhmann and Lyotard.

10 Cf. Abendroth et al., *Die Linke antwortet Jürgen Habermas*. See also Peter Hohendahl's useful article in *New German Critique* (1979), and his introduction to Habermas's article on 'The public sphere', *New German Critique*, 3 (1974).

11 Jäger, *Öffentlichkeit und Parlamentarismus*.

12 Luhmann, *Soziologische Aufklärung* (1977), p. 67, quoted by Hohendahl, *New German Critique* (1979), p. 101.

13 Negt and Kluge, *The Public Sphere and Experience*.

14 Young, 'Impartiality and the civic public', p. 398. See also the useful discussion of these issues in Felski, *Beyond Feminist Aesthetics*.

15 Habermas and Luhmann, *Theorie der Gesellschaft oder Sozialtechnologie*; also 'Können komplexe Gesellschaften eine vernünftige Identität ausbilden?', in Habermas, *Zwei Reden*.

16 Stamm, *Alternative Öffentlichkeit*, p. 259. Cf. Habermas, *Faktizität und Geltung*, ch. 8.

17 Habermas, Introduction to *Strukturwandel*, 2nd edn, p. 17.

18 Pateman, 'The fraternal social contract' and *The Sexual Contract*.

19 The abridged English version of *Theory and Practice*, translated from the fourth edition of 1971, lacks the essays on Schelling, Ernst Bloch and Karl Löwith, a long survey article 'On the philosophical discussion around Marx and Marxism' and an essay on 'Critical and conservative tasks of sociology'. It includes, however, the important essay on 'Labour and interaction' from *Technik und Wissenschaft als Ideologie*. Page references in parentheses in the text are to the English edition except where otherwise indicated.

20 This reference, as well as anticipating one of Perry Anderson's theses in *Considerations on Western Marxism* (and partially justifying the turn

to cultural phenomena in terms of their having become an important locus of repression), should probably also be read as a discreet but fundamental rejection of a major part of Adorno's work.

21 In the following pages, Habermas argues, in a way which anticipates the argument of *Knowledge and Human Interests*, for the existence of a parallel between Marx's critique of idealist philosophy and critical theory's critique of positivist social theory: 'a critical self-enlightenment of positivism leads into the same dimension at which Marx arrived, so to speak, from the opposite direction.'

22 As a nearby footnote indicates, Habermas is referring to the neutral concept of ideology in Soviet *Diamat* (dialectical materialism). For an interesting attempt to demonstrate that Marx, too, uses ideology in a neutral sense, see McCarney, *The Real World of Ideology*.

23 Habermas's subsequent abandonment of the philosophy of history as a foundation or orienting basis for his theory is prefigured in his rather anxious remarks about it here, though he retains for some time the concept of a practically oriented philosophy of history.

24 Axel Honneth, in *The Struggle for Recognition*, provides an excellent account of this concept in Hegel's work, going on to apply it in an extremely creative way to the analysis of social conflict and social movements.

25 Habermas has subsequently returned to this theme in the development of his own 'discourse ethic'. See, in particular, the essay in *Moral Consciousness and Communicative Action*, 'Morality and ethical life: Does Hegel's critique of Kant apply to discourse ethics?', and 'Moral und Sittlichkeit', in *Zur Rekonstruktion des historischen Materialismus*, ch. 3, n. 75.

26 Cf. McCarthy, *The Critical Theory of Jürgen Habermas*, p. 36.

27 Giddens, 'Labour and interaction', in Thompson and Held (eds), *Habermas: Critical Debates*. It is interesting to note that Habermas introduces here the distinction, crucial to his later work, between strategic action within a given rule-governed system and 'communicative actions under common traditions' (p. 151). The context here is Kant's moral theory: this abstracts from the social context of interaction which, rather than an abstract practical reason, is the real source of ethical norms.

28 Habermas, 'Technology and science as ideology', in *Toward a Rational Society*, p. 91. Cf. McCarthy, *The Critical Theory of Jürgen Habermas*, pp. 24–6.

29 Habermas, 'A reply to my critics', in Thompson and Held (eds), *Habermas*, p. 267.

30 Axel Honneth, 'Work and instrumental action', *New German Critique*, 26 (1982), pp. 31–54.

31 Nor does his later concept of 'action oriented to success'.

32 See Offe, *Arbeitsgesellschaft*; see also Offe's important article 'Binding, shackles, brakes: on self-limitation strategies', in Honneth et al. (eds), *Cultural-Political Interventions*.
33 Honneth, 'Work and instrumental action', p. 54.
34 McCarthy, *The Critical Theory of Jürgen Habermas*, p. 36.

Chapter 2   Scientism in Theory and Practice

1 This is also of course the period of the student protest movements, whose anti-technocratic orientation forms a kind of backdrop to Habermas's writing on scientism. I shall not directly address his essays on the student movement, but some of the issues recur in his later work.
2 Habermas, *Theory and Practice*, p. 254.
3 Stockman, 'Habermas, Marcuse and the *Aufhebung* of science and technology'.
4 Schelsky, quoted by Habermas, *Toward a Rational Society*, p. 59.
5 Ibid., p. 59.
6 Ibid., p. 115.
7 Ibid., p. 85, Cf. Claus Offe, 'Technik und Eindimensionalität'.
8 Marcuse, *One Dimensional Man*, pp. 166–7.
9 Habermas, *Toward a Rational Society*, p. 88. For a less negative view, see Leiss, *The Domination of Nature*.
10 Habermas, *Toward a Rational Society*.
11 Ibid., p. 90.
12 Ibid., p. 111.
13 Habermas, *Theory and Practice*, p. 255.
14 Ibid., p. 75.
15 Adorno et al., *The Positivist Dispute in German Sociology*.
16 Habermas, *Autonomy and Solidarity*, p. 150. It is significant that the final essay in *Theory and Practice*, 'Dogmatism, reason and decision', is largely devoted to a preliminary discussion of these issues.
17 Habermas, *Theory and Practice*, p. 265.
18 Habermas, *Zur Logik der Sozialwissenschaften*, 2nd edn (1971), p. 7. Hereafter cited as *LSW*.
19 Habermas, *On the Logic of the Social Sciences*, p. 2. Hereafter cited as *LSS*.
20 Ibid., ch. 2 and p. 43.
21 Habermas, 'Objektivismus in den Sozialwissenschaften', p. 549.
22 *LSS*, p. 95.
23 Apel, *Analytic Philosophy of Language* (1967).
24 Winch, *The Idea of a Social Science and its Relation to Philosophy*.

25 Gadamer, *Truth and Method.*

26 Schutz, *The Phenomenology of the Social World* (1972).

27 Schutz, *Collected Papers*, 3 vols (1962–6).

28 Habermas, *LSS*, p. 117.

29 Ibid., p. 136.

30 Habermas, 'The hermeneutic claim to universality', in Bleicher (ed.), *Contemporary Hermeneutics*, p. 190.

31 Habermas, *LSS*, p. 172.

32 Ibid., p. 174.

33 Ibid., p. 186.

34 Ibid., p. 172.

35 Thus the preface to the 2nd edition of *LSW* (p. 7) anticipates further clarification from a 'grounding of the social sciences in a theory of language'. The preface to the 5th edition, abridged in the English version (p. xiv), takes this back; the theory of communicative action is now not to be construed in terms of epistemological foundations.

36 *LSS*, pp. 174–5.

37 Cf. McCarthy, *The Critical Theory of Jürgen Habermas*, p. 16.

38 Cf. R. J. Bernstein, 'The relationship of Habermas' views to Hegel', p. 233ff.

39 *LSW*, p. xiii.

40 'In retrospect, I sometimes have the impression that a student can recreate a segment of the critical theory of the thirties if he systematically works his way from Kant through Hegel, including Schelling, and then approaches Marx via Lukács' (interview in Dews (ed.), *Habermas*, p. 95).

41 Cf. p. 15 above.

42 Habermas, *Knowledge and Human Interests* (hereafter *KHI*), p. 5. Conversely, philosophical reflection has tended to neglect science and technology; Habermas criticizes Karl Löwith, whose *From Hegel to Nietzsche* covers roughly the same time-period, for this neglect ('Karl Löwith's stoic retreat from historical consciousness', in Habermas, *Philosophical-Political Profiles*, p. 96; *Theorie und Praxis*, p. 369.

43 *KHI*, p. vii.

44 Ibid., p. 309.

45 Ibid., p. 310.

46 Ibid., p. 311.

47 Ibid. The English translation expresses this universal character with the term 'human interests'.

48 *LSS*, p. 155. See also the 'fragment' on objectivism in *LSW*, 5th edn.

49 Husserl, *The Crisis of the European Sciences and Transcendental Phenomenology.*

50 Cf. 'Does philosophy still have a purpose?' ('Wozu noch

Philosophie?'), in Habermas, *Philosophical-Political Profiles*, esp. pp. 17–18.

51   Habermas's friend Karl-Otto Apel, with whom he worked closely in relation to this topic (and also in his later work on language), tends to characterize the cognitive-interest model as an 'anthropology of knowledge' (Apel, *Towards a Transformation of Philosophy*, ch. 2). For Habermas's objection to the term, see his 'Postscript to *Knowledge and Human Interests*', pp. 160–1. I discuss the substantive issue below, pp. 32–34.

52   *KHI*, p. 313.

53   Cf. Giddens, *The Constitution of Society*, pp. 14ff and *passim*.

54   *KHI*, p. 314.

55   *KHI*, p. vii.

56   *KHI*, p. 4. Cf. Richard Rorty's more cynical view of the primacy of the theory of knowledge in Western philosophy from the seventeenth century onwards: 'It is supposed to explain how knowledge is possible, and to do that in some a priori way which both goes beyond common sense and yet avoids any need to mess about with neurons, or rats, or questionnaires': *Philosophy and the Mirror of Nature*, p. 151.

57   *KHI*, p. 5.

58   *KHI*, p. 24.

59   *KHI*, p. 63.

60   *KHI*, p. 89.

61   C. S. Peirce, 'Scientific method', quoted in *KHI*, p. 94.

62   Dilthey, *Gesammelte Schriften*, vol. 7, pp. 70–1.

63   *KHI*, p. 95. Habermas's footnote cites Peirce's definitions of truth and reality: 'The opinion which is fated to be ultimately agreed to by all who investigate, is what we mean by the truth, and the object represented in this opinion is the real.' As we shall see, Habermas's own consensus theory of truth follows that of Peirce.

64   *KHI*, p. 95.

65   *KHI*, p. 139.

66   *KHI*, p. 137.

67   *KHI*, p. 156.

68   *KHI*, p. 176.

69   Dilthey, *Gesammelte Schriften*, vol. 7, p. 137.

70   *KHI*, p. 181.

71   Cf. Gadamer, *Truth and Method*, p. 341. Habermas refers to Gadamer only three times in footnotes, but he also refers back to his own discussion in *LSS*.

72   *KHI*, p. 194.

73   Ibid.

74   *KHI*, pp. 197–8. Kant's definition of enlightenment is the emergence from self-imposed immaturity (*Unmündigheit*). Why, though, is self-

reflection necessarily emancipating? Habermas, as we shall see, later concedes that it isn't.

75   *KHI*, pp. 210–11.

76   *KHI*, p. 218.

77   *KHI*, p. 266.

78   *KHI*, p. 270.

79   *KHI*, p. 286.

80   *KHI*, p. 289. This connection must not, however, be concerned, *à la* Nietzsche, as a reduction of knowledge to interest. Nietzsche's consequent denial of self-reflection in science and life provides a further basis for the reduction of epistemology to methodology.

81   See, for example, Dallmayr (ed.), *Materialien zu Erkenntnis und Interesse* and Dallmayr, 'Critical theory criticised'; see also Russell Keat's *The Politics of Social Theory*. General works on Habermas also contain relevant material; see e.g. McCarthy, *The Critical Theory of Jürgen Habermas*, pp. 91–125; Thompson and Held (eds.), *Habermas*, esp. chs 4 (Ottman) and 5 (Hesse), and Habermas's 'Reply to my critics'.

82   Habermas, 'Reply to my critics', in Thompson and Held (eds), *Habermas*.

83   In *LSW*, 5th edn, pp. 541–607.

84   Habermas, 'Reply to my critics', p. 233.

85   McCarthy, *The Critical Theory of Jürgen Habermas*, pp. 110–11. Habermas had earlier described 'the formula "quasi-transcendental" [as] a product of an embarrassment which points to more problems than it solves' (*Theory and Practice*, p. 14).

86   Habermas and Luhmann, *Theorie der Gesellschaft oder Sozialtechnologie*, p. 212.

87   Habermas, 'Objektivismus'. *LSW*, 5th edn, pp. 578ff. The greater weight placed on language in the next period of Habermas's work will be discussed in the next chapter. Paradoxically, an approach in terms of formal pragmatics 'may help to ground a theory of cognitive interests, but itself can only indirectly be assigned to one of the knowledge-guiding interests' (p. 592).

88   Habermas, *Theory and Practice*, pp. 19–20. Cf. 'Postscript', pp. 166 and 168–74. This, too, points ahead to Habermas's preoccupations with pragmatics and the theory of truth.

89   *KHI*, appendix, p. 310.

90   Habermas, 'Postscript', p. 182.

91   Habermas, *Theory and Practice*, pp. 23–31.

92   Ibid., p. 33. On the related issue of Habermas's interpretation of Freud, see in particular Keat, *The Politics of Social Theory*. Also relevant are Lorenzer, *Die Wahrheit der psychoanalytischen Erkenntnis*, Roy Schafer, 'Narration in the psychoanalytic dialogue', in W. J. T.

Mitchell (ed.), *On Narrative* (Chicago, Ill., University of Chicago Press, 1981), and Jay Bernstein, 'Self-knowledge as praxis: narrative and interpretation in psychoanalysis', in Cristopher Nash (ed.), *Narrative in Culture*, London, Routledge 1989.

93   Habermas, *Vergangenheit als Zukunft*, p. 133.

94   Keat, *Politics of Social Theory*, p. 7.

95   Cf. ibid., p. 168.

96   Ibid., esp. pp. 95–109. Cf. Kessler, *Identität und Kritik*, pp. 1–2, 35. Habermas's account of Freud was, as he acknowledges, strongly influenced by Alfred Lorenzer's ambitious reinterpretation of psychoanalytic theory in relation to critical hermeneutics, philosophy of science and historical materialism.

97   Keat, *Politics of Social Theory*, pp. 144–59.

98   Fay, *Social Theory and Political Practice*.

99   For a good account, see Halfpenny, *Positivism and Sociology*.

100   Cf. Barry Barnes, *Interests and the Growth of Knowledge* (London, Routledge & Kegan Paul, 1977).

101   Cf. Bhaskar, *A Realist Theory of Science*; Outhwaite, *New Philosophies of Social Science*.

102   Stockman, 'Habermas, Marcuse, and the *Aufhebung* of science and technology' and *Anti-Positivist Theories of the Sciences*; Keat, *Politics of Social Theory*; Outhwaite, *Concept Formation in Social Science*, chs 2 and 3; Outhwaite, *New Philosophies of Social Science*, ch. 5.

103   Habermas, 'Postcript', p. 180.

104   Habermas, *Communication and the Evolution of Society*, p. 16. Cf. the passage from his Gauss lectures in *Vorstudien and Ergänzungen zur Theorie des Kommunikativen Handelns*, pp. 18–19.

105   Cf. Outhwaite, *New Philosophies of Social Science*, ch. 2.

106   'Philosophy of history' is mentioned in *KHI* only with reference to past intellectual contexts.

107   Habermas, 'Does philosophy still have a purpose?' (1971), in *Philosophical-Political Profiles*, p. 18.

108   'Philosophy as place-holder and interpreter' (1981), repr. in Habermas, *Moral Consciousness and Communicative Action*.

109   *KHI*, p. vii.

Chapter 3   Communication and Discourse Ethics

1   As noted above, in relation to *LSS*, Habermas gave up the idea of grounding the social sciences in the theory of language, and he now insists that the theory of communicative action is not a metatheory (*TCA*, vol. 1, p. xxxix). Despite this shift, there is a substantial continuity in his work throughout the decade.

2   *KHI*, p. 314.
3   'The hermeneutic claim to universality', in Bleicher, *Contemporary Hermeneutics*, pp. 181–211.
4   Ibid., p. 185.
5   Ibid., p. 205.
6   Habermas, 'Vorbereitende Bemerkungen zu einer Theorie der kommunikativen Kompetenz', in Habermas and Luhmann, *Theorie der Gesellschaft*, pp. 101–41.
7   Habermas, 'Wahrheitstheorien', in H. Fahrenbach (ed.), *Wirklichkeit und Reflexion* (Pfullingen, Neske, 1973), pp. 211–66; repr. in Habermas, *Vorstudien und Ergänzungen*, pp. 127–83.
8   Habermas, 'Vorlesungen zu einer sprachtheoretischen Grundlegung der Soziologie', in *Vorstudien und Ergänzungen*, pp. 11–126.
9   Ibid., p. 11.
10 In Habermas, *Communication and the Evolution of Society* (hereafter cited as *CES*).
11 Ibid., pp. 30ff. Cf. R. J. Bernstein (ed.), *Habermas and Modernity*, p. 14.
12 Habermas, *Vorstudien und Ergänzungen*, p. 82.
13 Habermas, *CES*, p. 1. John Thompson, 'Universal pragmatics', in Thompson and Held (eds), *Habermas*, pp. 116–33, examines the problems of this assumption.
14 He does not discuss 'non-verbal communication'.
15 Habermas later withdraws this further claim: Thompson and Held (eds), *Habermas*, pp. 261–2.
16 Habermas, *Vorstudien und Ergänzungen*, p. 126.
17 Ibid., p. 105.
18 Ibid., p. 107.
19 Ibid., p. 109
20 Ibid., p. 113. Cf. Harbermas, *Legitimation Crisis*, part 3, p. 2.
21 Habermas, *Vorstudien und Ergänzungen*, p. 115. One example of such a choice might be that between Habermas and Luhmann; the latter's systems theory is, despite its considerable intellectual merits, in Habermas's view also an expression of a 'new ideology' of self-regulating social systems (Narr et al., *Theorie der Gesellschaft*, pp. 266–7).
22 *TCA*, vol. 1, p. 41.
23 Ibid., p. 42.
24 Ibid., p. 19.
25 Habermas, 'Überlegungen zur Kommunikationspathologie', *Vorstudien und Ergänzungen*, pp. 226–70.
26 Ibid., p. 255.
27 Ibid., pp. 231–2. Whereas the 'value premises' of cognitive and moral development are 'truth' and 'moral judgement' respectively, those of interactive competence are consciousness and insight.

28 Ibid., p. 242.
29 Habermas counts this as a shift from communicative to strategic action (ibid., p. 252); the latter concept appears in a descriptive sense in this text but plays a more systematic role in *TCA*.
30 Cf. *TCA*, Preface.
31 See, for example, the two essays on ethical topics in Habermas, *Moral Consciousness and Communicative Action*.
32 Thompson and Held (eds), *Habermas*, p. 273.
33 'Wahrheitstheorien', in Habermas, *Vorstudien und Ergänzungen*, p. 126.
34 See Ilting, 'Geltung als Konsens', pp. 22–50, and Benhabib's useful summary (*Critique, Norm and Utopia*, pp. 287–8).
35 Benhabib, *Critique, Norm and Utopia*, p. 293, n. 43; cf. Apel, *Towards a Transformation of Philosophy*, pp. 225–301. See also Martin Jay, 'The debate over performative contradiction', in Honneth et al. (eds), *Philosophical Interventions*.
36 *TCA*, vol. 1, p. 287. Cf. Benhabib, *Critique, Norm and Utopia*, pp. 294–5.
37 *TCA*, vol. 1, p. 287.
38 Austin, *How to Do Things with Words*.
39 *TCA*, vol. 1, pp. 294ff. By this phrase Habermas intends to rule out 'latently strategic action'.
40 Ibid., p. 297.
41 Ibid., p. 240.
42 He later (*TCA*, vol. 1, p. 325) adds imperatives to this list.
43 In *TCA*, vol. 1, pp. 310–19, he discusses various technical objections to his position.
44 Ibid., p. 327.
45 Ibid., p. 328. Habermas does not spell out the relationship between this model and the earlier discussion in chapter 1 of *TCA* (vol. 1, pp. 85–6), in which dramaturgical and normatively regulated action are contrasted with communicative action.
46 See *TCA*, vol. 1, p. 332, n. 84.
47 Ibid., p. 333.
48 Ibid., p. 334, fig. 19.
49 Benhabib, *Critique, Norm and Utopia*, pp. 294–5.
50 Habermas, *CES*, ch. 2.
51 These are printed in Habermas, *Moral Consciousness and Communicative Action*.
52 Habermas, 'What is universal pragmatics?', *CES*, p. 68.
53 Here, as elsewhere in Habermas's theory, there is something strained about his presentation of the nature/society distinction; do we not make truth-claims about society? Habermas is concerned with a particular function of speech in relation to society: the establishment of

interpersonal relations as opposed to the representation of states of affairs in an 'objectivating attitude'. The latter is, however, possible 'not only toward inanimate nature but toward all objects and states of affairs that are directly or indirectly accessible to sensory experience' (*CES*, p. 66).

54 McCarthy, *The Critical Theory of Jürgen Habermas*, pp. 338–9.
55 Ibid., p. 348.
56 Ibid., p. 350.
57 Ibid., pp. 344–5. As McCarthy notes (p. 350), the key link is the concept of reciprocity; a relationship is completely reciprocal if each party may expect the other to behave in the same way in a comparable situation, in virtue of certain general principles. Reciprocity can be applied to moral conflicts because 'the point of view of reciprocity belongs eo ipso to the interactive knowledge of speaking and acting subjects' ('Moral development and ego identity', in *CES*, p. 88).
58 It should be noted that stage 7 is Habermas's addition to Kohlberg's six-stage model ('Moral development and ego identity', in *CES*, p. 90, cf. McCarthy, pp. 250–1). Kohlberg's stage 6 focuses on individual conscience, whereas in Habermas's stage 7 'the principle of justification of norms is no longer the monologically applicable principle of generalizability but the communally followed procedure of redeeming normative validity claims discursively.'
59 Kohlberg had problems documenting the sixth stage; cf. Thompson and Held (eds), *Habermas*, p. 260.
60 Kohlberg, quoted by Habermas, in ibid., p. 259.
61 'Does philosophy still have a purpose?', in Habermas, *Philosophical-Political Profiles*; 'Philosophy as stand-in and interpreter', in Baynes et al. (eds), *After Philosophy: End or Transformation?*
62 Habermas, 'Reply to my critics', in Thompson and Held (eds), *Habermas*, p. 259. Cf. *Moral Consciousness and Communicative Action*, pp. 37ff, 117ff.
63 Habermas, 'Reply', pp. 260–1; *Moral Consciousness and Communicative Action*, pp. 184ff. Cf. S. Lukes, 'Of gods and demons: Habermas and practical reason', Thompson and Held (eds), *Habermas*, ch. 7.
64 Habermas, *Moral Consciousness and Communicative Action*, p. 175. Cf. Benhabib, 'The generalized and the concrete other'; Fraser, 'Toward a discourse ethic of solidarity'.
65 Cf. White, *The Recent Work of Jürgen Habermas*, p. 65. See also Habermas, 'Moral und Sittlichkeit'; 'Morality and ethical life: does Hegel's critique of Kant apply to discourse ethics?', *Moral Consciousness and Communicative Action*.
66 Habermas, *Moral Consciousness and Communicative Action*, p. 116.
67 Ibid., p. 68.
68 McCarthy, *The Critical Theory of Jürgen Habermas*, p. 326.

69   Habermas, *Moral Consciousness and Communicative Action*, p. 103.
70   Ibid., p. 108.
71   Habermas, *Legitimation Crisis*, p. 87. I shall return to this issue in the context of Habermas's discussion of legitimation.
72   Habermas, *Moral Consciousness and Communicative Action*, p. 180.
73   Ibid., p. 180.
74   White, *Recent Work of Jürgen Habermas*, p. 85.
75   Habermas, 'Moral und Sittlichkeit', pp. 1042. Cf. *Moral Consciousness and Communicative Action*, p. 197.
76   Ibid., p. 1042.
77   Ibid. This is the familiar argument from universal pragmatics; Habermas qualifies, in a footnote, his earlier formulations in the title essay of *Moral Consciousness and Communicative Action*.
78   Habermas, 'Moral und Sittlichkeit', p. 1046. Cf. MCCA, p. 203. For a restatement of the Hegelian view that one cannot separate questions of justice from those of the good life, see Charles Taylor, 'Language and society', in Honneth and Joas (eds), *Communicative Action*.
79   Habermas, 'Moral und Sittlichkeit', p. 1048. Cf. MCCA, pp. 207–8.
80   *TCA*, vol. 1, p. 108.
81   Ibid.
82   S. Benhabib, in Benhabib and Dallmayr (eds), *The Communicative Ethics Controversy*, p. 331.
83   This would of course be one way of implementing a rejection of the Kantian emphasis on notions of justice and right; cf. Benhabib, in ibid., pp. 346–51.
84   Wellmer, *Ethik und Dialog*, p. 34. See also Benhabib's response to this interpretation, and the related critique by Agnes Heller, in Benhabib and Dallmayr (eds), *The Communicative Ethics Controversy*, pp. 343–6.
85   Cf. Habermas, *Justification and Application*, p. 17.
86   This is the direction he takes in *Faktizität und Geltung*, though *Justification and Application*, in which he continues to 'defend the primacy of a deontological conception of justice over the good', contains over 100 pages of responses to twelve critics on thirteen (relatively) separate issues.

Chapter 4   Social Evolution and Legitimation

1   Cf. Giddens, *The Constitution of Society*, pp. 227–43, esp. n. 32.
2   As we have seen, their status shifts from 'metatheory' to 'theory', but they remain in some sense basic.
3   Although Habermas has moved away from an identification of his own work with the philosophy of history as traditionally conceived, this can be seen as radicalizing rather than just abandoning it (*Kultur*

und Kritik, pp. 395–6; Gripp, *Jürgen Habermas*, p. 63).

4 There has of course been considerable discussion within Marxism about whether it should be seen as an evolutionary theory. Habermas at least believes it is. Cf. *Theory and Practice*, p. 1; *CES*, p. 126.

5 Strydom, 'The ontogenetic fallacy', p. 86.

6 Arnason, 'A review of Jürgen Habermas, p. 215, cited by Strydom, 'The ontogenetic fallacy', p. 70. This transfer from the individual to the societal level is what Strydom, following Klaus Eder, calls the ontogenetic fallacy.

7 Strydom, 'The ontogenetic fallacy', p. 68.

8 Michael Schmidt, 'Habermas' theory of social evolution', in Thompson and Held (eds), *Habermas*, pp. 162–80. Habermas's 'Reply' does not address this critique; see p. 220.

9 Honneth and Joas, *Social Action and Human Nature*. Honneth's later assessments, in his *Critique of Power*, are more critical of Habermas's evolutionism.

10 Habermas, 'Historical materialism and the development of normative structures', *CES*, pp. 98–9. Habermas notes that his programme also requires the investigation of the same parallels 'in the domain of ego development and the evolution of world views on the one hand, and in the domain of ego and group identities on the other' (*CES*, p. 99). The ensuing pages (99–116) outline some possible themes of such a programme.

11 *CES*, p. 98.

12 Ibid.

13 *CES*, p. 95. He goes on: 'This is the normal way (in my opinion normal for Marxists too) of dealing with a theory that needs revision in many respects but whose potential for stimulation has still not been exhausted.'

14 *CES*, p. 126.

15 *CES*, pp. 134–8. As Tom Bottomore noted (*The Frankfurt School*, p. 66), Habermas does not fully develop the implications of this idea.

16 *CES*, p. 139.

17 *CES*, p. 140.

18 *CES*, p. 142.

19 *CES*, p. 143. Cf. Karl Kautsky, *The Materialistic Conception of History*, pp. 229–30.

20 *CES*, p. 148.

21 *CES*, p. 155.

22 Habermas draws heavily here on the work of Klaus Eder on the development of state structures, and Rainer Döbert's work on that of world-views.

23 *CES*, p. 177.

24 *CES*, p. 146: 'the great endogenous, evolutionary advances that led to the first civilizations or to the rise of European capitalism were not conditioned but followed by significant development of productive forces. In these cases the development of productive forces could not have led to an evolutionary challenge.'

25 *CES*, p. 124. Cf. my discussion of *Legitimation Crisis*, p. 63 below.

26 *CES*, p. 123. Cf. Rockmore, *Habermas on Historical Materialism*.

27 See in particular 'Geschichte und Evolution', in Habermas, *Zur Rekonstruktion des historichen Materialismus*, ch. 6. Cf. McCarthy, *The Critical Theory of Jürgen Habermas*, pp. 267ff.

28 Cf. Bottomore, *The Frankfurt School*, pp. 66–7 and 72ff.

29 Honneth and Joas, *Social Action and Human Nature*, p. 164.

30 Ibid., p. 166. Compare Barrington Moore, *Injustice*, and Honneth, *The Struggle for Recognition*.

31 Cf. McCarthy, *The Critical Theory of Jürgen Habermas*, p. 423, n. 54. Habermas would of course claim that this horizon is an inevitable result of the Enlightenment and modernity. I shall return to this theme later. For a sceptical view, see Lassman, 'Social structure, history and evolution'.

32 Frankenberg and Rödel, *Von der Volkssouveränität zum Minderheitenschutz*.

33 See Strydom, 'The ontogentic fallacy', pp. 80–9; Klaus Eder, *Geschichte als Lernprozess?* (Frankfurt, Suhrkamp, 1985). Niedenzu, *Die Entstehung von herrschaftlich organisierten Gesellschaften*, takes a similar line, arguing also that the importance of exogenous influences on the development of ancient Egypt conflicts with Habermas's (and Eder's earlier) model.

34 Habermas, *Postmetaphysical Thinking*, ch. 6, pp. 137–8.

35 Habermas, *Autonomy and Solidarity*, pp. 203ff.

36 *TCA*, vol. 1, p. 66. McCarthy (*The Critical Theory of Jürgen Habermas*) translates *allgemein* with the more modest 'general'.

37 *TCA*, vol. 1, pp. 48–9.

38 McCarthy, *The Critical Theory of Jürgen Habermas*, p. 264.

39 Ibid., p. 270. It is in this spirit that Axel Honneth reads Habermas as reworking the theme of the *Dialectic of Enlightenment* (Honneth, *Critique of Power*, esp. ch. 9).

40 Habermas, *Legitimation Crisis*, Preface, p. xxv. This should be read in conjunction with 'Legitimation problems in the modern state', ch. 5 of *CES*. The article 'What does a crisis mean today?', repr. in Connerton (ed.), *Critical Sociology*, and Connolly (ed.), *Legitimacy and the State*, is a summary version of *Legitimation Crisis*.

41 Offe, *Contradictions of the Welfare State* and *Disorganized Capitalism*.

42 See, for example, Berger, 'Changing crises-types in Western societies', pp. 230–9.

43 On Weber, see Merquior, *Roussean and Weber*; Outhwaite, *Concept Formation*, ch. 4. See also Luhmann, *Legitimation durch Verfahren*.

44 Habermas, *Legitimation Crisis*, p. 1. Cf. Adorno, 'Späkapitalismus oder Industriegesellschaft?'

45 Habermas, *Legitimation Crisis*, pp. 3–4.

46 Ibid., p. 7. After his extensive polemic with Luhmann in 1971, Habermas has repeatedly returned to discuss his work – most recently in *Faktizität und Geltung*.

47 Habermas, *Legitimation Crisis*, p. 8. Habermas suggests that two features of this learning process are central: whether learning is reflexive, i.e. involves the discursive thematization of validity-claims, and whether theoretical and moral-practical questions are, as they usually are in the modern period, differentiated (ibid., p. 15).

48 Ibid., p. 22.

49 Ibid., p. 20.

50 Ibid., p. 27.

51 Ibid., p. 30.

52 Ibid., p. 33.

53 Ibid., p. 36.

54 Ibid., p. 40.

55 The concept of motivation crisis, which Habermas now sees as misleadingly broad in its formulation, spans such diverse phenomena as the withdrawal of motivation from the occupational system, e.g. a decline of the work ethic, and individual psychopathology on the other. (Cf. Thompson and Held (eds), *Habermas*, pp. 280–1).

56 Habermas, 'Legitimation problems in the modern state', *CES*, p. 193.

57 Claus Offe, in particular, has traced these convergences in theories of the welfare state, 'ungovernability', etc. See, for example, 'Ungovernability: on the renaissance of conservative theories of crisis', and 'Some contradictions in the modern welfare state', pp. 219–29; Berger, 'Changing crisis-types', pp. 230–9. For recent discussions, see Pierson, *Beyond the Welfare State?*, and Beck, *Risk Society*.

58 Held, 'Crisis tendencies, legitimation and the state', in Thompson and Held (eds), *Habermas*, ch. 10, p. 188.

59 Mann, 'The ideology of intellectuals and other people in the development of capitalism'.

60 Honneth 'Moral consciousness and class domination'; pp. 12–24. See also Honneth, *The Struggle for Recognition*.

61 On state socialism, see Andrew Arato, 'Critical sociology and authoritarian state socialism', in Thompson and Held (eds), *Habermas*. See also Habermas, *Die nachholende Revolution* and *Vergangenheit als Zukunft*.

Chapter 5   Rational Action and Societal
Rationalization

1   *TCA*, vol. 1, p. 140. Hereafter references to vol. 1 of *TCA* will be given
    in the text of this chapter by page numbers in parentheses. Parsons
    did of course have a similarly major substantive preoccupation, the
    'Hobbesian' problem of social order, but this became somewhat ef-
    faced by the flood of pure theory.

2   Habermas sees the theory of communicative action as belonging in
    the latter category. As he puts it in his Preface: 'The theory of com-
    municative action is not a metatheory but the beginning of a social
    theory concerned to validate (*ausweisen*) its own critical standards. I
    do not conceive of my analysis of the general structures of action
    oriented to reaching understanding as a continuation of the theory of
    knowledge by other means' (*TCA*, vol. 1 p. xcxix).

3   For some problems with this conception, see Herbert Schnädelbach's
    comments in Honneth and Joas (eds), *Communicative Action*, pp. 10ff,
    and my discussion in chapter 7 below.

4   Habermas is taking up a clear position here against emotivist theories
    of ethics, in which 'murder is wrong' means no more than 'murder:
    yuck', and against Nietzschean accounts of truth in which it is what
    does us good. More crucially, he objects to what he calls the 'reifying
    idea' in modernity that only the objective world, and not the social
    and the subjective world as well, can be subject to rational consensus
    (*TCA*, vol. 1, p. 74).

5   Max Weber did of course have a category of value-*rational* action.

6   Weber, *Economy and Society*, vol. 1, ch. 1.

7   Fundamental objections to theories of this type 'are themselves based
    on empiricist assumptions that are open to question' (*TCA*, vol. 1,
    p. 105).

8   This, he notes, is 'a very strong requirement for someone who is
    operating without metaphysical support and is also no longer confi-
    dent that a rigorous transcendental-pragmatic program, claiming to
    provide ultimate grounds, can be carried out' (*TCA*, vol. 1, p. 137).

9   In fact, as Habermas notes, Weber sees natural law as largely super-
    seded; he tends to equate legitimacy with (a belief in) formally correct
    procedural legality and he sees the 'substantive rationalization' of
    law, like that of the economy, as a threat to its formal qualities.

10 'This growing autonomy of self-regulated subsystems in relation to
    the communicatively structured lifeworld has less to do with the
    rationalization of action orientations than with a new level of system
    differentiation. This problem will provide us with an occasion, not to
    expand the action-theoretic approach in the direction of a theory of

communicative action, but to combine it with the systems-theoretic approach. Only the integration of both approaches makes the theory of communicative action a sound foundation for a social theory with any hope of success in tackling the problem of societal rationalization first dealt with by Max Weber' (*TCA*, vol. 1, pp. 270–1).

11 Or at the very least for Lenin, who insisted on the importance of reading Hegel in order to understand Marx and claimed that most Marxists, having not done this, had failed to understand Marx.

12 Habermas then offers his own typology of action, aiming 'to capture in action-theoretic terms the complex concept of rationality that Weber did employ in his cultural analyses' (*TCA*, vol. 1, p. 284). We can thus incorporate Weber's insights into the differentiation of forms of knowledge and action in European modernity, without following him in his selective focus on the rationalization of purposive-rational action (pp. 332, 335).

13 In Habermas's words: 'they submitted subjective reason to an unrelenting critique from the ironically distanced perspective of an objective reason that had fallen irreparably into ruin' (*TCA*, vol. 1, p. 377).

14 Habermas endorses Albrecht Wellmer's comment that the idea of the proletariat as the subject–object of history 'was in some respects equivalent to a return to objective idealism' (*TCA*, vol. 1, p. 365). See also Wellmer's penetrating discussion of Marxist humanism in his *Endspiele* (Frankfurt, Suhrkamp, 1993).

Chapter 6   The Colonization of the Lifeworld

1 Habermas, *TCA*, vol. 2, p. 3; hereafter references to vol. 2 of *TCA* will be given in the text of this chapter by page numbers in parentheses.

2 Logical empiricism, even in its original crude version, focused on the form of scientific *statements*, and this developed into a broader, though partial, interest in the language of science (see Outhwaite, *Concept Formation in Social Science* and *New Philosophies of Social Science*). On speech-act theory, developed out of the work of Ludwig Wittgenstein and J. L. Austin, see Searle, *Speech Acts*. For Mead, see *Mind, Self and Society*, p. 244. Habermas approvingly quotes Mead's assertion that 'In man the functional differentiation through language gives an entirely different principle of organization which produces not only a different type of individual but also a different society' (*TCA*, vol. 2, p. 4).

3 The ambiguity of the French word *conscience*, which means both conscience and consciousness, marks the dual status of the concept in Durkheim's thought, expressing a group identity which is both cognitive and moral.

4 Cf. Francis McHugh, 'Christian social theory', in Outhwaite and Bottomore (eds), *The Blackwell Dictionary of Twentieth-Century Social Thought*, pp. 70–3.

5 Something similar happens in the case of art.

6 Joas, who is the author of a major recent study of Mead, suggests that, although Mead did not in fact theorize military/industrial/political relations, his theoretical model is not limited in the way Habermas implies and his 'democratism' is more radical than Habermas realizes.

7 It is interesting to compare the present version of this claim with the final section of *On the Logic of the Social Sciences*.

8 Habermas summarizes Durkheim's account of mechanical and organic solidarity thus (*TCA*, vol. 2, p. 115): 'Whereas primitive societies are integrated via a basic normative consensus, the integration of developed societies comes about via the systematic interconnection of functionally specified domains of action.'

9 Habermas incorporates Talcott Parsons's trichotomy of culture, society and personality. 'I use the term culture for the stock of knowlege from which participants in communication supply themselves with interpretations as they come to an understanding about something in the world. I use the term society for the legitimate orders through which participants regulate their memberships in social groups and thereby secure solidarity. By personality I understand the competences that make a subject capable of speaking and acting, that put him in a position to take part in processes of reaching understanding and thereby to assert his own identity' (*TCA*, vol. 2, p. 138). He stresses, however, that, whereas Parsons analyses culture, society and personality 'as action systems constituting environments for one another', he himself insists on the dualism of internalist (lifeworld) and externalist (system) perspectives (ibid., p. 153).

10 Hence the appeal in social anthropology of functionalism, 'because in tribal societies systemic interdependencies are directly mirrored in normative structures', but also of hermeneutic approaches, since the processes studied take place in the lifeworld and are intelligible to members, though not (initially) to observers.

11 Cf. Godelier, *Perspectives in Marxist Anthropology*.

12 State socialist societies combined (in principle) central control of all aspects of economy and society with considerable differentiation in detail.

13 'Basic institutions' such as 'family status, the authority of office, or bourgeois private law' can only develop 'if the lifeworld is sufficiently rationalized, above all if law and morality have reached a corresponding stage of development' (*TCA*, vol. 2, p. 173). See also pp. 174–5 and fig. 26, and the earlier formulation in *CES*, chs 3 and 4.

14 In Weberian terms, the distinction is, once again, between interest-based action (*Interessenhandeln*) and a rationally based (and, from Weber's standpoint, somewhat idealized) conception of action based on agreement (*Einverständnishandeln*), though Habermas augments this with the further distinction between system integration and social integration. Cf. Martin Albrow, *Max Weber's Construction of Social Theory*, esp. chs 8 and 9.

15 In the words of the Christian hymn:

> The rich man in his castle,
> The poor man at the gate
> God made them high or lowly
> And ordered their estate.

16 I shall not discuss in any detail Habermas's reformulation of central elements of Parsons's theory, such as the account of steering media (*TCA*, vol. 2, fig. 27).

17 Cf. *TCA*, vol. 2, p. 343: 'Reification effects can result in like manner from the bureaucratization and monetarization of public and private areas of life.'

18 Habermas uses the term 'condensation' (*Verdichtung*) (*TCA*, vol. 2, p. 357).

19 Habermas notes that the first phase of juridification was also ambiguous, since it freed (but also forced) people to sell their labour power (*TCA*, vol. 2, pp. 361–2).

20 Cf. Moore's rather one-dimensional analysis of fascism, in his *Social Origins of Dictatorship and Democracy*, as a pathological outcome of a variant of the modernization process.

21 The word 'Marxist' is added in the translation.

22 This critique of early critical theory is brilliantly developed in Honneth's *Critique of Power*.

23 McCarthy's translation of *überliefert* as 'traditional' is misleading here, since the bourgeois ideals which Horkheimer wanted to radically realize were precisely not traditional.

24 This might seem a plausible account not only of capitalist societies but of what happened to state socialism in the 1980s, but Habermas argues that the processes are different in 'bureaucratic socialism', where 'instead of the reification of communicative relations we find the shamming of communicative relations in bureaucratically dessicated, forcibly "humanized" domains of pseudopolitical intercourse in an overextended and administered public sphere' (in Thompson and Held (eds), *Habermas*, p. 283). See also *TCA*, vol. 2, p. 386.

25 Inglehart, *The Silent Revolution*.

26 See Habermas, 'The unity of reason in the diversity of its voices', *Postmetaphysical Thinking*, and chapter 8 below.

Chapter 7 The Theory of Communicative Action: An Assessment

1   In this chapter I shall refer a good deal to the excellent collection of essays edited by Honneth and Joas, *Communicative Action*, including Habermas's reply in the same volume. Page numbers in parentheses in the text of this chapter refer to this publication.

2   The ancillary critique of state socialism, which Habermas never did more than outline, has now lost much of its application, with the almost complete extinction of these regimes. See, however, Habermas, *Die nachholende Revolution* and *The Past as the Future*; also Andrew Arato, 'Critical theory and authoritarian state socialism', in Thompson and Held (eds), *Habermas*; and Ray, *Rethinking Critical Theory*.

3   See Habermas's comments on classical social theory, referred to at the end of chapter 6.

4   It would be too easy to say that theories of this sort only apply to market societies and the ideologies to which they give rise, since we can hardly deny the evidence of strategic action in non-market societies.

5   Habermas, *Vergangenheit als Zukunft*, pp. 142–3. (*Faktizität und Geltung*, which I discuss in chapter 9 below, is substantially concerned with this issue.)

6   Ibid. pp. 146ff. Cf. Karl-Otto Apel's criticisms, from a transcendentalist point of view, of this form of justification, in the Habermas Festschrift, Honneth et al. (eds), *Philosophical Interventions in the Unfinished Project of the Enlightenment*.

7   Habermas, *Vergangenheit als Zukunft*, p. 148.

8   Cf. Charles Taylor's contribution in Honneth and Joas (eds), *Communicative Action*.

9   His latest formulation 'amends' (ibid., p. 254, n. 85) that in his 1982 lecture (in *Vorstudien und Ergänzungen*, p. 603), but there is clearly a residual area which requires further specification in both theoretical and empirical terms.

10 Herbert Schnädelbach makes a similar point in 'The face in the sand: Foucault and the anthropological slumber', in Honneth et al. (eds), *Philosophical Interventions in the Unfinished Project of the Enlightenment*, pp. 332–3.

11 Habermas, *TCA*, vol. 2, pp. 148–9. On the issue of non-intervention in traditional lifeworlds, see the discussion of pre-colonial India and of the American South in 'Life-forms, morality and the task of the philosopher', in Peter Dews (ed.), *Habermas: Autonomy and Solidarity*, 2nd edn (London, Verso, 1992), pp. 203–5.

12 Günther Dux, 'Communicative reason and interest', in Honneth and Joas (eds), *Communicative Action*, pp. 74–96.

13 Cf. Thomas McCarthy, 'Complexity and democracy: or the seducements of systems theory', in Honneth and Joas (eds), *Communicative Action*, p. 137.

14 Cf. Habermas's Hegel Prize speech: 'Können komplexe Gesellschaften eine vernünftige Identität ausbilden?'

15 This is another instance of Habermas's attachment to a neo-Kantian approach to metatheory. A philosophical realist would take more seriously the claim that it is '*the same* society', and the resulting ontological commitments of such theories. On this, see Outhwaite, *New Philosophies of Social Science*, esp. ch. 5.

16 Contra his earlier references to 'systems of purposive-rational action' (Honneth and Joas (eds), *Communicative Action*, p. 258).

17 See, for example, his response to Hans-Peter Krüger that one must distinguish between the facilitation of public communication and the restriction of information by steering media (ibid., p. 262).

18 Habermas, *The New Conservatism*, p. 51.

19 Cf. Offe, *Arbeitsgesellschaft – Strukturprobleme und Zukunftsperspektiven*. See also Offe's important article 'Binding, shackles, brakes: on self-limitation strategies', in Honneth et al. (eds), *Cultural-Political Interventions*.

20 Habermas, *The New Conservatism*, p. 56.

21 Ibid., p. 58.

22 Kunneman, *Der Wahrheitstrichter*.

23 Ibid., p. 205.

24 Ibid., p. 212. Kunneman cites (p. 211) Abraham de Swaan's account of the shift from *Befehlsreglement* to *Verhandlungsreglement*, from a system of commands to one of negotiation.

25 Ibid., p. 233.

26 Ibid., p. 280.

27 See Stephen White's excellent monograph, *The Recent Work of Jürgen Habermas*.

28 Cf. Beck, *Risk Society*.

29 Habermas, *Vergangenheit als Zukunft*, pp. 143–5. See also, for example, Eder, *The New Politics of Class*, and Ray, *Rethinking Critical Theory*.

Chapter 8   Modernity and Philosophy

1 Reprinted in Hal Foster (ed.), *Postmodern Culture* (London, Pluto, 1985).

2 Jean-François Lyotard, *The Postmodern Condition*, was first published in French in 1979 and in German translation in 1982. For useful

overviews of the debates, see Wellmer, 'On the dialectic of modernism and postmodernism'; Richard Rorty, 'Habermas and Lyotard on postmodernism', in R. J. Bernstein (ed.), *Habermas and Modernity*; and Dews, *Logics of Disintegration*.

3 Habermas, *The Philosophical Discourse of Modernity* (Cambridge, Polity, 1990). References to this edition hereafter appear in the text of this chapter by page numbers in parentheses.

4 Hegel, *Lectures on the Philosophy of Religion*, Part III, p. 297.

5 By this term Habermas means not only neo-Marxists but also thinkers such as Alfred Schutz, Helmuth Plessner, Martin Heidegger and Jacques Derrida. Carlos Castoriadis, who is the subject of an excursus following ch. 11 of *Philosophical Discourse of Modernity*, is of particular interest because of his intermediate position between the two camps. Habermas argues (p. 330) that his over-general account of the 'imaginary institution' of society 'leaves no room for an intersubjective practice for which socialized individuals are accountable' (p. 330). Habermas's own alternative, however, as Chantal Mouffe has noted, remains undeveloped.

6 This account, which may seem rather forced, should be read in conjunction with section 1 of Habermas's 'Reply' in Thompson and Held (eds), *Habermas*.

7 Cf. Habermas, *Philosophical Discourse of Modernity*, p. 408, n. 28.

8 See the essay on the novelist Italo Calvino in *Moral Consciousness and Communicative Action* ('Philosophy and science as literature').

9 Habermas, *Philosophical Discourse of Modernity*, p. 270; see also pp. 254 and 261, and note 7 on pp. 415ff.

10 His later stress on self-formation, of which Habermas cites only a very early expression, may be understood not just as a much-needed qualification to his earlier theories, but as an indirect way of grounding his own programme of resistance.

11 Habermas concludes with a similar critique of Foucault's one-sided account of sexual regulation, which anticipates Foucault's own subsequent 'turn' in the second and third volumes of the *History of Sexuality*.

12 Richard J. Bernstein, 'Foucault: critique as a philosophical ethos', in Honneth et al. (eds), *Philosophical Interventions*. Since the rhetorical aspect of language in general is one of the themes at stake in the whole debate, I should emphasize that I am using these terms in the very banal sense in which one can distinguish, say, claims about the power relations built into all use of language from assertions such as 'all language is fascist'.

13 Cf. Honneth, *Critique of Power*.

14 There is of course something in this charge in relation to Nietzsche and Heidegger and, in a different way, Adorno, but one should remember that all three have also inspired a massive body of reflec-

tion on the theme of everyday life – notably in the work of Michel de Certeau and Michel Maffesoli. See, for example, Maffesoli's edited collection on 'The sociology of everyday life', *Current Sociology*, 37, 1 (1989).

15　Thus, Habermas suggests, the ideologies which conceal these antagonisms are not reducible to the false consciousness of collectives such as classes; they must rather be analysed as systematically distorted structures of everyday communication (note 5, p. 419).

16　Luhmann's theory, he goes on, makes the reverse mistake, overlooking the class effects of system differentiation. See my discussion below.

17　Habermas, 'Remarks on the discussion', p. 127; *Postmetaphysical Thinking*, pp. 25–6, and cf. p. 45. This is, of course, somewhat disingenuous, since Habermas was himself largely responsible for raising the temperature of the debate. The term 'postmodern' too has been so broadened as to have lost what meaning it ever had. See, for example, Arthur Frank, 'Only by daylight: Habermas's postmodern modernism'.

18　Habermas, 'Untiefen der Rationalitätskritik', in *Die neue Unübersichtlichkeit*, p. 133.

19　Ibid., p. 134.

20　Ibid.

21　Habermas, *Postmetaphysical Thinking*, p. 13 and *passim*.

22　Ibid., pp. 135–9.

23　Ibid., p. 141.

24　Ibid., p. 141.

25　Ibid., p. 142.

26　For a critique, see Bhaskar, *Philosophy and the Idea of Freedom*.

27　Manfred Frank, *Die Grenzen der Verständigung*, p. 64.

28　*Theory, Culture and Society*, special issue on critical theory, p. 127.

Chapter 9　Law and the State

1　Habermas, *Law and Morality: The Tanner Lectures on Human Values*, p. 219.

2　Habermas, *Faktizität und Geltung* (*Facticity and Validity*), p. 547; page references hereafter appear in the text in parentheses.

3　He notes however (p. 10) that he now sees the 'complementary' relationship between morality and law in different terms, i.e. as a rather more distant one.

4　Moreover, legal structures preserve a social solidarity which is currently endangered and in need of regeneration.

5　This 'weak force of rational motivation' (p. 19) is, however, more open-ended than the direct force of an old-style rule of action (p. 18).

Thus the theory of communicative action has 'to explain how the reproduction of society can take place on such a fragile basis as that of . . . validity-claims' (p. 23).

6 Habermas distinguishes between fully universalistic moral claims and 'ethical-political' ones which express the shared undestandings of a specific political community (p. 139).

7 Arendt's phrase comes from her *Vita Activa*, p. 1940. See also Habermas, 'Hannah Arendt: on the concept of power', *Philosophical-Political Profiles*, pp. 171–87.

8 In Habermas, *Justification and Application*, pp. 1–17.

9 These examples seem to raise more problems of demarcation than they resolve.

10 Whereas a rational agreement (*Einverständnis*) is based on grounds which convince all parties in the same way, a compromise can be acceptable to different parties for different reasons.

11 One promising approach is the current work on social movements' cultural impact on the redefinition of issues which can then be processed in more formal political channels. Cf. Eder, *The New Politics of Class*.

12 Cf. *Faktizität und Geltung*, pp. 236–7, where Habermas discusses the loose relation between principles of the *Rechtsstaat* (such as the division of powers) and their precise institutional embodiment.

13 This is the paradox which Habermas identifies at the heart of the welfare state – see pp. 100–1 above. In the following pages of *Faktizität und Geltung* he goes on to discuss ways in which the modern welfare state needs to strengthen the collective rights of disadvantaged groups (notably women) as well as improving individual life-chances.

14 Cf. the quotations from Becker, *Die Freiheit, die wir meinen*, in *Faktizität und Geltung*, p. 355, n. 6, and pp. 356–7, n. 7.

15 Charles Larmore, review symposium on *Faktizität und Geltung*, in *Deutsche Zeitschrift für Philosophie*, 41, 2 (1993), pp. 321–64.

16 Ibid., p. 327.

17 Habermas, *Faktizität und Geltung*, p. 503.

18 Peter Dews, in *Deutsche Zeitschrift für Philosophie*, p. 363.

19 Gillian Rose's work is a brilliant exception.

20 As Dews notes, Habermas has himself stressed the interdependence of justice and solidarity (*Erläuterungen zur Diskursethik*, p. 70).

Conclusion: Habermas and the Future of Critical Theory

1 As noted by Dubiel, *Kritische Theorie der Gesellschaft*, p. 85.

2 I do not question the usefulness, nor the continued applicability of

the term, only its role as an all-purpose shibboleth.

3 Cf. Luhmann, *Soziologische Aufklärung 4*, pp. 5ff.

4 Cf. Bottomore, *The Frankfurt School*, pp. 71–81.

5 See Rose, *Dialectic of Nihilism*, ch. 1; J. M. Bernstein, *The Politics of Transfiguration*. As we saw in chapter 3, a more diffuse Hegelianism pervades the discussion of Habermas's moral theory.

6 Charles Taylor, in Honneth et al. (eds), *Philosophical Interventions*.

7 Habermas, *Erläuterungen zur Diskursethik*, p. 47.

8 Ibid., p. 48. See Habermas, *Moral Consciousness and Communicative Action*, pp. 199–203; Wellmer, *The Persistence of Modernity*; and Benhabib, in Benhabib and Dallmayr, *The Communicative Ethics Controversy*, p. 346. Without wishing to be accused of what a British opposition politician once described as 'stirring up complacency', I take the interesting point to be, not that there may be a drafting error in Habermas's formulation of his moral theory, but that it forms an integral part of a broader outline of a desirable form of life. See Habermas, *Justification and Application*, p. 17.

9 Thomas McCarthy, 'Philosophy and social practice: avoiding the ethnocentric predicament', in Honneth et al. (eds), *Philosophical Interventions*, p. 259.

10 See for example *The Past as the Future*.

Bibliography

The following abbreviations have been used in references to works by Habermas:

CES   *Communication and the Evolution of Society*
KHI   *Knowledge and Human Interests*
LSS   *On the Logic of the Social Sciences*
LSW   *Zur Logik der Sozialwissenschaften*
TCA   *The Theory of Communicative Action*

Abendroth, Wolfgang, et al., *Die Linke antwortet Jürgen Habermas*, Frankfurt, Europäische Verlagsanstalt, 1968.

Adorno, T. W., 'Spätkapitalismus oder Industriegesellschaft?', *Gesammelte Schriften*, vol. 8, Frankfurt, Suhrkamp, 1972.

Adorno, T. W., Albert, H., Dahrendort, R., Habermas, J., Pilot, H., and Popper, K. R., *The Positivist Dispute in German Sociology*, London, Heinemann, 1976.

Albrow, Martin, *Max Weber's Construction of Social Theory*, London, Macmillan, 1990.

Anderson, Perry, *Considerations on Western Marxism*, London, New Left Books, 1976.

Apel, Karl-Otto, *Analytic Philosophy of Language and the Geisteswissenschaften*, Dordrecht, Reidel, 1967. First published 1965.

Apel, Karl-Otto, *Towards a Transformation of Philosophy*, abridged edn, London, Routledge & Kegan Paul, 1980. First published in 1972.

Apel, Karl-Otto, *Understanding and Explanation: A Transcendental-Pragmatic Perspective*, abridged edn, Cambridge, Mass., MIT Press, 1984. First published 1979.

Apel, Karl-Otto, Habermas, J., Gadamer, H. G., von Bormann, C., Bubner, R., and Giegel, H. J., *Hermeneutik und Ideologiekritik*, Frankfurt, Suhrkamp, 1971.

Arendt, Hannah, *Vita Activa*, Stuttgart, Kohlhammer, 1960.

Arnason, Johann, 'A review of Jürgen Habermas, *Zur Rekonstruktion des historischen Materialismus*', *Telos*, 39 (1979), pp. 201–18.

Assoun, Paul-Laurent, and Roulet, Gérard, *Marxisme et théorie critique*, Paris, Payot, 1978.

Austin, J. L., *How to Do Things with Words*, Oxford, Clarendon Press, 1962.

Baynes, K., Bohman, J., and McCarthy, T. (eds), *After Philosophy: End or Transformation?*, Cambridge, Mass., M.I.T. Press, 1987.

Beck, Ulrich, *Risk Society*, London, Sage, 1992.

Becker, Werner, *Die Freiheit, die wir meinen*, Munich, Piper, 1992.

Benhabib, Seyla, *Critique, Norm and Utopia*, New York, Columbia University Press, 1980.

Benhabib, Seyla, 'The generalized and the concrete other: the Kohlberg–Gilligan controversy and feminist theory', *Praxis International*, 5, 4 (1986).

Benhabib, Seyla, and Cornell, Drucilla (eds), *Feminism and Critique: Essays on the Politics of Gender in Late-Capitalist Societies*, Cambridge, Polity, 1987.

Benhabib, S., and Dallmayr, F. (eds), *The Communicative Ethics Controversy*, Cambridge, Mass., M.I.T. Press, 1990.

Berger, Johannes, 'Changing crises-types in Western societies', *Praxis International*, 1, 3 (1981), pp. 230–9.

Berger, Peter, and Luckmann, Thomas, *The Social Construction of Reality*, Harmondsworth, Penguin, 1967.

Bernstein, J. M., *The Fate of Art: Aesthetic Alienation from Kant to Derrida and Adorno*, Cambridge, Polity, 1993.

Bernstein, J. M., *The Politics of Transfiguration*, London, Routledge, 1994.

Bernstein, R. J., 'The relationship of Habermas' views to Hegel', in D. P. Verene (ed.), *Hegel's Social and Political Thought*, Brighton, Harvester, 1980.

Bernstein, R. J., *Beyond Objectivism and Relativism*, Oxford, Blackwell, 1983.

Bernstein, R. J., (ed.), *Habermas and Modernity*, Oxford, Blackwell, 1985.

Bernstein, R. J., *Philosophical Profiles*, Cambridge, Polity, 1986.

Bernstein, R. J., *The New Constellation: The Ethical Horizons of Modernity/Postmodernity*, Cambridge, Polity, 1991.

Bhaskar, Roy, *A Realist Theory of Science*, 2nd edn, Brighton, Harvester, 1978.

Bhaskar, Roy, *Philosophy and the Idea of Freedom*, London, Verso, 1991.

Bleicher, J. (ed.), *Contemporary Hermeneutics*, London, Routledge, 1980.

Bonss, Wolfgang, and Honneth, Axel (eds), *Sozialforschung als Kritik*, Frankfurt, Suhrkamp, 1982.

Bottomore, Tom, *The Frankfurt School*, Chichester, Ellis Horwood, 1984.

Braaten, Jane, *Habermas' Critical Theory of Society*, Albany, SUNY Press, 1991.

Brand, Arie, *The Force of Reason: An Introduction to Habermas' 'Theory of Communicative Action'*, Sydney, Allen & Unwin, 1990.

Calhoun, Craig (ed.), *Habermas and the Public Sphere*, Cambridge, Mass., MIT Press, 1992.

Cohen, Jean, and Arato, Andrew, *Civil Society and Political Theory*, Cambridge, Mass., MIT Press, 1992.

Connerton, Paul (ed.), *Critical Sociology*, Harmondsworth, Penguin, 1976.

Connolly, W. (ed.), *Legitimacy and the State*, Oxford, Blackwell, 1984.

Current Sociology, 37, 1 (1989), *The Sociology of Everyday Life*, ed. M. Maffesoli.

Dallmayr, F. R., 'Critical theory criticised: Habermas' *Knowledge and Human Interests* and its aftermath', *Philosophy of the Social Sciences*, 2 (1972).

Dallmayr, F. R. (ed.), *Materialien zu Erkenntnis und Interesse*, Frankfurt, Suhrkamp, 1974.

Deutsche Zeitschrift für Philosophie, review symposium on *Faktizität und Geltung*, 41, 2 (1993), pp. 321–64.

Dews, Peter, *Logics of Disintegration: Post-Structuralist Thought and the Claims of Critical Theory*, London, Verso, 1987.

Dilthey, W., *Gesammelte Schriften*, 18 vols, Leipzig and Berlin, B. Teubner, 1962–77.

Dubiel, Helmut, *Kritische Theorie der Gesellschaft*, Weinheim, Juventa, 1988.

Eder, Klaus, *Die Entstehung staatlich organisierter Gesellschaften*, Frankfurt, Suhrkamp, 1976; 2nd edn, 1980.

Eder, Klaus, *The New Politics of Class: Social Movements and Cultural Dynamics in Advanced Societies*, London, Sage, 1993.

Fay, Brian, *Social Theory and Political Practice*, London, Allen & Unwin, 1975.

Felski, Rita, *Beyond Feminist Aesthetics*, London, Hutchinson Radius, 1989.

Ferry, Jean-Marc, *Habermas: l'éthique de la communication*, Paris: Presses Universitaires de France, 1987.

Forrester, John (ed.), *Critical Theory and Public Life*, Cambridge, Mass., MIT Press, 1985.

Frank, Arthur, 'Only by daylight: Habermas's postmodern modernism', *Theory, Culture and Society*, 9, 3 (1992).

Frank, Manfred, *Die Grenzen der Verständigung: Ein Geistergespräch zwischen Lyotard und Habermas*, Frankfurt, Suhrkamp, 1988.

Frankenberg, G., and Rödel, U., *Von der Volkssouveränität zum Minderheitenschutz*, Frankfurt, Europäische Verlagsanstalt, 1981.

Fraser, Nancy, 'Toward a discourse ethic of solidarity', *Praxis International*, 5, 4 (1986).

Gadamer, Hans-Georg, *Truth and Method*, London, Sheed & Ward, 1975. First published 1960.

Geuss, Raymond, *The Idea of a Critical Theory. Habermas and the Frankfurt*

School, Cambridge, Cambridge University Press, 1981.

Giddens, A., *The Constitution of Society*, Cambridge, Polity, 1984.

Godelier, Maurice, *Perspectives in Marxist Anthropology*, Cambridge, Cambridge University Press, 1976.

Gripp, Helga, *Jürgen Habermas*, Paderborn, Schöningh, 1984.

Habermas, Jürgen, von Friedeburg, L., Oehler, C., and Weltz, F., *Student und Politik*, Neuwied, Luchterhand, 1961.

Habermas, Jürgen, *Strukturwandel der Öffentlichkeit*, Neuwied/Berlin, Luchterhand, 1962; 2nd edn, Frankfurt, Suhrkamp, 1989. Tr. as *The Structural Transformation of the Public Sphere*, Cambridge, Polity, 1989.

Habermas, Jürgen, *Theorie und Praxis*, Neuwied/Berlin, Luchterhand, 1963. Tr. as *Theory and Practice*, Cambridge, Polity, 1986.

Habermas, Jürgen, *Technik und Wissenschaft als Ideologie*, Frankfurt, Suhrkamp, 1968. Part translated in Jürgen Habermas, *Toward a Rational Society*, Cambridge, Polity, 1986.

Habermas, Jürgen, *Erkenntnis und Interesse*, Frankfurt, Suhrkamp, 1968. Tr. as *Knowledge and Human Interests*, Cambridge, Polity, 1986.

Habermas, Jürgen, *Zur Logik der Sozialwissenschaften*, 2nd edn, Frankfurt, Suhrkamp, 1971. Tr. as *On the Logic of the Social Sciences*, Cambridge, Polity, 1990.

Habermas, Jürgen, 'A postscript to *Knowledge and Human Interests*', *Philosophy of the Social Sciences*, 3, 2 (1973).

Habermas, Jürgen, *Legitimationsprobleme im Spätkapitalismus*, Frankfurt, Suhrkamp, 1973. Tr. as *Legitimation Crisis*, London, Heinemann, 1976.

Habermas, Jürgen, 'What does a crisis mean today?', *Social Research* (Winter 1973), repr. in P. Connerton (ed.), *Critical Sociology*, Harmondsworth, Penguin, 1976.

Habermas, Jürgen, *Kultur und Kritik*, Frankfurt, Suhrkamp, 1973.

Habermas, Jürgen, 'The public sphere', *New German Critique*, 3 (1974).

Habermas, Jürgen, 'Können komplexe Gesellschaften eine vernünftige Identität ausbilden?', in J. Habermas and D. Henrich, *Zwei Reden*, Frankfurt, Suhrkamp, 1974.

Habermas, Jürgen, *Zur Rekonstruktion des historischen Materialismus*, Frankfurt, Suhrkamp, 1976. Part translated in *Communication and the Evolution of Society*, Cambridge, Polity, 1991.

Habermas, Jürgen, *Theorie des kommunikativen Handelns*, 2 vols, Frankfurt, Suhrkamp, 1981. Tr. by Thomas McCarthy as *The Theory of Communicative Action*, vol. 1, London, Heinemann, 1984, repr. Cambridge, Polity, vol. 2, Cambridge, Polity, 1987.

Habermas, Jürgen, *Philosophical-Political Profiles*, London, Heinemann, 1983.

Habermas, Jürgen, *Vorstudien and Ergänzungen zur Theorie des kommunikativen Handelns*, Frankfurt, Suhrkamp, 1984.

Habermas, Jürgen, 'Objektivismus in den Sozialwissenschaften', in *Zur*

Logik der Sozialwissenschaften, 5th edn Frankfurt, Suhrkamp, 1982.

Habermas, Jürgen, 'The entwinement of myth and enlightenment', *New German Critique*, 26 (1982), pp. 13–20.

Habermas, Jürgen, *Moralbewusstsein und kommunikatives Handeln*, Frankfurt, Suhrkamp, 1983. Tr. as *Moral Consciousness and Communicative Action*, Cambridge, Polity, 1990.

Habermas, Jürgen, 'Moral und Sittlichkeit: Hegels Kantkritik im Lichte der Diskursethik', *Merkur*, 39, 12 (Dec. 1985).

Habermas, Jürgen, 'Modernity – an incomplete project', repr. in Hal Foster (ed.), *Postmodern Culture*, London, Pluto, 1985.

Habermas, Jürgen, *Die neue Unübersichtlichkeit*, Frankfurt, Suhrkamp, 1985. Tr. as *The New Conservatism*, Cambridge: Polity, 1989.

Habermas, Jürgen, *Der Philosophische Diskurs der Moderne*, Frankfurt, Suhrkamp, 1985. Tr. as *The Philosophical Discourse of Modernity*, Cambridge, Polity, 1990.

Habermas, Jürgen, *Autonomy and Solidarity*, ed. Peter Dews, London, Verso, 1986; 2nd edn, London, Verso, 1992.

Habermas, Jürgen, *Nachmetaphysisches Denken*, Frankfurt, Suhrkamp, 1988. Tr. as *Postmetaphysical Thinking*, Cambridge, Polity, 1992.

Habermas, Jürgen, 'Towards a communication concept of rational will formation', *Ratio Juris*, 2 (July 1989), pp. 144–54.

Habermas, Jürgen, 'Volkssouveränität als Verfahren', *Merkur*, 43, 6 (1989), pp. 465–77.

Habermas, Jürgen, *Die nachholende Revolution*, Frankfurt, Suhrkamp, 1990.

Habermas, Jürgen, 'Remarks on the discussion', *Theory, Culture and Society*, 7 (1990).

Habermas, Jürgen, *Law and Morality: The Tanner Lectures on Human Values*, VIII, 1988, pp. 217–279.

Habermas, Jürgen, *Erläuterungen zur Diskursethik*, Frankfurt, Suhrkamp, 1991. Tr. as *Justification and Application*, Cambridge, Polity, 1993.

Habermas, Jürgen, *Vergangenheit als Zukunft*, ed. Michael Heller, Zurich, Pendo, 1991; 2nd, expanded edn Munich, Piper, 1993. Tr. as *The Past as Future*, Lincoln, University of Nebraska Press, 1994.

Habermas, Jürgen, *Faktizität und Geltung*, Frankfurt, Suhrkamp, 1992.

Habermas, Jürgen, and Luhmann, Niklas, *Theorie der Gesellschaft oder Sozialtechnologie: Was leistet die Systemforschung?*, Frankfurt, Suhrkamp, 1971.

Halfpenny, Peter, *Positivism and Sociology*, London, Allen & Unwin, 1982.

Hegel, G. W. F., *Lectures on the Philosophy of Religion*, London, Routledge, 1968.

Held, David, *Introduction to Critical Theory: Horkheimer to Habermas*, London, Hutchinson, 1980.

Hohendahl, Peter, 'Habermas' critique of the Frankfurt School', *New German Critique*, 35 (1985), pp. 3–26.

Holub, Robert C., *Jürgen Habermas: Critic in the Public Sphere*, London, Routledge, 1991.

Honneth, Axel, 'Communication and reconciliation in Habermas' critique of Adorno', *Telos*, 39 (1979), pp. 45–61.

Honneth, Axel, 'Moral consciousness and class domination: some problems in the analysis of hidden morality', *Praxis International*, 2, 1 (1982), pp. 12–24.

Honneth, Axel, 'Work and Instrumental Action', *New German Critique*, 26 (1982), pp. 31–54.

Honneth, Axel, 'Diskursethik und implizites Gerechtigkeitskonzept', in Emil Angehrn and Georg Lohmann (eds), *Ethik und Marx*, Königstein, Hain Verlag, 1985.

Honneth, Axel, *Critique of Power*, Cambridge, Mass., MIT Press, 1992. First published 1985.

Honneth, Axel, *The Struggle for Recognition*, Cambridge, Polity, 1994.

Honneth, Axel, and Joas, Hans, *Social Action and Human Nature*, Cambridge, Cambridge University Press, 1988. First published 1980.

Honneth, Axel, and Joas, Hans (eds), *Communicative Action*, Cambridge, Polity, 1991.

Honneth, Axel, et al. (eds), *Philosophical Interventions in the Unfinished Project of the Enlightenment*, Cambridge, Mass., MIT Press, 1992.

Honneth, Axel, et al. (eds), *Cultural-Political Interventions in the Unfinished Project of the Enlightenment*, Cambridge, Mass., MIT Press, 1992.

Horkheimer, Max, and Adorno, Theodor W., *Dialectic of Enlightenment*, London, Verso, 1972, 1979. First published 1947.

Horster, Detlef, *Habermas zur Einführung*, Hanover, SOAK (Sozialistischer Arbeitskreis), 1984.

Husserl, Edmund, *The Crisis of the European Sciences and Transcendental Phenomenology*, Evanston, Ill., Northwestern University Press, 1970. First published 1938.

Ilting, Karl-Heinz, 'Geltung als Konsens', *Neue Hefte für Philosophie*, 10 (1976).

Inglehart, R. F., *The Silent Revolution: Changing Values and Political Styles among the Western Mass Publics*, Princeton, NJ, Princeton University Press, 1977.

Ingram, David, *Habermas and the Dialectic of Reason*, New Haven, Conn., Yale University Press, 1987.

Jäger, Wolfgang, *Öffentlichkeit und Parlamentarismus: Eine Kritik an Jürgen Habermas*, Stuttgart, Kohlhammer, 1973.

Kautsky, Karl, *The Materialistic Conception of History*, ed. John H. Kautsky, New Haven, Conn., Yale University Press, 1988. First published in German, 1927.

Keat, Russell, *The Politics of Social Theory: Habermas, Freud and the Critique of Positivism*, Oxford, Blackwell, 1981.

Kellner, Douglas, *Critical Theory, Marxism and Modernity*, Cambridge, Polity, 1989.

Kessler, Alfred, *Identität und Kritik: Zu Habermas' Interpretation des psychoanalytischen Prozesses*, Würzburg, Königshausen & Neumann, 1983.

Kortian, Garbis, *Metacritique*, Cambridge: Cambridge University Press, 1980.

Kuhn, Thomas S., *The Structure of Scientific Revolutions*, Chicago, Ill., University of Chicago Press, 1962, 1970.

Kunneman, Harry, *Der Wahrheitstrichter: Habermas und die Postmoderne*, Frankfurt, Campus, 1991.

Lassman, Peter, 'Social structure, history and evolution', *Economy and Society*, 13, 1 (1984).

Leiss, W., *The Domination of Nature*, New York, George Braziller, 1972.

Lorenzer, Alfred, *Die Wahrheit der psychoanalytischen Erkenntnis*, Frankfurt, Suhrkamp, 1976.

Löwith, Karl, *From Hegel to Nietzsche*, London, Constable, 1965.

Luhmann, Niklas, *Legitimation durch Verfahren*, Berlin and Neuwied, Luchterhand, 1969; Frankfurt, Suhrkamp, 1983.

Luhmann, Niklas, *Soziologische Aufklärung*, Opladen, Westdeutscher Verlag, 1977.

Luhmann, Niklas, *Soziologische Aufklärung 4*, Opladen: Westdeutscher Verlag, 1987.

Lyotard, Jean-François, *The Postmodern Condition: A Report on Knowledge*, Manchester, Manchester University Press, 1984.

Mann, M., 'The ideology of intellectuals and other people in the development of capitalism', in L. N. Lindberg, R. Alford, C. Crouch and C. Offe (eds), *Stress and Contradiction in Modern Capitalism*, Lexington, Mass., D. C. Heath, 1975.

Marcuse, Herbert, *One Dimensional Man*, Boston, Mass., Beacon Press, 1964.

McCarney, Joe, *The Real World of Ideology*, Brighton, Harvester, 1980.

McCarthy, Thomas, *The Critical Theory of Jürgen Habermas*, Cambridge, Polity, 1978.

Mead, George Herbert, *Mind, Self and Society*, Chicago, Ill., University of Chicago Press, 1962. First published 1934.

Merquior, J. G., *Rousseau and Weber. Two Studies in the Theory of Legitimacy*, London, Routledge, 1980.

Moore, Barrington, Jr, *Social Origins of Dictatorship and Democracy*, Harmondsworth, Penguin, 1967.

Moore, Barrington, Jr, *Injustice*, London, Macmillan, 1978.

Narr, Wolf-Dieter, et al., *Theorie der Gesellschaft oder Sozialtechnologie: Neue Beiträge zur Habermas–Luhmann-Diskussion*, Frankfurt, Suhrkamp, 1974.

Negt, Oskar, and Kluge, Alexander, *The Public Sphere and Experience*, Minneapolis, Minnesota University Press, 1993. First published 1972.

Niedenzu, Heinz-Jürgen, *Die Entstehung von herrschaftlich organisierten Gesellschaften*, Frankfurt, Haag & Hercken, 1982.

Offe, Claus, 'Technik und Eindimensionalität. Eine Version der Technokratiethese?', in Jürgen Habermas (ed.), *Antworten auf Herbert Marcuse*, Frankfurt, Suhrkamp, 1968.

Offe, Claus, 'Ungovernability: on the renaissance of conservative theories of crisis', in Jürgen Habermas (ed.), *Observations on the Spiritual Situation of the Age*, Cambridge, Mass., MIT Press, 1984. First published 1979.

Offe, Claus, 'Some contradictions in the modern welfare state', *Praxis International*, 1, 3 (1981), pp. 219–29.

Offe, Claus, *Contradictions of the Welfare State*, London, Hutchinson, 1984.

Offe, Claus, *Arbeitsgesellschaft – Strukturprobleme und Zukunftsperspektiven*, Frankfurt, 1984.

Offe, Claus, *Disorganized Capitalism*, Cambridge, Polity, 1985.

Outhwaite, William, *Concept Formation in Social Science*, London, Routledge, 1983.

Outhwaite, William, *New Philosophies of Social Science: Realism, Hermeneutics and Critical Theory*, London, Macmillan, 1987.

Outhwaite, W., and Bottomore, T. (eds), *The Blackwell Dictionary of Twentieth-Century Social Thought*, Oxford, Blackwell, 1993.

Pateman, Carole, 'The fraternal social contract', in John Keane (ed.), *Society and the State*, London, Verso, 1988.

Pateman, Carole, *The Sexual Contract*, Cambridge, Polity, 1988.

Pierson, Chris, *Beyond the Welfare State?*, Cambridge, Polity, 1991.

Pusey, Michael, *Jürgen Habermas*, Chichester, Ellis Horwood, 1987.

Rasmussen, David M., *Reading Habermas*, Cambridge, Mass., Blackwell, 1990. (Includes bibliography of recent works on Habermas.)

Ray, Larry, *Rethinking Critical Theory: Emancipation in the Age of Global Social Movements*, London, Sage, 1993.

Rockmore, Tom, *Habermas on Historical Materialism*, Bloomington and Indianapolis, Indiana University Press, 1989.

Roderick, Richard, *Habermas and the Foundations of Critical Theory*, London, Macmillan, 1986.

Rorty, Richard, *Philosophy and the Mirror of Nature*, Princeton, NJ, Princeton University Press, 1979.

Rose, Gillian, *Hegel contra Sociology*, London, Athlone Press, 1981.

Rose, Gillian, *Dialectic of Nihilism: Post-Structuralism and Law*, Oxford, Blackwell, 1984.

Schafer, Roy, 'Narration in the psychoanalytic dialogue', in W. J. T. Mitchell (ed.), *On Narrative*, Chicago, Ill., University of Chicago Press, 1981.

Schutz, Alfred, *Collected Papers*, 3 vols, The Hague, Martinus Nijhoff, 1962–6.

Schutz, Alfred, *The Phenomenology of the Social World*, London, Heinemann, 1972. First published 1932.

Searle, John, *Speech Acts*, London, Cambridge University Press, 1969.

Sensat, Julius, *Habermas and Marxism*, Beverly Hills, Cal., Sage, 1979.

Stamm, Karl-Heinz, *Alternative Öffentlichkeit: Die Erfahrungsproduktion neuer sozialen Bewegungen*, Frankfurt and New York, Campus, 1988.

Stockman, Norman, 'Habermas, Marcuse and the *Aufhebung* of science and technology', *Philosophy of the Social Sciences*, 8 (1978).

Stockman, N., *Anti-Positivist Theories of the Sciences*, Dordrecht, Reidel, 1983.

Strydom, Piet, 'The ontogenetic fallacy: the immanent critique of Habermas' developmental logical theory of evolution', *Theory, Culture and Society*, 9, 3 (1992).

Theory, Culture and Society, 7 (1990) special issue on critical theory.

Therborn, G., 'Jürgen Habermas: a new eclectic', *New Left Review*, 67 (May–June 1971), pp. 69–83.

Thompson, John B., *Critical Hermeneutics: A Study in the Thought of Paul Ricœur and Jürgen Habermas*, Cambridge, Cambridge University Press, 1981.

Thompson, J. B., and Held, D. (eds), *Habermas: Critical Debates*, London, Macmillan, 1982.

Weber, Max, *Economy and Society*, Berkeley, University of California Press, 1978.

Wellmer, Albrecht, *Critical Theory of Society*, New York, Seabury, 1974. First published 1969.

Wellmer, Albrecht, 'On the dialectic of modernism and postmodernism', *Praxis International*, 4, 4 (1985).

Wellmer, Albrecht, *Ethik und Dialog: Elemente des moralischen Urteils bei Kant und in der Diskursethik*, Frankfurt, Suhrkamp, 1986.

Wellmer, Albrecht, *The Persistence of Modernity*, Cambridge, Polity, 1991.

White, Stephen, *The Recent Work of Jürgen Habermas: Reason, Justice and Modernity*, Cambridge, Cambridge University Press, 1988.

Wiggershaus, Rolf, *The Frankfurt School*, Cambridge, Polity, 1994. First Published, 1986.

Winch, Peter, *The Idea of a Social Science and its Relation to Philosophy*, London, Routledge & Kegan Paul, 1958.

Young, Iris Marion, 'Impartiality and the civic public: some implications of feminist critiques of moral and political theory', *Praxis International*, 5, 4 (1986), p. 398. Repr. in Seyla Benhabib and Drucilla Cornell (eds), *Feminism and Critique: Essays on the Politics of Gender in Late-Capitalist Societies*, Cambridge, Polity, 1987.

Index